WATCH

*wide-awake faith
in a world fast asleep*

D1114409

WATCH

wide-awake faith in a world fast asleep

Rick James

A NavPress resource published in alliance
with Tyndale House Publishers, Inc.

NavPress is the publishing ministry of The Navigators, an international Christian organization and leader in personal spiritual development. NavPress is committed to helping people grow spiritually and enjoy lives of meaning and hope through personal and group resources that are biblically rooted, culturally relevant, and highly practical.

For more information, visit www.NavPress.com.

Watch: Wide-Awake Faith in a World Fast Asleep

Copyright © 2016 by Rick James. All rights reserved.

A NavPress resource published in alliance with Tyndale House Publishers, Inc.

NAVPRESS and the NAVPRESS logo are registered trademarks of NavPress, The Navigators, Colorado Springs, CO. *TYNDALE* is a registered trademark of Tyndale House Publishers, Inc. Absence of ® in connection with marks of NavPress or other parties does not indicate an absence of registration of those marks.

The Team:
Don Pape, Publisher
Caitlyn Carlson, Acquisitions Editor

Cover photograph of rooster copyright © aluxum/Getty Images. All rights reserved.

Unless otherwise indicated, all Scripture quotations are taken from *The Holy Bible*, English Standard Version® (ESV®), copyright © 2001 by Crossway, a publishing ministry of Good News Publishers. Used by permission. All rights reserved.

Scripture quotations marked DLNT are taken from *Disciples' Literal New Testament: Serving Modern Disciples by More Fully Reflecting the Writing Style of the Ancient Disciples*, copyright © 2011 Michael J. Magill. All rights reserved. Published by Reyma Publishing.

Scripture quotations marked MSG are taken from *THE MESSAGE* by Eugene Peterson, copyright © 1993, 1994, 1995, 1996, 2000, 2001, 2002. Used by permission of NavPress Publishing Group. All rights reserved.

Scripture quotations marked NASB are taken from the New American Standard Bible,® copyright © 1960, 1962, 1963, 1968, 1971, 1972, 1973, 1975, 1977, 1995 by The Lockman Foundation. Used by permission.

Scripture quotations marked NIV are taken from the Holy Bible, *New International Version,*® *NIV.*® Copyright © 1973, 1978, 1984, 2011 by Biblica, Inc.® Used by permission. All rights reserved worldwide.

Scripture quotations marked NKJV are from the New King James Version,® copyright © 1982 by Thomas Nelson, Inc. Used by permission. All rights reserved.

Scripture quotations marked NLT are taken from the *Holy Bible*, New Living Translation, copyright © 1996, 2004, 2015 by Tyndale House Foundation. Used by permission of Tyndale House Publishers, Inc., Carol Stream, Illinois 60188. All rights reserved.

Scripture quotations marked NRSV are taken from the New Revised Standard Version Bible, copyright © 1989, Division of Christian Education of the National Council of the Churches of Christ in the United States of America. Used by permission. All rights reserved.

Some of the anecdotal illustrations in this book are true to life and are included with the permission of the persons involved. All other illustrations are composites of real situations, and any resemblance to people living or dead is purely coincidental.

For information about special discounts for bulk purchases, please contact Tyndale House Publishers at csresponse@tyndale.com or call 800-323-9400.

Cataloging-in-Publication Data is available.

ISBN 978-1-63146-508-6

Printed in the United States of America

22	21	20	19	18	17	16
7	6	5	4	3	2	1

To my precious ones—
Avery, Whitney, and Will

CONTENTS

FOREWORD

IN HIS BOOK *A Million Ways to Die*, Rick wrote about what it means to "carry the cross" and "die to self." I particularly liked this quotation:

> Death has exactly zero intrinsic value. It's just that death is the only road that happens to be headed to resurrection, transformation, and transfiguration. By definition, resurrection can only be experienced by something dead, and this is what inflates the value of death. "Death has been swallowed up in victory" (1 Cor. 15:54), "swallowed up by life" (2 Cor. 5:4). Death is just something for eternal life to consume, digest, and metabolize into life.

This is a great insight into what it means to die with Christ. I enjoy that about Rick's writing—it's insightful, and he look at familiar truth in unfamiliar ways.

In *Watch*, Rick explores the corollary to "carrying the cross": living out the resurrected life of our Lord Jesus—Christ in us, for us, through us. There are plenty of motivating Christian books, but what's unique is that Rick has strung together all of the biblical motivations to spiritual wakefulness. In tracing all of the "stay-awake," "be-alert" teachings of Jesus and of the rest of the New Testament, what we see is the consistent, compelling theology of wakefulness that courses through Scripture. This is not a book encouraging Christians to live more awake and alive to Christ; it's a book expounding the biblical charge to live more awake and alive to Christ. It highlights Scripture's teachings, warnings, and motivations—Scripture's reasons for staying awake and Scripture's instructions on how.

Jesus has called us, as believers, to be awake and alert to his word, his will, and the opportunities to serve that are all around us. This teaching pulses through the entirety of the New Testament: Stay awake! Be alert! Beware! Be on guard! Make the most of every opportunity! But Scripture does not merely tell us to be vigilant; it also instructs us in how, and that's what Rick pulls from the texts and illustrates in very practical ways.

Rick says that "the daily goal of the Christian life is to stay spiritually awake—as awake as possible, for as long as possible" and that "this is the most ecumenical of Christian pursuits, something every follower of Christ shares with every other, no matter what their denomination." This seems resonantly true; it's true in my life. I get up each day with a desire to be alive and awake to the Lord—"as awake as possible, for as long as possible." And if that's your desire, you're going to get a lot out of *Watch*. I'm excited for you.

Mark Batterson
New York Times bestselling author of *The Circle Maker*,
lead pastor of National Community Church

Encephalitis Lethargica
The Great Sleeping Sickness

The tragic case of a man being in the world and yet out of it was described to me yesterday. This man, workless and homeless, more than three years ago walked into the West Highland Rest Home. He complained of being terribly tired, and it was obvious that his complaint was genuine. He simply could not stay awake. When the doctor examined him he found he was suffering from sleepy sickness, and he was put to bed right away. He is still sleeping.
THE DAILY POST, 1927

THIS MEDICAL CONDITION is known as *encephalitis lethargica,* which means "inflammation of the brain that makes you tired." The symptoms start with a fever, sore throat, and headache, and move to lethargy, sleep inversion (night becomes day), catatonia, and—many times—death. It has a 35 percent mortality rate. Those who survive are usually left in a catatonic state that bears a creepy resemblance to sleep, which is where the illness gets its more common and pronounceable name: "sleeping sickness."[1]

While *encephalitis lethargica* is extremely rare, from 1915 to 1926 an epidemic of it spread across the globe, killing more than five million people. That would be like twenty million today, allowing for inflation (which I imagine is not quite the right term to apply to such a statistic). Think about it: twenty million people suddenly nodding off and never waking up. There has never been anything like it before or since.

Many who survived the epidemic never fully recovered, spending the rest of their lives in a dreary netherworld somewhere

between life and death, real and unreal, asleep and awake—
and "these patients were put away in chronic hospitals, nursing
homes, lunatic asylums, or special colonies; and there, for the
most part, they were totally forgotten."[2]

In 1973, Oliver Sacks published *Awakenings*, a book that
detailed his treatment of several dozen survivors of the epidemic
who were still alive in 1969, still in cognitive slumber in some
rundown mental institution in Brooklyn, New York. Here's how
Sacks described the patients prior to treating them with the wonder drug L-DOPA:

> They would be conscious and aware—yet not fully awake;
> they would sit motionless and speechless all day in their
> chairs, totally lacking energy, impetus, initiative, motive,
> appetite, affect, or desire; they registered what went on
> about them without active attention, and with profound
> indifference. They neither conveyed nor felt the feeling of
> life; they were as insubstantial as ghosts, and as passive as
> zombies. . . . They were ontologically dead, or suspended,
> or "asleep"—awaiting an awakening.[3]

It's hard to imagine anyone living in that condition. But I'm
afraid *we* might be.

Sleep Is Not Your Friend

Sleep is a peculiar state, in that you're not aware when you're
doing it, which is why sleep aids like Ambien carry warnings not
to "operate heavy machinery," of which I can't help but picture
forklifts and bulldozers and such. To be aware of the moment you
fall asleep isn't physically possible; once you've woken up, you're
only aware you were asleep. This defining aspect of sleep is what
makes it so applicable or analogous to spiritual life.[4]

The Bible is filled with spiritual metaphors for every illness known to antiquity: blind, deaf, lame, leprous. But sleep and its related cognates (dull, drunk, drowsy) are far and away the most common in the New Testament—and the terms usually attributed to us, Jesus' would-be disciples, not the unbelieving world.

> And they went to a place called Gethsemane. And he said to his disciples, "Sit here while I pray. . . . Remain here and watch." . . . And he came and found them sleeping, and he said to Peter, "Simon, are you asleep? Could you not watch one hour?" . . . And again he went away and prayed. . . . And again he came and found them sleeping, for their eyes were very heavy, and they did not know what to answer him. And he came the third time and said to them, "Are you still sleeping and taking your rest? It is enough; the hour has come." MARK 14:32, 34, 37, 39-41

It's a fitting metaphor. I mean, what better way to describe someone who has been quickened by God's Spirit but remains oblivious and unresponsive to spiritual reality? They're not dead, but they're certainly not alive. They're asleep, or drowsy, or drunk, or dull, or slow . . . and the biblical metaphors go on.

To be asleep is to be oblivious to being oblivious. The danger of sleep is the danger of carbon monoxide: It's colorless and odorless, and you're anesthetized before you know it—before you ever hit the floor. And this is why sleep (spiritual unreceptivity) received the sternest and most-repeated warnings from Jesus: "And what I say to you I say to all: Stay awake" (Mark 13:37).

It's difficult not to see something prophetic in the disciples falling asleep in Gethsemane. Why the sudden narcolepsy? Why does Jesus go away, leaving them until he *returns*? Why do the disciples fall asleep, not once or twice, but three times? What of Jesus' parable about his return—"If he comes in the second watch, or in the third, and finds them awake, blessed are those servants!" (Luke 12:38)? There are certainly hallmarks here of an enacted prophecy or parable. The warning is clear enough: Sleep is a very grave danger to the church and to the disciple. If anything will be our undoing, sleep will.

The Silver Chair

[Jill] was very angry because she could feel enchantment getting hold of her every moment. But of course the very fact that she could still feel it, showed that it had not yet fully worked. . . .

[Jill said,] "*We* come from another world." . . .

"Tell us, little maid, where is this other world? What ships and chariots go between it and ours?" [said the Witch.] . . .

Jill couldn't remember the names of the things in our world. And this time it didn't come into her head that she was being enchanted, for now the magic was in its full strength; and of course, the more enchanted you get, the more certain you feel that you are not enchanted at all.

She found herself saying (and at the moment it was a relief to say): "No. I suppose that other world must be all a dream."

"Yes. It *is* all a dream," said the Witch. . . .

"Yes, all a dream," said Jill.

"There never was such a world," said the Witch.

"No," said Jill and Scrubb, "never was such a world."

"There never was any world but mine," said the Witch.

"There never was any world but yours," said they.[5]

In this scene from C. S. Lewis's *The Silver Chair*, the children slowly, imperceptibly fall under the witch's spell, an enchantment that turns reality into a dream and dream into reality. In the story, Prince Rilian has already come under the spell and no longer knows that he's prince of Narnia. But each night Rilian is tied to a silver chair while the enchantment wears off, and for an hour Rilian is Rilian again. Prince of Narnia. Fully aware of his identity and bondage, and loath to begin another mindless twenty-three-hour cycle.

This is my day and, I assume, yours, too. A struggle against sleep—spiritually speaking, that is. The day begins prayerful and usually ends that way, but in the hours between—*oh the hours between*. The world and its celebrities and trends and news and Netflix and caffeine and Wolf Blitzer: It's all so bewitching, as are my gadgets, my apps, my shows, my photos, my music, my posts, and did I already mention Wolf Blitzer? It's beguiling. We are brought inside the City Gates, strolling about the Great City, striding among People of Purpose . . . we are absolutely out of our minds.

And then at some point in the day, we return to ourselves, to prayer, to Scripture, and to God. Looking back on the day, it's hard to place when nap time began; but somehow we entered the world mindful, and before the day was done our minds had become the world, and God and Christ and sheep and angels all seemed so out of place, like a crèche in Macy's. Another day, another cycle.

Now, you wouldn't want to say that distractions were any less of a problem for Christians living in the past or at least before the iPhone, but I'm going to say it anyway because I think it's true: A less distracted spiritual life *was* easier for non-wired Christians. That's a totally fair statement. Just as it would be fair for a fourth-century believer to whine about us having Christian podcasts. There are challenges unique to every age. Let me give you three of ours.

1. The Modern World

[H]ark! there is the whistle of the locomotive,—the long shriek, harsh above all other harshness, for the space of a mile cannot mollify it into harmony. It tells a story of

busy men, citizens, from the hot street, who have come
to spend a day in a country village,—men of business,—
in short, of all unquietness; and no wonder that it gives
such a startling shriek, since it brings the noisy world
into the midst of our slumbrous peace.[6]

That reflection comes from 1844 (the word *hark* was your clue).
Nathaniel Hawthorne wrote this in his journal as a train arrived
in Connecticut from New York City, interrupting Nathaniel's
afternoon of quiet repose. He was none too happy about the dis-
ruption to his usual peace. Oh dear, sweet, ignorant Nathaniel,
if you only knew what was coming.

In *Understanding Media*, Marshall McLuhan insightfully
noted that "the new media and technologies by which we amplify
and extend ourselves" have a "numbing or narcotic effect . . . that
lulls attention."[7] The clock, for example, took away our sense of
time, just as maps replaced our sense of direction. But only in the
past decade have tools replaced some major brain functions. It's
not worth enumerating the number of calls, texts, and e-mails we
get or the number of hours we spend online. It's a lot. Probably
better not to know. But what makes it all the more disturbing is
that we have no idea of the long-term effects.

The one side effect that *is* readily apparent is that technological
connectivity aggressively conspires against spiritual connectivity.
"The Net," says Nicholas Carr in *The Shallows*, "is, by design, an
interruption system, a machine geared for dividing attention."[8]
It chops our attention into bits and parcels it out the same way
it sends e-mail: "The Net seizes our attention only to scatter it."[9]

There's no precedent for what we're experiencing. None. The
distraction of our modern world is an overwhelming obstacle to
keeping our minds "on things above" (Colossians 3:1, NIV) and
hearing God's voice within. And this is not the only challenge
facing us.

2. Long for This World

I was recently reading *Long for This World: The Strange Science of Immortality*, a book on the science of gerontology (aging), and was struck by this provocative statement from Aubrey de Grey, one of the leading figures in gerontology, and by the resulting implication:

> [De Grey said,] "Of course, if you live a thousand years, driving will be outlawed! It could be a highly risk-averse world." . . . If you hope to live a thousand years and you are struck by a cab at twenty-five, you lose an awful lot.[10]

De Grey was speaking to the relationship between the length of our lifespan and our outlook on life. His speculation is that a thousand-year lifespan would lead to a risk-averse society, but that's not so much provocative as just a little crazy. What's provocative is the idea that the length of our lifespan affects our outlook—how little or how much time we have left.

In 2006, Stanford professor Laura Carstensen published "The Influence of a Sense of Time on Human Development," which has been enormously influential in the social sciences. What Carstensen's research showed is that the perception of how much longer we have to live, and not chronological age, is the primary factor affecting human motivation:

> The subjective sense of future time plays an essential role in human motivation. Gradually, *time left* becomes a better predictor than chronological age for a range of cognitive, emotional, and motivational variables.[11]

Among other revelations, Carstensen discovered that the risk and experimentation of youth is not so much about age as about the perception that death is a long way off. Who knew? That's a big thought with enormous spiritual implications, because you and I *already* have an enhanced lifespan and it's *already* affecting our spiritual awareness. We just haven't given it any thought.

You and I approach the Christian life in a fundamentally different way than do believers in any other place at any other time. No one else reading their Bible in the past few thousand years has read it with the confident assumption that they'd still be alive and kicking in their nineties. Our minds unconsciously do the math with any Scripture calling for obedience: "be holy" (for another sixty years); "forgive your enemies" (for another sixty years); "avoid sexual immorality" (for another sixty years).

Two of my kids returned from a youth conference not too impressed with the program, so I asked what they didn't like about it. They said, "It was all about recruiting for missions," and I politely nodded my head. Then I said, "That's because you're freaks," because shocking non sequiturs are the only way to capture a teenager's attention. And into the created void, I said:

> A couple hundred years ago, if your father was a farmer, you were a farmer. End of story. How many people in human history have had the freedom to choose what they want to do for a living? You can also travel; you can pick any place on the planet and go there . . . today. When has anyone ever been able to do such a thing? And wherever you go in the developing world, your life expectancy will be about twenty years beyond the indigenous population's. Your situation is utterly unique, and *that's* why it was all about recruiting for missions.

My kids, however, reckon their own finish line to be about seventy years from now, so my words had all the gravitas of an adult in a *Charlie Brown* special.

Spiritual attentiveness, hope, perseverance, and self-control are all temporally bound, inseparable from the length of wait-ing. And here you and I are tasked to remain spiritually vigilant for almost twice as long as our brothers and sisters throughout history. To regard this as a *challenge* may be an understatement.

3. *Alternative Worlds*

It's a little abstract to point to a moment when escapism and fantasy came to dominate the American psyche, but I'd like to cast my vote for this moment right here:

> Someone asked, "How do you feel?" Tim couldn't speak. It was all too much. Everything around him started taking on the shimmer and glimmer of jeweled patterns. *How* do *I feel? Far away. Gone. Far. Far. Gone. Drifting off into a cavern of sea light.* Making his way back to the house, he fell on the bed, into the arms of another woman who had taken the mushrooms. *Bodies like warm foam rubber. Marshmallow flesh. Mermaids. Laughing. Poking fingers through bikini lace. Quicksand flesh. Dark hair. Ponytail. Cherokee princess. Humming-bird words buzz from mouth. Stop talking. Look outside. . . . The undulating sea! Deep. Plants twirling together. Not even the plants know which leaf, which stem, belongs to which. Interconnected. Giant jungle palm time. . . .*
>
> Everything was quivering with life, even inanimate objects. . . . Nile palaces, Hindu temples, Babylonian boudoirs.[12]

In 1960, seven psilocybin mushrooms and a bottle of beer took Timothy Leary on a psychedelic voyage beyond the lines of latitude, past the borders of sea monsters and westerly winds, and clear off the map. Leary was Columbus in the new age of exploration, and during a summer sabbatical in Cuernavaca,

Mexico, while experimenting with hallucinogenic mushrooms, Leary made landfall in the New World. News of the discovery spread across college campuses, and a generation eager to stake a claim tuned in, turned on, and dropped out.[13]

It's like any fantasy world—you can't really say it doesn't exist, but it certainly does in the mind of the person experiencing it. Escapism can be drug-induced, lust-induced, greed-induced, boredom-induced, media-induced, induced any number of ways—but what is induced is another reality, an alternative landscape that provides for us what the real world cannot or will not.

We were made to jostle between worlds, which is why it comes so naturally to us. Our minds naturally accommodate the perceptual commute between God's Kingdom *here* (in the physical world) and God's Kingdom *there* (in the spiritual world). There and back, there and back—we ride the rails all day long. Like looking at an object with the right eye closed and then the left, spiritual wakefulness is the ongoing alignment of two realities, two kingdoms.

If spiritual awareness consists in this ferrying between point A and point B, escapism is an alternate point B, a different destination. Today the destinations are so vast and varied, so immersive, addictive, and accessible, that I think we need to acknowledge this as a challenge unique to us. I mean, knowing Martin Luther as we do, if he were around today, wouldn't someone need to be checking the history on his web browser? I would think.

We could of course keep going, and for quite some time, surveying the unique challenges we face given that modernizing forces have been as vulgar and violent to the soul as Cortez's modernization was to Mexico.

But we have more important things to do. Jesus has instructed us to stay awake, so if everyone will please put their cellphone on vibrate, we'll get on with it. Sure, it'll be a challenge, but so what? What are you doing a week from next Thursday? What other grand pursuits do you have on the calendar? What else is worth the effort? So, if that's settled, I can tell you where we're going. Jesus told us to be awake, but what exactly does this mean?

The New Testament's Theology of Wakefulness

> Waves move a disturbance through a medium. . . .
> Paradoxically, [a wave is] both an object and a motion.
> When wave energy does move through a medium—
> water, for instance—the medium itself doesn't actually
> go anywhere. In other words, when a wave rises in the
> ocean and appears to race across the surface, that specific
> patch of water is not really advancing—the wave energy
> is. It's like cracking a whip. . . . In order to exist, waves
> require a disturbing force.[14]

Picture the powerful surge of a tsunami. Its force is generated by some concussive event on the ocean floor, and the energy from that event ripples through water in a wave, cresting, curling, and finally crashing on some unlucky shoreline. The physics of a wave is the physics of momentum, and it's important to see this in the pace and tempo of the New Testament: a wave. Jesus' death and resurrection would, I think, qualify as a concussive event. And from it, surging forward, verse to verse and book to book, is a wave of momentum, "like cracking a whip," ultimately crashing upon the shores of the New Heaven and New Earth.

As a book, the New Testament is not an exhaustive history like Chronicles or Kings, a collection of poetry like Psalms or Proverbs, or Ezekiel (whatever *it* is). Rather, its inspired genre is, more or less, the epistle: letters written on the run and on the lam, dispatched with urgency, sent by courier, signed with longing. Driving momentum forward are the constant reminders of the brevity of life and the temporal nature of this age: "the time is near" (Revelation 1:3); "the end of all things is at hand"

(1 Peter 4:7); "the days are evil" (Ephesians 5:16); "the hour has come" (Romans 13:11).

And though the Kingdom is inaugurated, it has yet to be consummated, and so the clock is always ticking. Alertness is unsustainable without reference to a clock, which is why Jesus constantly references it (Mark 13:35: "Therefore stay awake—for you do not know when the master of the house will come"), as do authors throughout the New Testament (1 Corinthians 7:29, NIV: "What I mean, brothers and sisters, is that the time is short").

Like any book, the New Testament has a tone and tempo, and this is its divinely inspired tempo. Now, you can pull out some Kingdom-y quotes and repackage it as a utopian manifesto telling us to stretch out, settle down, and build a better world; but that's not what it is. Twisting Scripture's tempo is still twisting Scripture.

The New Testament is written not to an audience in cultural ascendancy but to persecuted, temporarily displaced outcasts of this world who are waiting for their King to return and a new age to dawn. It is the instructions for how to live in this in-between time, this waiting between the ages; it is an eschatological handbook on how to survive while the lights are out.

As such, the New Testament is primarily concerned with keeping us awake, alert, undistracted, and motivated while we wait. In this age, we are the disciples in Gethsemane, and Scripture is constantly checking on us and poking at us to stay "awake" (Revelation 16:15) and "prepared" (Luke 1:17), always "watchful" (Colossians 4:2), "alert" (1 Peter 5:8, NIV), and "on guard" (Mark 13:33).

There is a very clear theology of wakefulness in the New Testament: biblical truths and teachings given by God to create in us—and sustain in us—spiritual alertness through the present age. In the rest of this book we will trace that theology, looking to those passages and teachings that speak directly to alertness and vigilance or warn of their absence. But before we start, we need to briefly distinguish between two types of alertness, or wakefulness, found in Scripture, because there are two different ways to be awake, and both are important.

Two Types of Attention

Human attention (awareness) has become one of the most intensely studied topics in psychology, sociology, and neuroscience, and current research indicates that we pay attention through two distinct processes: "top-down" attention and "bottom-up" attention.[15] Top-down attention is conceptual in nature—seeing the "big picture." Bottom-up attention is awareness of our more immediate physical environment. And yes, I'll explain.

Let's suppose that the peaceful inhabitants of Switzerland have finally come unhinged and declared war . . . on everyone. The nation is a seething cauldron of bankers. Now, imagine you're in charge of the American military. Your highest priority is to create a battle plan, and to do this you need a room full of medal-chested men in buzz-cuts; you need analysis of troop movements and weaponry; you need weather models and casualty projections; you need tactical scenarios with names like Broken Sparrow and Operation Bunny Rabbit. You need total awareness, but it's total *conceptual* awareness. This is top-down attention.

The second type, bottom-up attention, is what is needed by the soldier on the front lines, in the trenches. (Assume, for the sake of my anachronistic metaphor, that soldiers still fight in trenches, the Kaiser rules Germany, and the Hindenburg rules the skies.) For a combat soldier, awareness is perceptual, not philosophical: You're discerning the enemy not with your mind but with your eyes. You are trying to be *physically* alert. Strategizing generals don't need this sort of awareness; they don't need to be keenly aware of their conference table or the hands darting for snacks.

Because God made us this way, it's not surprising that Scripture speaks both to our big-picture, forward-looking awareness (like being ready for the Lord's return) and to our immediate awareness of God in our circumstances: "Suppose [you notice] a brother or a sister is without clothes and daily food . . . but [you do] nothing . . . what good is it?" (James 2:15-16, NIV). We need both top-down and bottom-up awareness, which is something of James's point here: What good is conceptual awareness of biblical doctrine if you are oblivious to the practical opportunities and application?

This is an important lens through which to see the New Testament's teaching on alertness and through which to read the chapters ahead. The most abstract thinker must see the importance of practical, in-the-moment attentiveness, and the most practical doer must see the relevance of big-picture doctrines like rewards or the return of Christ. Scripture addresses both because we need both. The Kingdom is already but not yet, and so it requires both top-down and bottom-up attention. In the present age, being either nearsighted or farsighted is not being fully alert.

And being fully alert? Well, that's being fully alive. When we live awake in our faith, our lives change, and the lives of everyone around us change. And that reminds me: There was a very happy ending for some of those patients treated for sleeping sickness. Dopamine, fittingly nicknamed *resurrectamine*, demonstrated an amazing ability to reverse the symptoms of sleep and reanimate the slumberers:

The next day Mrs. Y "exploded" as the nursing-staff put it. . . . On Saturday 17 May, about half an hour after receiving her morning gram of L-DOPA, Mrs. Y suddenly jumped to her feet, and before incredulous eyes walked the length of the ward. "What do you think of that, eh?" she exclaimed in a loud, excited voice. "What do you think of that, what do you think of that, what do you think of that?" . . .

Throughout the course of this amazing weekend, Mrs. Y walked excitedly all around the hospital, starting conversations with fellow-patients who had never heard her talk before, rejoicing ebulliently in her new-found freedom. Her capacity to chew and swallow were suddenly increased, and so too was her appetite: "Don't give me any of that slush! . . . I want a steak, well done!"[16]

Sensory Data
Discerning the Will of God

IT WAS TWO O'CLOCK on a Tuesday afternoon, and I was sitting in my living room. I work from home some days, and I was going through e-mails when my friend Shane came in through the back door. He walked over to me, dumped a pocketful of heroin in my lap, and said, "Can you flush this for me? I didn't have any, but I can't get myself to throw it away."

I'm just your average suburban minister—a late-night trip to the Wendy's drive-through is living on the edge for me. So how I found myself on this particular Tuesday with a cache of heroin nesting in my lap is an interesting story and not a bad segue to the subject of God's will.

Some years back, one of my daughter's high-school friends, Blake, said he wanted to introduce me to a guy he met on Facebook—some nineteen-year-old kid who had just started walking with God. I figured, sure, why not? So I told Blake to bring him by the house.

Shane showed up at the door with a Bible and *The Life and*

Diary of David Brainerd in his hand. That was it, the near sum of his worldly possessions at the time, and you have to respect his selectiveness—I mean, if you can own only two things, right? He had grown up in a godly home, had wonderful parents, and had gone to Christian schools, but these speed bumps hadn't slowed him any. Three weeks before I met him, he was shooting heroin daily, like having a grapefruit with breakfast, quite cognizant that such an aggressive embrace of the "good life" usually terminates within a year. Shane knew he was going to die. But he didn't.

Instead, Shane gave his life to Christ and, without aid of medication or rehab, went through a hellish week of detox under the loving care of his parents. Everything about drugs is at some level ironic, and so, not surprisingly, light is excruciating to the eyes during withdrawal. But everything about spiritual life is also ironic, so after six days Shane was up walking in the sun. A few weeks later he was back in Philadelphia, trying to put his life together and in need of a place to stay. That's when my wife (Katie) and I met him, and he came to stay with us.

What I remember of Shane's first weeks was a lot of Kim Walker singing "How He Loves Us." I used to like that song—until I'd heard it all the way through fifty-three times in a row. Shane didn't sleep or dream well, so he kept the same songs playing through the night. During the day he studied and memorized Scripture; at night he slept to a noise machine of "How He Loves Us."

When I decided to take Shane to an overnight ministry event, it was a dawning moment as I realized how much our lives were changing:

"Can we take Big Nick with us?"

"Who's Big Nick?"

"A friend from high school; he's a pretty major drug dealer now."

"So would he stay with us? In the hotel room?"

"Is that okay?"

"Does he have a gun?"

"Probably, but he wouldn't bring it."

"Shane, I was joking. You can't be serious . . ."

We did take Big Nick. He was big and his name was Nick, so no surprises there, and for the next couple of days I was Elvis traveling with my own personal bodyguard and pharmaceutical supplier.

Our home became a strange intersection between worlds. Most nights there were four, six, eight people in our living room until two, three, four in the morning. There were Bible studies on different nights of the week, and many who came were in drug recovery (or should have been). We took in another kid similarly in recovery. Big Nick trusted Christ. I baptized a handful of guys in a swimming pool in the freezing cold of November. Ashtrays overflowed, and Katie and I learned a new vocabulary: *zanies* (Xanax), *percs* (Percocet) . . .

A lot of kids came in and out. Some hung around, some dropped out, some went away to rehab, some overdosed, one went to prison, many of them relapsed, and some are still following Jesus. It's now a few years later, and people seem to be moving on; but who knows? I can no longer see that far in front of me. But we'll come back to that . . .

Lotsa Luck

In the book of Acts, toward the end of the first chapter, the disciples are hoping to replace Judas and put a full starting twelve back out on the field. That all seems normal enough until they literally roll dice to choose his successor: "They cast lots, and the lot fell to Matthias; so he was added to the eleven apostles" (Acts 1:26, NIV). This is a little disturbing—like throwing-a-witch-into-a-pond-to-see-if-she-floats kind of disturbing. As a means of discerning God's providence, casting lots was common enough in the Old Testament, but what's odd is watching the disciples do it: *Okay boys, rock, paper, scissors for who goes to the Gentiles.*

That oddness? You're supposed to feel that. Casting lots *is* out of place, and the story is situated here to show us exactly why and what changed. For recorded in Acts 2—immediately following the casting-lots incident—is Pentecost, the coming of the Holy Spirit. From this time forward, following the will of God will never be the same.

It's not that everyone in Israel was casting lots prior to Pentecost, but things were different. In his magisterial project *The Meaning of the Pentateuch*, John Sailhamer provides a consonant answer as to how the average Jewish man or woman understood "discerning God's will" in the centuries leading up to Christ.

The clues, according to Sailhamer, are found in the first chapter of Joshua and in the first psalm. In the threefold division that was the Hebrew Bible (Pentateuch, Prophets, and Writings), Joshua 1 introduced the "Prophets" and Psalm 1 introduced the "Writings." It's here, in the seams of the Old Testament, that linking themes are evident, as the inspired editors labored to turn three books into one.[1] So notice the similarity in Joshua 1 and Psalm 1:

Meditate on [the Book of the Law] day and night . . .
then you will make your way prosperous, and then you
will have good success.   JOSHUA 1:8

But his delight is in the law of the LORD,
    and on his law he meditates day and night. . . .
In all that he does, he prospers.
PSALM 1:2-3

Both passages emphasize meditating on the law of God as the means to a wise and fruitful life, as the means to living and discerning the will of God. Here is what's really interesting: The inspired editors of the Hebrew Bible believed that the direct leading of the Spirit had ceased (which is why no Scripture was added after Malachi in 420 BC) and would only resume at the coming of the Messiah. In the meantime, God's leading and direction was to be sought solely in the study of God's law: Scripture alone would continue "the office of prophecy."[2]

What the Gospels tell us is that the Messiah has arrived. What Acts 2 tells us is that the direct leading of the Spirit has resumed.

And with the coming of the Spirit, there is a distinct change in the narrative of Acts: a clear shift from *providence* (like casting lots) and biblical *principles* as the means of discerning God's will, to the active *presence* of God leading his people. Just look at these narrative clauses in contrast to casting lots:

The Spirit of the Lord suddenly took Philip away.
ACTS 8:39, NIV

The Spirit said to him, "Simon, three men are looking for you." ACTS 10:19, NIV

The two of them, sent on their way by the Holy Spirit, went down to Seleucia. ACTS 13:4, NIV

Something new was happening in these first centuries of the church, and even now something new is happening. For Katie and me, these past few years have been something new.

Prior to Shane, discerning God's will had become somewhat rote for us. Knowledge of Scripture, reason, a modicum of sanctification, and fifty years of living had left little to the imagination. Then the speed of life changed. Daily decisions had life-and-death consequences, and I couldn't find a chapter in any how-to-raise-your-kids-in-the-fear-and-admonition-of-the-Lord book that told me where to dispose of a cache of heroin or whether smoking cigarettes was an acceptable alternative to smoking crack.

Like the first-century church, we were operating without a manual, relying on God's Spirit moment by moment for wisdom and guidance. But to see how all this relates to being spiritually awake, I need to turn from the glamorous world of narcotics to the developing science of traffic psychology.

Driving Right

Had you been driving the roads of Stockholm in 1967, you would have been tapping your steering wheel to the song "Håll dig till höger, Svensson." In English this translates to "Let's All Drive on the Right, Svensson." The song's popularity was due to an upcoming change in Sweden—from driving on the left side of the road to driving on the right.

"H-Day," after the word *höger* (Swedish for "right"), was scheduled for September 3, 1967, when the entire country would get up in the morning, get in their cars, and drive on what was, to them, the wrong side of the road. As the day moved closer, prophecies of a traffic apocalypse multiplied: The *New York Times* reported, "What is going to happen . . . in September has cast many grotesque shadows all over Sweden." But what happened on September 3, no one saw coming: The roads in Sweden got safer. And not just for a day or a week. It took a full year for accident rates to climb back to where they were before the switch. The unintended consequence of H-Day was a revolution in traffic design, shifting focus from driver *safety* to driver *alertness*. On H-Day, the roads in Sweden became safer because driving became more dangerous.[3]

Gathering data, highway engineers found evidence of this counterintuitive phenomenon everywhere: When dangerous curves were marked with warning signs and safety reflectors, people drove faster. The more stop signs on a given road, the more drivers accelerated between signs. The wider the roads, the more cars tried to pass one another. The traffic system, designed for safety, had inadvertently produced recklessness.

Now, decades later, Europeans are driving on the fruit of that research. Long straightaways are bent every mile or so to keep drivers engaged. Safety signs have been taken down, forcing drivers to draw visual cues from the road and not signage. Curbs have been removed to take away the perceived security they provide, and the Russian roulette of roundabouts has replaced the predictability of four-way stops. Traffic signs still have a place, convicting the lawless and setting a general framework, but in these European towns, drivers are alert, negotiating the real world. They are no longer following mindlessly the regulatory signage that had done the driving for them.

So here let me propose that God has been laying down curved stretches of highway in our lives with a view toward spiritual alertness, prayerful engagement, attentive listening, continued reliance, and yielded submission. I'll also propose that perhaps we've been viewing God's will the way people used to view driving. I'm suggesting that the revolution in traffic safety is the revolution of Acts 2: discernment shifting from impersonal principles and providence (road signs) to active engagement with God and his Spirit.

This new awakeness and awareness to God is what we're probing here. This searching out of God's will is a major aspect of New Testament wakefulness: "Look carefully then how you walk, not as unwise but as wise, making the best use of the time, because the days are evil. Therefore do not be foolish, but understand what the will of the Lord is" (Ephesians 5:15-17).

This is a particular type of awareness, and to see it perhaps we ought to distinguish it from alternatives—different models of tracing divine direction.

1. Follow the Signs

"The view put forth in this book is that the Bible is *fully sufficient* to provide all guidance needed for a believer to know and do God's will."[4] This is the provocative thesis of Garry Friesen's classic study *Decision Making and the Will of God*, and I think it's a fair summary of this approach to discernment. Yet even in this short description, the correspondence between this view and the way traffic engineers used to view driving is fairly obvious. In fact, it's identical to the way believers approached God's will before Pentecost. But something *did* happen at Pentecost.

If you think of Paul's missionary adventures in the book of Acts, even if he had a copy of the New Testament (which he obviously didn't), what verse would have told him to go to Macedonia rather than to Asia, or to remain another few years in Corinth? Life has too many twists and turns for generic signage.

The New Testament's emphasis on wisdom centers on its location (it's found in Christ), not its attainment, and that's because intimacy, not autonomy, is the goal of New Testament spirituality. God wants us to be awake to him, processing our decisions with him, not walled off in *our* own thoughts, hashing out for *ourselves* what godly course *we* think seems sensible.

2. Ignore the Road

On his blog, popular writer Donald Miller addressed the question "Does God have a plan for your life?" His answer? "Probably not."[5] What he finds problematic about God having "a plan" is clear from the analogy he gives:

> Imagine visiting a friends [sic] house for dinner for the
> first time. You sit down at the table and the father, who
> sits at the head of the table, tells each of the kids, and
> the wife for that matter, what and when to eat. Then

he tells them what to wear to bed, when they will be getting up, where they will be going to college and who they will be married to. Later, you tell your friend you thought their dad might be a bit controlling.[6]

This critique is a view of intimate involvement (intimacy) distorted by a *fear* of intimacy. I mean, from a certain point of view, sex looks like a wrestling match, but that's exactly what it's not. Intimacy longs to share every facet of life and being out of an impulse to know, to be known, to care, and to please, not to control. Control has nothing to do with it.

Since our relationship with God is the most intimate of our relationships, it's difficult to see how God (who possesses full knowledge of us and our gifts and all outcomes of our choices) could *not* have an opinion about our decisions and direction, could *not* have a plan.

Angst and passivity can mire the discernment process, and that, I think we can all agree, is a problem. But this attempts to fix the "driving" problem by removing the road altogether—there's simply no plan to be followed. It's a logical solution, just not a biblical one. The scriptural idea of God's will repeated chapter after chapter is to "be careful [to] walk" (Ephesians 5:15, NASB) in the works God "prepared beforehand" for us to walk in (Ephesians 2:10). That sounds a lot like a plan.

During his lifetime, G. K. Chesterton was probably better known for his Father Brown detective novels than for his theological reflections, but the two are not disconnected. In the late 1920s, Chesterton wrote a series of essays on the art and science of the detective story. They're insightful, particularly for the way they illuminate the unfolding of God's plan:

The true object of an intelligent detective story is not to baffle the reader, but to enlighten the reader; but to enlighten him in such a manner that each successive portion of the truth comes as a surprise.[7]

The story is written for the moment when the reader does understand, not merely for the many preliminary moments when he does not understand. The misunderstanding is only meant as a dark outline of cloud to bring out the brightness of that instant of intelligibility.[8]

This is the beauty of God's will. This is what keeps us awake. It's the sleuthing, the discovery, the progressive illumination of his will, and the unfolding plot of our lives. Any view of God's will that suggests that such sleuthing is unnecessary, or that there is no grand plan to uncover, misses the point and beauty of the story.

In the end, we have our relationship with God's will pretty much the way we want it. Twin beds, two cars, separate bank accounts . . . as in marriage, it's possible to live with considerable autonomy, but that doesn't mean a more shared existence isn't possible and preferable. The real answer to the question "Does God have a wonderful plan for your life?" is, "Do you want him to?"

3. Just Follow the Wind

At this point it might seem I'm advocating a rather hippie-ish approach to God's will: top down, Jefferson Starship playing on the radio, the Spirit blowing through your hair as you drive to the dictates of vibes and impressions. But this isn't responsible driving.

Now you could ask, "What's wrong with being led by the Spirit's voice alone?" To which I'd say, "Several things." First, apart from Scripture, God's voice isn't super clear, and our own voice can sound a lot like his. Second, of all means by which

God speaks to us, Scripture alone is perspicuous, inerrant, and verifiable. And third, God wants to speak to us in all kinds of ways (Scripture, circumstances, wise counsel, etc.), and in taking a hyper-spiritual approach we tune in only to the most mystical modes of communication because—let's be honest—why would you comb the Scripture when you're expecting a vision or prophecy to arrive at any moment? You wouldn't. You don't.

To be fair, there's more nuance to each of these approaches, and in being brief I'm being a bit dismissive; but we've got a lot to cover. I think the Bible suggests something different, and to appreciate the genius of Scripture's approach, we need to jump to another seemingly unrelated field: the science of memory.

Eyes, Ears, and Nose

In *Moonwalking with Einstein*, Joshua Foer turns his considerable writing talents to the subject of memory and how we remember things. To that end, he begins his book quite memorably:

> Dom DeLuise, celebrity fat man . . . , has been implicated
> in the following unseemly acts in my mind's eye: He has
> hocked a globule of spittle . . . on Albert Einstein's thick
> white mane . . . and delivered a devastating karate kick . . .
> to the groin of Pope Benedict XVI.[9]

This is how Joshua Foer remembers the order of a deck of cards. Visually. Each graphic image summons to mind a particular card. If you were curious, the "globule of spittle" is somehow the nine of clubs.

The mind is an amazing mechanism, but it is notoriously bad at remembering names and dates and precise wording in general. This is no slight against the mind; it's simply accustomed to taking in words like pistachios: consuming the concept and discarding the shell of syllables it came wrapped in. And so the way orators and actors and politicians have bolstered their memories over the past few thousand years is by soliciting the aid of their other senses. This is known as "elaborative encoding," and it is to "remember . . . multisensorily."[10]

Oddly enough, there are professional mnemonists who compete each year at the World Memory Championship, an olympiad that includes among its challenges fifteen minutes to memorize three hundred random words, five minutes to memorize one thousand random digits, and five minutes to learn the order of a shuffled deck of playing cards. And these are just the stretching exercises.

Because our visual and spatial faculties are the strongest of our senses, these "mental athletes" (as they like to call themselves) employ a device called a memory palace. A memory palace is a mental landscape, someplace easily pictured (your kitchen, your street) that's used to store the objects being memorized. One guy, Dr. Yip Swee Chooi, memorized the entire 56,000-word, 1,774-page Oxford Chinese-English dictionary by using his body, and its sundry parts, as his mental landscape.[11]

Placed in the memory palace are sensory-rich representations of the objects, thus Foer's memorable introduction. Former world memory champion Ben Pridmore assigned a humorous, crude, scandalous, sentimental, animated, pungent, tragic, or tasty image to every numeral when he memorized the first fifty thousand digits of the mathematical constant *pi*. Memory is a matter of bringing to bear *all* of the input from *all* of the senses.

Here's where I'm going with this. Scripture takes a multisensory approach to discerning God's will, from miraculous visions to proverbial wisdom and everything in between. There's an array of spiritual senses at our disposal. But the problem, as with our memory, is that we lean heavily on one sense and ignore the others.

Younger Christians tend to fixate on the fantastical—ignoring wisdom, Scripture, and godly counsel. Mature believers, having left behind the carefree days of choosing a career or mate on the basis of a cloud formation, tend to winnow their senses to the most concrete. But to be discerning of God's will we require our other senses, processing the input prayerfully, in conversation with God.

We know our spiritual senses as we know our physical senses: more intuitively than scientifically, which is why a Nobel Prize still awaits the scientist who can explain how the human nose identifies ten times the number of smells for which it has receptors. So while you may not agree with my particular inventory of spiritual senses, a survey seems warranted.

The Many Senses

A reasonably thorough search of Scripture reveals at least the following means (or senses) for discerning God's leading.

Emotions

As in every other area of life, emotions have an important voice. It's just a really whiney voice. Amidst a crowded room of pressing factors, emotions can throw a tantrum and manipulate other faculties of judgment. So, if emotions are to be invited into big-boy conversations, they need to behave, and that requires separating the little hellions. For example, the feeling that says, "I don't know if I want to marry you" could mean: *I don't know if I like your family*; *I was planning on grad school*; *I don't want kids*; or *I simply don't like you*. When feelings are carefully handled and identified, we find God's Spirit at work, gently persuading at the level of emotion.

Logic and Reasoning

Like eyesight, reasoning is our default sense, and we rely on it a thousand times a day: "Look, a piece of the sun is stuck on my windshield. No, wait, the sun is super hot and really far away—it must be a reflection." There's nothing freaky, mysterious, or subjective here, and when it comes to discerning God's will, this is a positive thing, not a negative one.

Wisdom

Wisdom is practical, applied knowledge: "Is not wisdom found among the aged? Does not long life bring understanding?" (Job 12:12, NIV). Wisdom operates upon our knowledge base of how life works, how God works (Scripture), how people work, and how we work. But wisdom is like geometry, in that knowing the theorems doesn't solve the problem—you have to know which theorem applies.

So let's just say I'm consistently unable to pay my bills. It's a problem, but what principle applies? Is it a time to wait on God, a time to ask for a raise, a time to change jobs, or a time to rethink my lifestyle? Is God telling me to budget, save, resign, repent, tithe, work, pray, or trust? Or is this a spiritual attack? Wisdom discerns the right theorem.

Circumstances

Imagine I start singing the theme song to *Sesame Street*—"Sunny day, everything's . . ."—and then abruptly stop. That familiar arrangement of notes should lead you to anticipate the notes that are coming. This is how the purposeful arrangement of circumstances functions in our lives.

How has God used me in the past? Why this string of related events? Why do I keep hearing the same advice? Why this opportunity at this time? These are the types of patterns we notice, patterns hinting at God's involvement, notes on a page thoughtfully arranged, anticipating a general course of direction and precluding many others.

Such careful observation is in contrast to seizing upon a

singular event and taking it to be a "sign," like, *This burn mark on my grilled-cheese sandwich looks like the boot of Italy; God must be telling me to move there.* God's prolonged involvement in our lives is not something Satan can easily duplicate. Anyone, on the other hand, can make a grilled-cheese sandwich.

Wise Counsel

Proverbs 19:20, along with many other proverbs in Scripture, implores us to "listen to advice and accept instruction, that you may gain wisdom in the future." Mature believers are trained detectives who have traced God's purposes and pathways for a generation or two. When you lay before them the clues you've collected, they notice patterns—patterns they've seen but maybe you haven't.

There are lots of reasons we don't seek out godly counsel. I know why I don't. It's the same reason I don't stop for directions when I'm lost. My wife thinks it's pride. She's wrong. It's just pure laziness.

Impressions

When I started writing today, I opened the Word program on my Mac. Immediately the Word icon, a big blue W, began hopping up and down, exuberant to be picked over the other programs. I have rows of programs on my computer, but I notice Microsoft Word because it's the one hopping up and down. Sometimes a sermon is like that, sometimes a verse of Scripture is like that, and sometimes a scene in a movie is like that: God's Spirit animates a word or a thought or an idea and says, "Pay attention! This phrase, this place, this person is significant."

Scripture

As the Starbucks employee opened the cash register, I prayed, "Oh Lord, is it your will that I club the barista and steal that stack of twenties?" This didn't happen at Starbucks today because stealing is addressed in Scripture—and discernment is superfluous where God's will is explicit.

However, it's not only in the explicit statements of Scripture that God's will is revealed. God's Word brings us into contact with the person, the heart, the character of God, and that informs a whole lot of issues unaddressed in the Bible. For example, in my marriage, I've never once heard Katie say, "Don't bring a dead billy goat into the house," but I'm pretty sure how that would go down if I did.

The Mind

Dreams, divine visions, and prophetic words are all quite exciting to read about in Scripture, so perhaps we could just leave them there. Because in real life, deciphering people's private revelations and picking through the mystery stew of meaning is not exciting at all. Still, such things happen—at least I believe they do—and they can be exceedingly meaningful and encouraging to people. The giving of dreams and visions demonstrates God's ability to bypass our normal reasoning faculties and communicate directly to our minds, and it seems that certain cultures, situations, and individuals may require this.

The everyman school of parenting would say, "Don't give your teen a Maserati for his sixteenth birthday. It would stunt the development of patience, perseverance, and responsibility and, at the same time, foster passivity, entitlement, and immaturity." I think the same reasoning holds true for why God's direct communication is more of an exception than a rule.

How the Senses Work Together

How our spiritual senses all work together is pretty much how our physical senses all work together. There is, first, a predominant sense, and in the physical world that's sight. I didn't need to smell, touch, or taste my way to work today. In the spiritual realm a renewed mind, saturated in prayer and Scripture, is as all-purpose as a set of eyes.

The second principle is convergence. We experience the sensation of flavor mostly by smell, partly by taste, and a little by sight. And so when we really need discernment in following God's leading, we rely on a multisensory approach, looking for the overlap and alignment of our senses.

There is a third principle we want to explore in slightly more detail: The processing of sensory information, whether physical or spiritual, is essentially a process of pattern recognition.

Prospecting for Patterns

Gerald Edelman, founder of the Neurosciences Institute and recipient of the Nobel Prize, states rather bluntly that "brains operate . . . not by logic but rather by pattern recognition."[12] So when we look at the stars, we see constellations; when we see random numbers, our minds look for a meaningful sequence; and when a basketball player makes a few consecutive shots, our brain immediately wakes to the pattern that he's on a hot streak.

Intelligence itself is pattern recognition: Some of us quite naturally intuit the patterns of logic, music, economics, math, and mechanics, while others recognize the patterns of communication, design, emotions, ideas, and human behavior. Our quick recognition, intuitive understanding, and insightful projections of certain patterns are where our particular genius lies.

James Geary, in his book *I Is an Other*, observes,

> Our brains are always prospecting for pattern. . . . The brain is so fanatical about pattern that it will gladly generate patterns even where none exist. . . . The brain's pattern recognition circuits take raw data from the

senses, sort through it for apparent patterns, and use those patterns to determine a response.[13]

Like all analytical thinking, discerning God's activity involves this same "prospecting for pattern." Though our specific question may not be answered in Scripture, we look for biblical principles and *patterns* to apply. We consider the patterns of how God has used us in the past. We consider the strategies or patterns that Satan has employed against us—patterns of temptation, weakness, and sin (2 Corinthians 2:11; Ephesians 6:11). We analyze the patterns of our circumstances and notice what's out of sequence. We summon the patterns of our heart—its history of passions, desires, and ambitions. This is not spooky. This is how God made our minds—this is how we think. And because God is active in our lives and circumstances, lo and behold, there are many patterns to be discovered—many traces of intelligent activity.

Our intellect can thumb its nose at pattern finding because it's suspicious (and rightly so) of the reckless, deterministic, sloppy, and superstitious ways that patterns are often applied—for example, *They were the* seventh *person to apply for the job, so let's hire them!*

But intellectualism involves the same "prospecting for pattern," only searching for more subtle and "sophisticated" patterns. Intellectualism, for example, delights to find patterns of irony, metaphor, and chiastic structure in Scripture, but for some reason finds numeric patterns (3, 7, 40, 666) lowbrow and uncultured.

Yet pattern recognition is how all of us make sense out of nonsense. And since it plays such a significant role in spiritual discernment, we need to get better at it: more prayerful, more discerning, less superstitious, less snobbish. When our earthly minds see a correlation between our good works and how much

God loves us, or when patterns seem to indicate that God is angry or disinterested, we submit such observation (and all observation) to the truth of Scripture, which tells us no such patterns exist for believers. When we continue in sin and experience no correlating repercussions, we believe a correlation exists by faith in God's Word. This is how we grow in discernment: the reforming and refining of our pattern recognition according to the truth of God's Word.

Last, we should register in our minds that more patterns exist than ones we're aware of. My wife is an artist and can find beauty in things that others may find odd. And other artists tend to like these same things. Because I don't get it, I have two choices: believe art is a sham and artists pretend to see patterns when they don't; or believe there are ethereal patterns that I—and my friends at the bowling alley—don't see so well. I go with the latter.

Digression: Intuitive Thinking

In what *AdWeek* called the best ad campaign of the decade, a cool, laid-back hipster introduces himself as an Apple computer ("Hi, I'm a Mac") and stands next to a nerd claiming to be a PC ("And I'm a PC"). The ads resonated because there was something mildly true in the caricatures. The mildly true part is that people process information either intuitively or concretely (*intuitive* versus *sensing* on the Myers-Briggs Type Indicator).

We have an innate bias in processing spiritual information, an epistemological wiring toward the intuitive or concrete: Macs or PCs. Unless trumped by biblical conviction, our partiality will assert itself in a preferred style of worship, in doctrinal leanings, and—quite significantly—in how we discern God's will.

Discernment of God's will sorts out along this Mac-PC divide, and my intent here is not to choose sides or resolve the exegetical issues that cement that divide. I do, however, think a little clarity on intuitive thinking would be helpful all the way around.

Intuitive thoughts blink into the mind unannounced, poof, like Endora on *Bewitched*. This mysterious entrance leads some to identify these thoughts as the Spirit's leading and others to identify them as nonsense. Recent studies in neurology back neither assumption.

To keep us from cognitive overload, many of the smaller observations we take in from our surroundings—a person's shifty eyes, the perspiration on their forehead, the laundry bag in their hands, etc.—are processed at the unconscious level in the brain's limbic system. Having made its observations, the limbic system passes its evaluations to the conscious, reasoning side of the brain in the form of a singular impression, a gut feeling: *This guy's a bank robber.*[14]

This is what makes intuition seem both mysterious and emotional—*How did I just know he was a bank robber?*—when it's really the product of observation made at the subconscious level. This intuition, however, needs to be cross-examined by the reasoning mind, which might conclude, *This person is headed to the laundromat.*

Intuitive thinking is our own pattern prospecting done at the subconscious level. It is not inspired, but it is not irrational, either. It is simply more data to be culled by a Scripture-saturated, Spirit-filled mind. This is not to say we don't get impressions from God or that these impressions don't come to us through our intuitive faculties. It is only to say that impressions and intuition are not the same, and their striking similarity should cause us to be stingy with the phrase "the Lord told me."

Need to Know

We had just been to a funeral. One of Shane's friends had died of an overdose. A nineteen-year-old kid who had gotten high, nodded off, and never woke up. After the funeral, Shane, Mark (another of Shane's friends), and I went back to our house. Mark, an addict himself, had maintained a cool, disinterested presence throughout the funeral. Upon arriving home, Shane and I went inside while Mark stayed on the porch, sucking oxygen through his cigarettes as though the sudden drop into reality was a deep-sea dive.

I was sitting in the living room when I erupted out of my seat, tromped outside, and said, "Listen, Mark. You're going to be dead in a year. This time next fall, Shane and I will be at your funeral, and your only way out is Jesus. You know enough to know that Jesus is real and what I'm telling you is true."

Well, when I was done talking, tears ran down Mark's face from under his sunglasses, and with complete sincerity, Mark asked Jesus into his life. I've never been that blunt or rude, certainly not in communicating the gospel. But I felt constrained, propelled, as if I had no choice and could do nothing other. There was nothing debatable about the sensation.

Now, some believe that the direct guidance given by the Spirit in the book of Acts is due to the uniqueness of the apostolic age, an age without a New Testament to guide it. But I think the reason is simpler—less theological, anyway. I think the early Christians received special leading and direction because they needed it.

These men and women were actively proclaiming the gospel, aggressively pushing the boundaries of Christ's Kingdom. This requires real-time intelligence: whom to speak to, what to say, how to say it, where to go next. Quite honestly, our days don't require much of that: *Fries or onion rings, O Lord? Turn thine eyes to thy hungry servant.*

When our home became a mission, my approach to the day shifted from a mind-set of "What do I need to do today?" to "How does God want to use me today?" I was alert, seeking and initiating opportunities to disciple, encourage, correct, teach, witness to, love, listen to, and bless those around me. And in that mind-set, I really did experience that moment-by-moment empowerment and direction that animates the book of Acts.

There are warehouses of books written on God's will and how better to hear God's voice. But what if listening isn't the problem? What if it's a lack of involvement in the activities that require God to speak? It's possible, you know. The book of Acts is a record of the church on mission; we have no record of first-century believers going about the daily grind, still being moved about like chess pieces.

(Doing a final edit of this manuscript, I sadly note that Mark has since died of an overdose. At the funeral I was comforted not only by his response that day, but by the reality of the Spirit's promptings to speak with him.)

Where Are We?

We have been all over the map, literally, from roads in Sweden to memory palaces, but the inquiry into God's leading, and our being awake to it, is utterly irrelevant if not for one thing: that we desire God's will above all else and truly believe that his plan for us is better than our own aspirations. If not, our hearts can always find a way to subvert the process of discernment.

Personal bias can cause us to weight certain factors more than others, give significance to the insignificant, suppress evidence, and create patterns that validate desires. There's really no limit to the ways we can sabotage and slant our own investigations.

Because the heart sees what it wants to find, there is a singular safeguard in the discernment process: a heart that desires God's will above anything and everything else. This alone frees the compass to point where God wills. This is what makes the pursuit of God's will such a significant source of Christian wakefulness. The prerequisite need for objectivity in the investigation keeps us continually surrendering our will to his.

Powerball

I've borrowed quite a bit from the sciences in this chapter, so why not close with one more—from computer science.

In *The Unofficial Guide to Walt Disney World* there is a series of suggested tours designed to minimize waiting and maximize times on rides. But to be forthright, and perhaps just a little too thorough, the authors of the 2010 edition include this disclaimer:

> The 21 attractions in the Magic Kingdom One-day Touring
> Plan for Adults have a staggering 51,090,942,171,709,440,000
> possible touring plans. That's over 51 billion billion combina-
> tions, or roughly six times as many as the estimated number
> of grains of sand on Earth.[15]

Best-route problems are infamous in computer science, none more so than the "traveling salesman" who must find the fastest route between forty-eight cities. The equation to compute the options looks like this: $48 \times 47 \times 46 \ldots \times 2 \times 1$. That seems simple enough, but that equation yields 10^{61} permutations and would take a computer longer than the age of the universe to calculate. Google Maps and other programs only approximate.

These sorts of problems have a name: "NP Complete." The problem (or one aspect of it) is that without a simplifying algorithm (and one does not exist), future contingencies leave us with options beyond calculating. A mere string of forty-eight left 10^{61} possibilities.[16] This is how complicated the future is. This is how complicated *your* future is. God knows the future (and perhaps other possible futures), and we have here a hint of what such knowledge entails. We can trust him to lead us. We need to trust him: A near-infinite number of variables lie outside our control.

But, as it is, God is not the only one who has a plan for our lives, or ponders our future, or affects circumstances, or influences choices. His plans are not the only ones that call for our attention.

Homeland

In the Event of a Terrorist Attack

NORTH OF THE DANUBE and up the Olt River in Eastern Europe, the towns, farms, and people are sparse, rundown, and yet just a little bit quaint. Like Amish country under Soviet rule. But the sparseness and economic deprivation and communist hangover all disappear the moment you arrive in Râmnicu Vâlcea, about three hours northwest of Bucharest. It's Las Vegas in the Nevada desert.

Writer Yudhijit Bhattacharjee describes Râmnicu Vâlcea as something of a cross between Rodeo Drive and the Jersey Shore: "Expensive cars choke the streets . . . top-of-the-line BMWs, Audis, and Mercedes driven by twenty- and thirtysomething men sporting gold chains. . . . The streets are lined with gleaming storefronts—leather accessories, Italian fashions."[1]

When a town springs to life and everyone's pockets are bulging with cash and Lexus keys, it's usually because of the discovery of some new industry or natural resource. But that's not what's going on in Râmnicu Vâlcea.

> Among law enforcement officials around the world,
> the city of 120,000 has a nickname: Hackerville.
> . . . [Cybercrimes] have brought tens of millions of
> dollars into the area over the past decade, fueling the
> development of new apartment buildings, nightclubs,
> and shopping centers.[2]

The city's wealth is derived almost entirely from e-scams, identity theft, and corporate looting, a fact that can be identified by several dozen Western Unions within the radius of a few blocks. Day and night, hackers sit in the cafés, their stripped-down computers decaled like guitar cases as they troll back alleys of the Internet, looking for the smallest cracks to exploit. Once inside they'll steal anything, including you. Identity theft is the workhorse of the black-market economy.

Lion King

I think Râmnicu Vâlcea is a good picture of the machinations of spiritual evil: malevolent forces, heartless, soulless, unseen, and untraceable, everywhere and nowhere, never sleeping, always watching, baiting, probing, hunting for weakness, exploiting vulnerability—and always, always looking for a doorway in.

But while a cyber or terrorist attack captures a modern sense of fear and dread, it misses a nuance of the meaning in Scripture's metaphor, which likens Satan to a ravenous lion: "Be alert and of sober mind. Your enemy the devil prowls around like a roaring lion looking for someone to devour" (1 Peter 5:8, NIV).

A lot of posturing and image management goes on in the jungle, and lions do a lion's share of the trash talk. In reality, a few hyenas could dispose of a lion, and rather handily, if not for that bellicose roar. That roar is hype, spin, PR. You can hear it five miles in the distance. It's so terrifying that the lion's prey is literally paralyzed by fear—scared stiff. This is how the lion rules—not by power and majesty, but by fear and intimidation, like a third-world dictator, like a drug lord . . . like Satan.

And here's another nuance: The lion Peter describes does not consume people but faith, and that's a pretty awful prospect—ultimate and eternal identity theft.

But Scripture's warning is to "be awake," not scared, and a serious threat will wake you up. That's certainly been the case with cyber, as well as airport, security. You want to see vigilance? Try getting on your plane with more than four ounces of toothpaste in your carry-on. It's ironic that danger would be the means to greater watchfulness, but what about the Christian life is not ironic? If you think about it, no one is more responsible for the great creeds of the Christian faith than the heretics who inspired them.

So this is the prelude to our topic: spiritual battle. Amidst the calls to wakefulness and watchfulness in the New Testament, there is considerable urgency surrounding spiritual battle and the designs and intent of evil. In a word, we are *prey*. And because we have no idea of what's going on out there and no idea where "out there" is, we're going to follow very closely Ephesians 6:10-20, the apostle Paul's discourse on this battle. Here's a representative chunk:

> Finally, be strong in the Lord and in the strength of his might. Put on the whole armor of God, that you may be able to stand against the schemes of the devil. For we do not wrestle against flesh and blood, but against the rulers, against the authorities, against the cosmic powers over this present darkness, against the spiritual forces of evil in the heavenly places. Therefore take up the whole armor of God, that you may be able to withstand in the evil day, and having done all, to stand firm. EPHESIANS 6:10-13

The full text, verses 10-20, is by far the clearest description in the Bible concerning our war with evil. But even so, if you've experienced the battle, you can't help noticing the fifty or sixty thousand words that *aren't* there, that might explain to our satisfaction just what in the name of glory is going on down here. The Mick Jagger/Keith Richards line from "Sympathy for the Devil" comes to mind: "Pleased to meet you / Hope you guess my name / But what's puzzling you / is the nature of my game." *Puzzling* is an understatement. So is *game*. Hopefully our study will bring insight and clarity to both.

There's really no way to go through Ephesians 6:10-20 verse by verse in the space of a chapter. Not gonna happen. So what we'll do is pull out the main concepts and focus on them. Those concepts are as follows: The enemy and battle are *spiritual* in nature; the fight is *real*, as are casualties; there is *method* and *strategy* in the enemy's actions; and we are to *stand firm*, put on the full *armor of God*, and put to use our own *spiritual weapons*. Okay, one idea at a time . . .

The Opposite of Flesh and Blood

In Ephesians 6:12, Paul tells us that "our struggle is not against flesh and blood" (NIV). This seems self-evident, so why does Paul explain to us, as if we'd been left back in the third grade, that our enemy does not have a body? Surely we know this, right?

Well, here's something odd I've observed of myself. When my e-mail isn't working or the Internet is slow, I start punching— rather aggressively—the buttons on my keyboard. What's odd is that I *know* it's not a keyboard problem and I *know* that smashing the Return key is not going to fix it. The real problem is somewhere out there, somewhere in the universe of 1s and 0s and quarks and terabytes. *I know that.* But at the same time, I must not know it, or must not want to know it. Or maybe I want to believe that there's something I can do on a physical level to fix the problem, or maybe I want the problem to be the keyboard so I can retaliate. I can't very well punch the Internet, much as I would love to.

But hold those thoughts, because this reminds me of a story that I'm going to very much regret telling you.

As I mentioned in the last chapter, our home is unusual in that there tend to be quite a few interesting people hanging around ("interesting" being a euphemism for just about anything you'd like). We've been host to young people involved in some pretty dark things, and depending on who stops by, the spiritual climate changes very quickly. If you're one of those people who senses such things, you can feel the dark settle in like a cold front.

One evening there was a gathering going on downstairs, and Katie and I were upstairs in bed, almost asleep, when a group of kids stopped by—and I could feel that climate change. I just lay there in bed, somewhere between asleep and awake, dreaming and praying, when I heard ever-so-faint talking. It wasn't coming from downstairs. It wasn't really coming from anywhere. But I heard it.

Nothing rouses me when I'm half asleep, so I just dreamily thought to myself, *How interesting—those are probably demonic voices. I wonder what they're saying.* I tried to listen, but I was right in the ether between asleep and awake, a cognitive state somehow connected to my perception. I kept telling myself, *Remember a sentence, remember something*, but it was too late and I was asleep.

When I awoke I couldn't remember much, but somehow I had held on to a single sentence from the night before, so I wrote it down: "He doesn't, his enemy is."

I marveled at the brilliance: a language, fluently spoken, with intentional pronoun confusion, inverted sentence structure, words purposefully omitted, and carefully crafted ambiguity. It could be an arrogant boast ("He doesn't know who his enemy is"), a suspicious innuendo ("He doesn't know that someone he trusts is actually his enemy"), or a recriminating little mind game ("He is his own worst enemy"). The language was a conceptual rake: dragged across the mind, it was designed to snag loose threads of fear, mistrust, insecurity, and suspicion. It was evil in a dialectal form, which is simply fascinating.

"True story," as they say, but I didn't share it to illumine the goings-on in the spiritual world. Rather, I want to examine our posture toward these things. It's hard to believe. I'm not sure I believe me. Yet nothing is inconsistent with a biblical view of spiritual reality, so why is that? I think this is what Scripture is exposing in the statement "Our struggle is not against flesh and blood." We believe it, and we know it's true, but we are empiricists by default. That is, we intuitively think in terms of physical, mental, emotional, cultural, and circumstantial causation, but we must remind ourselves—quite intentionally—of the causative influence and interference of spiritual evil.

Evil will steal our joy, our sanity, our ministry, our money, our friends, our marriage, our kids—and we'll never see it coming. We'll simply chalk it up to a lousy day, lousy planning, lousy friends, lousy parenting, lousy job, lousy luck, lousy life. We'll simply see ourselves as tragic victims of Murphy's Law. And our response, rather than praying, will be banging the keyboard in the myriad ways we find to do that. On the plane of our experience, the real problems reside one flight down—and the real solutions reside one flight up. Our struggle is not against flesh and blood.

Real Battle, Real Blood
We Wish to Inform You That Tomorrow We Will Be Killed with Our Families. In 1999, Philip Gourevitch wrote a visceral account of the Rwanda genocide, and that's not a quote—that's the title. If you've ever received one of those formally written e-mails requesting a money transfer for the prince of Zaire or someplace, you have a context. In Rwanda, a group of Tutsis,

rounded up and awaiting massacre, dispatched this plea for government intervention in that stilted, formal, let-me-write-this-in-my-best-penmanship style. No one came to their aid. Not the government, not the UN, not the US—no one. And the Tutsi pastors who wrote the letter, along with 800,000 others, were massacred in the days that followed.[3]

Such news and such evil is commonplace in the world, which is why the world was indifferent to Rwanda's genocide. We're detached and desensitized; genocide is just one more heinous evil going on somewhere *out there*.

I think we tend to read Ephesians 6 with the same detachment. Persecuted believers in China, martyred saints in the Sudan, demonic activity in South America—obviously there's a battle, but it's somewhere *out there*. We sense we're viewing evil from the vantage point of safety, but it's more likely we're looking *out* from behind the barbed wire, not in. Prisoners and puppets lack the freedom to speak, and I don't feel particularly free. Not to speak about Satan or spiritual battle or demons or evil, not even with Christians. Why is that?

In the text, evil is described as an invading army, which is a wonderful metaphor, except that it's not a metaphor. If you don't believe in invisible armies, just look at a drop of water under a microscope. How exactly would you describe the monsters swimming around in there? Are they a metaphor? Or what about a virus—HIV or influenza? Turns out there are lots of nonmetaphoric invisible armies out there with the selfsame goal of infecting, colonizing, controlling, and ultimately using humans as incubators to replicate and spread to other living hosts. And if you consider doctors to be knowledgeable about such things, by faith, you'd get a vaccine. Ephesians 6:10-20 is saying that the war, the battle, and the army are real. Get a vaccine.

We haven't had the same face-to-face relationship with evil as the rest of the world. There's not much famine or plague on our side of the tracks, and it's left us adolescent in our grasp of evil. I know it's left me this way.

In the calendar year of campus ministry, December is a time to pull away from campus, to rest, and to attend to more domestic affairs. One particular December, no sooner had I taken my leave than our finances fell down a hole. No paycheck, no money to pay the bills, no presents for under the tree—*Merry Christmas, Bedford Falls, merry Christmas.*

I was in my study, irritated with God for allowing calamity to intrude on my vacation, when the television caught my eye with a story running on the local news. A town close by was preparing for the boat ride commemorating George Washington's crossing of the Delaware. The Brits, who had approached the war like a cricket match, had been caught completely off guard when Washington attacked on Christmas Eve. It's probably the biggest reason we don't have a picture of the Queen Mum hanging over the fireplace.

God used the newscast to realign my thinking. I had lost sight of the war. I had forgotten that in a war, unlike dodgeball, you don't get to call "time out." You don't get to tell the enemy you're on vacation. Lack of persecution and a strong belief in God's sovereignty had led me to think of the battle as staged—like one of those weekend Civil War reenactments.

Enduring engagement in this war hinges on the capacity to process real pain and loss. Someone with a naive view of the conflict—one that doesn't account for casualties or blames God for them—is headed for a rough go. Somehow, first-century believers retained an unshakable belief in God's sovereignty, yet experienced neither shock nor confusion when the clashing of kingdoms resulted in death . . . or worse. In writing Acts, for example, Luke feels no need to explain why Peter's friends watch him get rescued and Stephen's family watch him get buried. Very different stories. Side by side. No editorial comment.

Proceeding from Jesus' temptation in the wilderness, Scripture tells us that Satan "left him until an opportune time" (Luke 4:13, NIV), and by *opportune* it surely doesn't mean opportune for Jesus. Evil has a will and agenda of its own. Think of an angel needing to wake Joseph in the middle of the night to escape a massacre (Matthew 2:13-15). That sounds real, not staged. Sounds like he'd better do it.

Our choices and actions matter very much to the outcome, or why would Paul even write Ephesians 6:10-20? God has unlimited power, but there are contingencies in its exercise, some of which we are aware of (sin, prayer, unbelief, etc.) and some of which we are not (see Job 1). Although God reigns and the war with evil will ultimately be won, that doesn't imply or ensure that any particular battle will be.

Spiritual battle brings into conflict, at least in the human mind, certain theological truths: God's sovereign control, the reality of pain and suffering, the power of our actions and our inaction, the role of prayer, and the volition and influence of evil. The way wisdom solves such problems is to keep all truths in dynamic tension, not forcing a fit or disposing of one truth for another. In toggling truth, we keep all truth in play. And in spiritual battle we need all of it.

Well, we should move on to the battle itself, but having never been in a war myself, I want to call a quick time-out to fix our uniforms . . .

An Important Corrective: Scarier than God?

If you've ever looked up your symptoms on WebMD, you know that the journey from ignorance to paranoia is a short one—poison ivy and meningitis both start with a rash. It's a journey Paul wishes to avoid with this subject, and so woven into this text—and the letter as a whole—is what I'll call measured caution.

A spiritual atlas of the world would, I think, show some

locations as more wild and less tamed than others. During my time there, Rutgers University was one of those places, and the spiritual climate was sticky and oppressive, like humidity or bug spray or something. But as they say, it isn't paranoia if someone *really is* out to get you, and we were as paranoid as Ichabod Crane returning from the harvest party.

One night I had a horrible nightmare. I dreamed that something demonic had broken into our home, which my subconscious rendered as a circus clown or Christmas nutcracker. The thing was attacking me, and in the dream I simply knew that the only way to beat the thing off was to punch it in the stomach as hard as I possibly could. I woke up on top of Katie, my nine-months-pregnant wife, fist cocked, about to punch our unborn baby.

That certainly woke me to the spiritual battle but spun me out in the other direction. At night I'd patrol the hallways exorcising whatever was or wasn't there—"I banish thee to the abyss, foul spirit; I bind thee and roll thee in the blood of the Lord Jesus, and punt thee to the outer darkness, where thou shalt wail and gnash thy teeth."

I'm sure there are times to assert our authority in Christ, confronting something overtly demonic. The disciples did. But it's a fine line, and inclinations toward superstition or paranoia are clear signs of crossing it. I had crossed it, and as Paul penned Ephesians 6:10-20, there's reason to believe the Ephesians had as well.

The Ephesians were well acquainted with spiritual evil, and that's observable in their unique response to the gospel. Acts 19:19 (NIV) reports, "A number who had practiced sorcery brought their scrolls together and burned them publicly." Biblical scholar Bruce Metzger states that "of all ancient Graeco-Roman cities, Ephesus . . . was by far the most hospitable to magicians, sorcerers, and charlatans of all sorts."[4] Ephesus was the Salem, Massachusetts, of the ancient world.

This explains the emphasis on spiritual warfare throughout the letter, not just the final chapter. For example, when Paul declares the authority of Jesus to be "above every name that is named" (Ephesians 1:21), he's alluding to the practice of "naming [reciting] names," an ancient magic ritual for invoking spirits (seen popularly in the Harry Potter books, as Harry's mortal enemy, Lord Voldemort, bears the title "He-Who-Must-Not-Be-Named"). Using this imagery, Paul impresses upon the Ephesians that invoking any name against Jesus amounts to bringing a knife to a gunfight.

The need for such encouragement suggests that the Ephesians were intimidated by the powers of darkness that swirled about their city, powers no doubt connected to the cultic worship of the goddess Artemis. And who wouldn't be? The early Christians believed Artemis to be a demon, and her temple and statue were mammoth structures that towered over the city. It would be like living on Ellis Island if the Statue of Liberty were the Statue of Satan. What they needed to know was that Christ's power was "incomparably great[er]" (Ephesians 1:19, NIV) than all the evil in Ephesus.

It's often observed that Christians fall into the trap of either being too focused on Satan or ignoring him altogether. That's probably true, but as stated, it sounds as if the answer is to just "mellow out," and that's not Scripture's perspective. The problem is not in "seeing a demon behind every bush"; it's in not seeing the more powerful Son of God standing behind every demon. The corrective is recognition of the superior power of "the Lord and . . . the strength of his might" (Ephesians 6:10).

And now we can get on with the battle.

Satan's Schemes

Put on the whole armor of God, that you may be able to stand against the schemes of the devil.   EPHESIANS 6:11

In Ephesians 6:11, the word *schemes* is accurate but not very helpful because *schemes* sounds harmless, like *naughty* or *mischief*—the kind of trouble Garfield the cat might get into. But what *schemes* is intended to communicate is the intelligent, premeditated plans of evil: plans like Himmler's for the Jewish race or the plan of ISIS for its caliphate. In contrast to the mindless path of disease and tornadoes (natural evil), demonic evil is characterized by strategic thought.

A remarkable depiction of demonic "strategy" can be found in the second book of C. S. Lewis's space trilogy. In *Perelandra*, the Genesis account is recreated with a new Eve in a new Eden, and the new Eden is the planet Venus. The hero of the story, Ransom, finds himself marooned on Venus, locked in a struggle with Satan for the soul of Eve. Satan, sitting side by side with Ransom, is bound from physically harming him but nevertheless finds a means of torment.

> The Un-man began to speak. It did not even look in Ransom's direction; slowly and cumbrously, as if by some machinery that needed oiling, it made its mouth and lips pronounce his name.
>
> "Ransom," it said.
>
> "Well?" said Ransom.
>
> "Nothing," said the Un-man. . . .
>
> "Ransom," it said again.
>
> "What is it?" said Ransom sharply.
>
> "Nothing," said the Un-man. . . .
>
> Again there was silence; and again, about a minute later, the horrible mouth said:
>
> "Ransom!" This time he made no reply. Another minute and it uttered his name again; and then, like a minute gun, "Ransom . . . Ransom . . . Ransom," perhaps a hundred times.
>
> "What the Hell do you want?" he roared at last.
>
> "Nothing," said the voice. Next time he determined

not to answer; but when it had called on him a thousand times he found himself answering whether he would or no, and "Nothing," came the reply. . . . What chilled and almost cowed him was the union of malice with something nearly childish. . . . Indeed no imagined horror could have surpassed the sense which grew within him as the slow hours passed.[5]

Brilliantly, Lewis uses the smallest sample of evil to demonstrate just how evil evil is. And what betrays demonic intention is strategy. A method to the madness.

In the 1940s, Dutch psychologist Adriaan de Groot attempted to quantify the difference between a good chess player and a great chess player, and his research turned up something quite interesting. Chess masters, it turned out, weren't smarter than average chess players. They didn't think more moves ahead, and they didn't have better strategy. A chess master simply knew the right move to make, not so much thinking about the chessboard as reacting to it.

A study of the player's eye movements showed that the chess masters weren't staring at any particular place on the board, but rather absorbing the entire pattern of the chessboard. In fractions of seconds the new chess pattern was cross-referenced with a database of patterns stored from years of playing. The result of the internal data search was an intuitive sense of the "right" move. What de Groot discovered is that the brilliance of strategists lies in pattern recognition, fine-tuned by exhaustive practice.[6]

This is as true in the spiritual realm as anyplace else. The apostle Paul claimed to be well aware of the devil's schemes, and no doubt he was, for the longer you engage in the spiritual war, the more patterns you see. When a mature Christian looks around, sniffs the air, and suggests that something doesn't feel right, it's not really any different than a seasoned gunnery sergeant observing the same on a battlefield. It's inference based on pattern recognition, recognition heightened and honed by experience.

The patterns of spiritual warfare found in Scripture provide general templates: the pattern of Adam's temptation, David's, and Jesus'. From the Bible we can infer the patterns of sin and temptations each faced. But to this database we continually add our own experience—how evil tests and tempts *us*. This is another way God uses evil for good, bringing to our awareness areas of sin and arrested development.

I recently watched a documentary on the Cold War that centered on the life of Dieter Wendland, just a regular guy, now in his sixties, who grew up in Germany. Like most teenagers of the sixties, Dieter followed the cultural trends of the day, sporting Roy Orbison sunglasses and listening to the Beatles. But Dieter lived in *East* Germany, and when his enthusiasm for Western culture led him to hang a Woodstock poster on his wall, he came to the attention of the Stasi, East Germany's secret police. The Stasi controlled a web of some 90,000 agents and 200,000 informants. By the 1980s they had collected information on nearly a third of East Germany's citizens, eighty-one miles' worth of files—including Dieter's.

When the Cold War ended and the Berlin Wall came down, Dieter, like many East Germans, applied to see the contents of his Stasi file. What Dieter found was horrifying: a three-hundred-page dossier, the contents of which contained a meticulous plan to sabotage his adult life and infiltrate his most intimate relationships.[7]

Can you imagine that? Try, because it's doubtful the Stasi knew more about Dieter Wendland than evil knows about you. Evil thinks about you. No reason to be alarmed—just alert.

Between 1940 and 1941, C. S. Lewis cataloged thirty-one of the more familiar schemes employed by the enemy. They were eventually collected and published under the title *The Screwtape*

Letters. Lewis found *Letters* disturbing to write, stating he would never engage in another project that required so much reflection from evil's point of view. As a satire, the book offers the critique that we carry on our lives oblivious to the plans of evil and, failing to recognize them, fail to respond.

And it's to our "response" the text turns.

Stand Firm

> So that when the day of evil comes, you may be able to
> stand your ground, and after you have done everything,
> to stand. Stand firm then . . .   EPHESIANS 6:13-14, NIV

No fewer than three times, the above passage tells us to stand firm against the devil's schemes. This is our strategic objective, and it's a rather underwhelming one. But there's a method to the apparent mediocrity, and it's found in the grammatical train wreck that is Ephesians 6:13-14.

The awkward phrasing—essentially, "stand, and after standing, stand firm"—draws our attention to the fact that a passive verb (*stand*) is being used in a very active way. It would be like a crowd at a football game standing to their feet and roaring, "PLAY DEAD," "REMAIN INERT," "HIBERNATE." Quite intentionally, we find the word *stand* where the text would lead us to expect *march*.

In his dissertation on power and magic in Ephesus, Clinton Arnold suggests that this is meant to communicate something important about spiritual battle: that standing our ground *is* marching forward.[8] "When believers 'endure' in their faith," says Gregory Beale in his commentary on Revelation, "they are . . . 'conquering' by not compromising."[9] To put it in words as grammatically ungraceful as Paul's: The only thing accomplished in resisting temptation is not merely not sinning—something more is being accomplished.

In trial and testing, we feel the stain of actions merely contemplated. Rancor or desertion or rebellion well up within us, and at least for a moment we rally to its side. Win, lose, or draw—we're ashamed of that part of us willing to sell out. This is how it feels, anyway. The truth is, in holding our ground, we've won. We've actually marched forward. Why the victory feels hollow, like a fifth-place trophy, is because of the illusion that we control territory we merely occupy.

On a map, the Kurram Valley, Orakzai, and North Waziristan are all snugly within the northwest border of Pakistan. As the Pakistani government is an official ally of America in the war on terror, we could conclude that these regions are free from terrorists. But they are not free from terrorists; they are Disneyland for terrorists. Though these territories lay within the borders of Pakistan, it's a misnomer to say that they are under the government's control. The enemy is free here to do whatever he wants.

We likewise assume that our speech, appetites, thoughts, ambitions, and so forth are all safely within the borders of our control, and that we are controlled by Christ. But this just isn't so. As in Pakistan, territory owned and territory occupied are two different things. If the enemy can march in at any time and do whatever he pleases, it's just not true to say an area is under the Spirit's control. And most of us have these areas: areas in which, given certain circumstances, we'll capitulate to sin with little or no resistance.

When we say no to temptation, we do not simply keep the enemy out; we take control of the unsecured territories within our own borders. We march forward by standing still. And here again, we cross paths with God's purposive use of evil: It conscripts us into battle, leaving us no option but to fight. This is how God made an army out of Israel: He let the Philistines move next door. They had no choice *but* to fight for their borders and fully occupy the land.

If we only stood firm in those areas where we habitually surrender, if we could just hold out once, twice . . . we could establish a border, turn the tide, redraw the boundary line between evil and us. If we could just stand.

Let me make another observation about standing firm. Many years after his bestselling book *People of the Lie*, renowned psychiatrist M. Scott Peck returned to his study of ontological evil. The book *Glimpses of the Devil* follows Peck and a team of clinical researchers as they study two possible cases of demon possession, one of which was a woman named Beccah who lived in New York City. During the interviews, Beccah's head "started to move back and forth in a strange weaving pattern that looked remarkably like that of a cobra."[10] The woman, who had previously seemed weak and sick, became incredibly strong and fought against the team attempting to restrain her. "Our intuitive minds," Peck wrote, "were so powerfully affected that what we *saw* was a snake."[11]

When Peck and his team reviewed video of the sessions, little of what they experienced was observable, and such is the power of Satan to project on the mind and magnify fear. But unlike Peck's demonic encounter, Paul's instruction to the Ephesians on spiritual battle is curiously free of formula prayers, ritual, or drama.

Ephesus was the known center of magic in the ancient world, a Hogwarts of charms and incantations. Central to this reputation was the Ephesian *Grammatica*, a list of six magical names (*saki, kataski, lix, tetrax, damnameneus, aision*) that could be recited for any number of reasons, one of which was the exorcism of a person demonized.

So the Ephesians were familiar with exorcisms and formulaic prayers for deliverance—and yet Paul doesn't mention any of it. Doesn't suggest any of it. He rather gives the unremarkable instruction to pursue spiritual freedom and protection through vigilance in prayer, faith, and holiness.

Maybe we can pull things together with this analogy. We just had the Orkin pest guy out to our house because of a possible mice "infestation" (his lovely word, not mine). According to Mr. Orkin, rodent problems are best dealt with through prevention, not intervention. Keep your house clean and you won't get rodents and you won't need Orkin. Don't keep it clean and, well . . . just keep it clean.

Armor of God

> Therefore take up the whole armor of God, that you
> may be able to withstand in the evil day. . . . Stand
> therefore, having fastened on the belt of truth, and
> having put on the breastplate of righteousness . . . take
> up the shield of faith, . . . the helmet of salvation, and
> the sword of the Spirit. EPHESIANS 6:13-18

Throughout the letter to this point (Ephesians 1–5), Paul has emphasized the need for righteousness, truth, faith, and prayer. But he's done so with a positive spin, from the perspective of spiritual health: *Do these things and you'll be blessed!* At the end of the letter, he circles back to the same topics by way of review, but he examines them from the angle of liability: Ignoring these issues will make people vulnerable to evil. Sanctification is complicated by its wartime setting, a setting that makes any gap in spiritual development equivalent to a hole in one's armor.

Most teaching and commentary on this "spiritual armor" seems, in my opinion, to get overly entangled in military minutiae. Whether the Roman breastplate buckled in the front or had embossed abs like Batman's body suit doesn't address the most fundamental question. So we're going to skip through the particulars and address the pressing question: What does it mean to wear this stuff?

Insight comes from considering the specific nature of evil's attack. Consider the word *schism*. It's an ugly word, and it stands in contrast to its whole-grain antonym, *integrity*. *Integrity* refers to internal consistency, and it is a feature of God's design found throughout creation. *Schism* is the splitting apart or dividing of something created to be whole. Schism is evil's corrosive method of disintegrating godly integrity.

When Satan attacks the mind, the cracked doorway is a breach in the mind's integrity: Drugs fragment consciousness, anxiety and fear divide the mind, lies and deceit bifurcate reality, trauma disassociates mind from body, guilt and shame turn the mind against itself, and so on and so forth. The gaps in our integrity are where we are vulnerable to a splinter.

In the realm of relationships gossip, envy, slander, and unforgiveness sever relational ties, while isolation, rejection, and bitterness single us out and splinter us off. Satan exploits the gaps that compromise the integrity of the community.

In the moral realm it is our sin and hypocrisy that create the divide, forming a gulf between what we project and who we are—what we say and what we do. The greater the gap between perception and reality, beliefs and actions, truth and lies, the easier to splinter.

In the spiritual realm, the integrity of our identity in Christ is maintained by faith. Vulnerability exists in that gap between what is true of us in Christ and what we functionally believe to be true. We are forgiven, we are God's children, we have eternal life, and God's Spirit indwells us. The extent to which we shrink back and disbelieve is the gap between head and helmet.

Paul's letter to the Ephesians divides neatly in two. Chapters 1 through 3 are a call to *believe* rightly and live out our new identity in Christ. Chapters 4 through 6 are a call to *live* rightly. As a summary of the letter, the armor of Ephesians 6:13 is a call to "gapless" living in faith and in practice. Putting on the armor means closing the gaps. The gaps in our speech are closed by *speaking truth*; gaps of hypocrisy are eliminated through *righteous living*; gaps in the mind are protected by renewing in the *Word*; and gaps of doubt and disbelief are *shielded by faith*.

Clearly, we don't live sinlessly—no one's armor fits like spandex. This passage, rather, is a charge to *pursue* "gapless living," *repent* of glaring gaps and gaping holes, and *reconcile* (confess, forgive) immediately when and where gaps occur, affording Satan nothing to exploit.

Lastly, a walk of integrity in faith and practice avails us of God's empowerment. And here, if Paul were writing today, he might jump from the protective metaphor of armor to that of an electrified fence. Closing gaps doesn't merely prevent break-ins; it enables the Spirit's power to flow unhindered to us and through us.

The extent to which we trust in, walk in, and live out our new identity in Christ is the extent of our armor, the extent of divine empowerment and protection.

Guns of Our Own

Gentlemen, please. Give me a moment of your time. A man is going to come in. . . . We ask that you remain in your seats; the doors will close and nobody is allowed to leave. You will also not be allowed to use your mobile phones. Do not worry; if you do everything that is asked of you, nothing will happen. Continue eating and don't ask for your bill. The boss will pay. Thank you.[12]

This account is from patrons at the Las Palmas restaurant in Culiacan, Mexico. The important dinner guest that night was Mexico's chief drug lord, Joaquín Guzmán Loera, or "El Chapo." At the time of this writing he's in custody, in the process of being extradited to the US, because Mexican prisons are merely hotels for the truly wicked. Crime and corruption reign in Mexico. Many people believe that the war with evil has already been lost and that resistance is pointless, so they've chosen a strategy of accommodation. "The hope," says one US counter-drug official, "is that the people will rise up and say, 'No More!'"[13] Until then, evil reigns; it reigns whenever and wherever we accommodate it.

In the last verses of the Ephesians text, we are finally on the offense. Proactive instead of reactive.

> And take the helmet of salvation, and the sword of the
> Spirit, which is the word of God, praying at all times in
> the Spirit, with all prayer and supplication. To that end
> keep alert with all perseverance, making supplication for
> all the saints. EPHESIANS 6:17-18

Of all people who might presume upon God for special protection, you'd have to put the apostle Paul—writer of Scripture, apostle to the nations—at the top of that list. And yet, can you think of anyone who took it less for granted? Paul never presumes; he prays. He prays "unceasingly" (1 Thessalonians 5:17, DLNT) and bundles in his beefy arms as much prayer support as he can gather.

The reason I didn't set aside time to pray this morning is simple: I presumed upon God's protection and power—just figured it would be there like my breakfast cereal. That's spiritually reckless. Like careless driving, it presumes that an accident will never happen. Paul never assumed things would just work out, never assumed God's sovereignty ensured a favorable outcome, never assumed anything—and prayed about everything. I love that about him.

God has given us a significant "say-so" against the forces of chaos and darkness that press in on us. Prayer is that "say-so."[14]

In the text, prayer is paired with Scripture, not because they go nicely together (though they do) but because Scripture, like prayer, is an offensive endeavor—a preemptive activity, a drill practiced daily. When the "day of evil" (Ephesians 6:13, NIV) comes, it's too late to open your Bible, because power and protection are not in the Bible—they are in the transfer of its truth to our head and heart. Apart from daily intake of scriptural truth, there is no battle, only a beating.

While more could and should be said about both prayer and Scripture, I used up my words on aspects of the battle, and now I'm plumb out. So we'll leave things here and move to a not-so-unrelated topic: community. It's said that only modern evangelicalism, with its emphasis on autonomy, has dared pit the individual believer, all alone in his or her prayer closet, against the powers of darkness.

Something rings true there: There's a communal aspect missing from our faith, and that's a big problem because community is one of those things we need to stay awake. In a city, nobody sleeps.

4

Sleepless Cities
The Metabolism of Community

IN THE OPENING DECADES of the twentieth century, in the Bavarian town of Herzogenaurach, two brothers, Adi and Rudi Dassler, began making athletic shoes in the laundry room of their mother's basement. Adi was a shoe cobbler by trade.

He was also a sports enthusiast and recognized the marketing opportunity afforded by the 1936 Olympics being hosted in mother Germany. So he packed up a few pairs of running spikes, drove from Bavaria to the Olympic Village in Germany, and presented a pair to the international track star Jesse Owens. Owens won four gold medals wearing the Dasslers' shoes. Overnight, Adi and Rudi went from making clogs for the bürgermeister to running an international shoe company. This was a celebrity endorsement before celebrity endorsements.

In the years leading up to World War II, the Dasslers' shoe company grew aggressively, with Adi focusing on design and production and Rudi, the more outgoing of the two, working in sales. But as the company expanded, the brothers' relationship began to deteriorate. Maybe it was success or maybe it was rivalry, but they found they couldn't agree on anything—not politics, not the future of the company, and most certainly not on the other's choice of a spouse (the sister-in-laws couldn't stand each other either).

Tensions between brothers escalated during the war. Rudi was captured by the Americans, which, all things considered, was like being in protective custody—until, that is, the US military came to possess documents linking Rudi to the Nazi Party. Rudi wasn't in the Nazi Party, but that's the funny, not-so-funny part: Those documents were forged and supplied by his brother. A new low, even for Adi.

The last straw, which finally dissolved the company, was a misunderstanding that took place during the Allied bombing of the brothers' town of Herzogenaurach. Adi and his wife climbed into the family bomb shelter, only to find it occupied by Rudi and his family.

"Here are the bloody bastards again," Adi said, referring to the Allied warplanes. However, Rudi misunderstood. He thought his brother was talking about him and his family, and you can totally picture this, can't you?

In 1948 the business split, and on opposite sides of the river that runs directly through Herzogenaurach, Adi and Rudi set up rival shoe companies. Adi called his company Adidas; Rudi called his Ruda before later changing it to Puma, which in German means "cougar."[1]

The families, and the town, were torn apart by the feud (Adi and Rudi remained unreconciled; their graves are situated on opposite ends of the village cemetery). Everyone in Herzogenaurach sided with one brother or the other, one company or the other, one shoe or the other.

It's a fascinating story, and I'd like to say there's a moral to it, but there isn't. Fueled by personal ambition, a drive for autonomy, and a divisive spirit, Adidas and Puma became two of the most successful brands in the world, and today both are worth several billion dollars. Financially, it's an unbelievable success story and a good place to start this chapter, because the Bible doesn't have any stories like this. Biblically speaking, community is everything, and a lack of it, an indifference to it, a distaste for it, or the deterioration of it is responsible for most of what ails us. There are no independent, autonomous, brother-against-brother, go-it-alone Christian success stories.

There's probably little need to be reminded that this is not a book about biblical community any more than it's about spiritual battle. Our interest is in spiritual wakefulness, and this necessarily brings us to the topic of community, because the writer of Hebrews sees a link.

Let us consider how we may spur one another on toward love and good deeds, not giving up meeting together, as some are in the habit of doing, but encouraging one another—and all the more as you see the Day approaching. HEBREWS 10:24-25, NIV

See to it, brothers and sisters, that none of you has a sinful, unbelieving heart that turns away from the living God. But encourage one another daily, as long as it is called "Today," so that none of you may be hardened by sin's deceitfulness. HEBREWS 3:12-13, NIV

Spiritual lethargy, mediocrity, unbelief, moral compromise, unthankfulness, loss of zeal, and lack of perspective are signs of spiritual entropy. Entropy is the scientific law that any system, closed or cut off, without new energy pouring into it, will move to a less ordered, more chaotic state. Think of Tom Hanks's castaway on an island with his best friend, a volleyball. That's an isolated system moving to a disordered state. It's a law (of thermo-dynamics), so it's nonnegotiable and as applicable to faith as it is to physics. But like the writer of Hebrews, you don't need to know entropy to recognize it or recognize that community (the infusion of outside energy) is the spiritual solution.

People Walk Faster in Cities

Geoffrey West is a theoretical physicist who has devoted his aca-demic life to reducing vast complexity into bite-size equations—*elegant* is the word for them, I think. Like Einstein, his interest has been the fundamental laws that explain the world around us, a world that is now urbanized. "For the first time in history, the majority of human beings live in urban areas."[2] So West set out to find the equivalent of $e=mc^2$ for an urban metropolis: a simple equation that would describe how and why a city grows.

West compiled every mind-numbing data point, from the sum total of electrical wire in Frankfurt to the number of college graduates in Boise. He amassed stats on gas stations and personal income, flu outbreaks and homicides, coffee shops and the walk-ing speed of pedestrians.

After two years of research, what West discovered is that all the roads and buses and crosswalks and skyscrapers and gridlock and everything else that makes up a city can be reduced to "a few exquisitely simple equations." Given the population of a city, West can predict, with 85 percent accuracy, everything from the "average income [to] the dimensions of its sewer system."[3]

According to West, cities operate upon a golden ratio of 1.15. That is, if you moved Jane Smith from a city of 500,000 to a city of one million, she would earn 15 percent more money, have 15 percent more restaurants in her neighborhood, possess a 15 percent higher education, file for 15 percent more pat-ents, and be 15 percent more likely to be victimized by violent crimes—and "whenever a city doubles in size, every measure of economic activity, from construction spending to the amount of bank deposits, *increases* by approximately 15 percent per capita."[4] Even "pace of life" statistics bear out this ratio: People actually do walk faster and talk faster in cities.

What was startling about the findings is that it's completely anomalous for how the world works. Regardless of what the system is, the physics of motion, mass, and complexity dictates that the bigger it is, the slower it runs. The heartbeat of an elephant is way slower than a human's, and a human's way slower than a gerbil's. Bigger system, slower metabolism. Logically, a city should be a slow and lumbering beast, like the DMV or the US State Department or an overcrowded classroom, where learning lags at the rate of the slowest learner. But cities defy that—or at least growing cities do.

The spiritual dynamics of community operate along similar lines—meaning they are synergistic, where the sum is greater than the parts. In community, our walk with God walks faster. Cities never sleep, and neither do we—spiritually speaking—when we're surrounded by a community of committed believers.

But every rule has exceptions, and that would be a city like Detroit. Detroit (though it now seems to be turning around) has in recent years operated like that overcrowded classroom. For a city to operate at that 1.15 ratio—to reverse entropy—it needs multiple resource streams pouring into it. Detroit had one: automobiles. And when that floundered, so did the city.

It goes without saying, but many Christian communities—churches, Bible studies, prayer groups, schools, youth groups—are like Detroit. Built on a dynamic leader or preaching, there's but a single river that runs through the community, and when that dries up . . .

But before going further, I should clarify this word *community*, or at least what I mean by it. *Christian community* is like Great Adventure. There is an actual amusement park called Great Adventure, and there is also an experience we call having a "great adventure." Sometimes going to Great Adventure is a great adventure; sometimes it's a great letdown or great mistake or great rip-off. It's the same with community. There's *the place*, the community where we worship, and then there's *the dynamic* of community—that life-giving, synergistic, spiritual dynamic that fuels faith and accelerates growth.

It's the *dynamic* of community we're interested in, and in my experience this dynamic can occur in a gathering of "two or three" (Matthew 18:20) or be absent from a gathering of two or three thousand. In thirty years of ministry, I've seen a lot of communities, been to a lot of communities—well over a thousand, I'm sure. All types, sizes, denominations, configurations, ethnicities, and states except Hawaii, Alaska, and Utah.

Why any particular community (the structure) lacks community (the dynamic) is indeed vexing, but where community flourishes, certain dynamics clearly are in place. We'll look at a few of those dynamics with the caveat that, for all I know, snake handling or duck hunting could be the key to community in Hawaii, Alaska, and Utah. After looking at dynamics, we'll circle back, and I'll tell you why I *hate* community.

Common Mission

So last year I was invited to a small Jesuit university in the Midwest to speak evangelistically on the subject of Jesus and religion. As it turned out, I hadn't actually been invited, but I didn't know that until I got there.

When I showed up on campus, I was met by three student leaders from the Christian fellowship, but not really. There was no Christian fellowship, no officers, no bylaws; just three guys named Grant, Kyle, and Ryan. Apparently, they had heard me speak at some conference and figured they'd have me come to their campus and "you know, do whatever."

At 7:00 p.m. we were all sitting in the student center, and as far as I knew I was speaking at a campus-wide event in an hour. But clearly something wasn't right: There was no publicity and no sign of an impending event, and Grant, Kyle, and Ryan were glancing around the student center as if a heist were in progress. Then Grant, I guess spotting someone, cryptically said to the others, "They know we're going to try to meet tonight."

And they finally explained the situation: Over the previous month, a drama had unfolded between the young men and the parochial administration. The university's policy was that only an approved Catholic priest could speak on matters of faith, and in light of the wife and children mentioned in my bio, I was clearly not a priest—or at least not a very good one.

And so the administration had expressly forbidden my coming to campus: no meeting room, no publicity, no sound system, no invitations, no event, period. But these guys had decided to do it anyway, and so I found myself hunkered down with an underground church of sorts: a few passionate believers who met together, prayed together, and purposed to proclaim the gospel in an environment hostile to their efforts and their faith.

Well, in for a dime, in for a dollar. I asked Grant, "What are we going to do?"

Grant said—and as I picture it now, he's speaking out of the side of his mouth, but really he wasn't—"There are meeting lounges in the basement of a building on the other side of campus. We'll try there."

"But how are students going to know about the meeting?" I asked Grant.

He said, "We're going to text everyone we know, tell them where and when, and see who shows up."

I liked this idea because I didn't have another one. So we walked across campus and down into the basement of some seventies-era building—forged in the architectural train-wreck of Catholic Modernism, when crucifixes were sleeked down to hood ornaments and Jesus took on the appearance of an Easter Island totem. There in the catacombs of Alfred E. Neuman Hall, the boys texted, and we waited to see who would come. By eight o'clock seventy to eighty students had packed the room. Grant was going to give it another ten minutes because people were still trickling in, but Bobby—who'd been standing lookout in the hall—rushed in looking panicked and said, "Mrs. Woodrow is coming."

Mrs. Woodrow was the dean of students. She wasn't a nun, but she had the biceps of one. Very intimidating. We all peeked out into the hallway, and sure enough, the Wicked Witch of the West was clomping down the linoleum runway, not looking pleased, no sir, not pleased at all. So Grant looked at me and said, "Just start. Just start the talk. It will be too awkward for her to stop the meeting if you're already talking." I liked this idea because I didn't have another one.

So I hopped up in front of everyone and just began talking. Ten seconds later I could see Mrs. Woodrow outside in the hallway. Grant was right: She wasn't going to interrupt me while I was talking. So I kept talking and didn't stop for an hour, and when I did, it was to give the students an opportunity to place their faith in Christ. During the entire talk, Mrs. Woodrow paced outside in the hallway.

When I finished and the students started to get up from their seats, Mrs. Woodrow plowed into the room. "Excuse me, excuse me. What is your name and who invited you here?"

"I'm just a friend of Grant, Kyle, and Ryan." That's all I said, and as it turned out, a lawyer couldn't have crafted it any better, because there were no rules about students having friends visit on campus. I mean, it was weird they had a fifty-year-old friend, but weird wasn't against school policy.

Afterward, we went back to one of their rooms to see what students had written on the comment cards.

"No way, April says she wants to hear more about Christ."

"Check this out, Mark says he trusted Christ."

"He did not!"

"Read it yourself."

It went on like that for a while, and I sat there listening, experiencing the Christian church as it was in the beginning, as it has come down to us today, and as it still is in many parts of the world. I experienced the church as a missional community.

By *missional*, I mean that Grant, Kyle, and Ryan were actively engaged in expanding Christ's Kingdom through spreading the message of the gospel. In the cosmic struggle, no good deed goes unpunished, so they were experiencing persecution in response to their evangelistic efforts. These two ingredients together—mission and persecution—create first-century, 1.15, biblical community.

I'm sure if ISIS or Al Qaeda took over America, much of the church's commitment and community problems would evaporate overnight (as well as a sizable chunk of "professing" Christians). But persecution is not within our control, and it's hard to imagine anyone requesting it. Mission is in our control, though. We can do something about that.

Grant, Kyle, and Ryan were not an official church or members of the Fellowship of Christian Something-or-Another. They were a tiny community of committed believers on a mission, or whatever your ecclesiology permits you to label such things. They had staked a Kingdom claim, like adopting a stretch of highway, and had taken ownership of their campus—fought for it, prayed for it, invested in it, and strategized how best to bring the gospel to the people around them.

Rallying a community together toward some unified effort to expand the Kingdom is the daunting challenge of spiritual leadership. Spiritual leaders have a task like Nehemiah in building the Kingdom wall: initiating the project, gathering people to the cause, setting the goals, dividing the labor, overcoming administrative and geographic hurdles, dispatching spiritual attack, and ultimately getting it done. Grant, Kyle, and Ryan weren't pastors, but they were spiritual leaders—and their community was unlike anything we're likely to experience until ISIS arrives.

Shared Bed

In a *New Yorker* article titled "Group Think," Malcolm Gladwell described the communal lifestyle of the original cast of *Saturday Night Live*, a relational dynamic responsible for the renaissance of modern comedy. Gladwell wrote:

> In the early days of "S.N.L." . . . everyone knew everyone and everyone was always in everyone else's business, and that fact goes a long way toward explaining the extraordinary chemistry among the show's cast. [John] Belushi would stay overnight at people's apartments, and he was notorious for getting hungry in the middle of the night and leaving spaghetti-sauce imprints all over the kitchen. . . . [Gilda] Radner would go to Jane Curtin's house and sit and watch Curtin and her husband, as if they were some strange species of mammal. . . . [Laraine] Newman would hang out at Radner's house, and Radner would be eating a gallon of ice cream and Newman would be snorting heroin. . . . "There we were," Newman recalls, "practicing our illnesses together."[5]

The cast members lived in an immersive community, which is an odd way to live for anyone except a college student. College is a brief experiment in communal living, but all of the hanging out and sharing "illnesses," to quote Newman, ends abruptly at graduation, with little or nothing to replace it. Christians engaged with campus ministry often have a terrible time acclimating to church in the real world, which may meet only once or twice a week.

But something could replace it—something needs to—and maybe that's "the home." It seems to me that in flourishing communities, housing and living situations play a creative role. The terms *parlor* or *salon* date back to when the home was a communal center, where people hung out, slept over, and shared illnesses, which at that time was probably the bubonic plague.

If you want a snapshot of the home as community and spiritual center, read Martin Luther's *Table Talk*. The household of Martin Luther (1483–1546) piled in dozens of boarders, students, houseguests, and colleagues, and if you can imagine, dinners were an open forum. The conversations and monologues were so interesting that no fewer than twelve individuals took to writing down the banter, capturing endearing moments like this:

> When Luther's puppy happened to be at the table,
> looked for a morsel from his master, and watched with
> open mouth and motionless eyes, [Luther] said, "Oh,
> if I could only pray the way this dog watches the meat!
> All his thoughts are concentrated on the piece of meat.
> Otherwise he has no thought, wish, or hope."[6]

The downside of publishing every spoken word at your dinner table is that there's no hiding your lesser insights, such as "Many devils are in woods, in waters, in wildernesses, and in dark pooly places." Oh, and just a heads-up, "Some are also in thick black clouds."[7] (Luther "unplugged" is like Kanye West "unplugged.") It's easy to imagine how animated those meals and discussions must have been. Yes sir, back before McMansions, and before pool tables and barbells demanded their own bedrooms, the home was a community center—and it could be again.

I remember clearly a very Lutheresque moment in our own

home. It was 3:02 a.m. when I came downstairs, and I remember because neon digits never let you forget. There was a group of about six or seven boys talking loudly and smoking cigarettes on the back porch. It was a Thursday night, and at the time, this wasn't unusual. We had two guys living with us who should have been in college but were instead getting their lives back on track. My son and several of his friends were enrolled in cyber-school, so every night was a weekend for them. A few more were just kind of wedged in that ever-yawning gap year.

For some reason the kids all smoked. It probably started with the ones who had been drug users, but the dominoes fell, including my precious son, and it still traumatizes me to see him with a cigarette propped in his mouth.

So anyway, it was 3:02 a.m., and things were noisier than usual downstairs, so I went down to check, and at the center of the commotion was a guy named Sam, who was a major dealer and drug supplier in town. Sam was panicked. He said he was experiencing some kind of demonic attack, and the boys were trying to pray with him, or for him, or against him, or whatever. It was confusing.

So I said to Sam, "Do you want to ask Jesus to come into your life?" Sam said yes, and I walked him through a simple prayer that we all prayed together, with the boys laying their hands on him. The radio was playing, and as we prayed, John Lennon's "Give Peace a Chance"—the stoners' anthem—came on. It was Sam's favorite song, so when it started everyone went a little crazy. I find it theologically painful to imagine that God had anything to do with it, but knowing him, he probably did.

It was an amazing moment, but that moment was 3:02 a.m. A lot happens in the human heart between midnight and dawn.

A couple of decades ago, a men's movement called Promise Keepers was going strong, and a lot of guys from a lot of churches went to their weekend conferences. If you went to one, you know that the program wasn't anything special; I'm sure pastors marveled at the commitments and recommitments made and wondered, *What on earth did you hear there that you didn't hear at church?* The answer is probably *nothing*, but there is *something* to that dynamic—that staying overnight.

Missionaries, church interns, college students, international students, exchange students—lots of people need a spare bedroom. Thankfully, John had one.

> When Jesus saw his mother there [at the cross], and the
> disciple whom he loved standing nearby, he said to her,
> "Woman, here is your son," and to the disciple, "Here is
> your mother." From that time on, this disciple took her
> into his home.   JOHN 19:26-27, NIV

Adopting, taking in boarders, living at single Christian guys' and girls' houses, staying overnight, taking part in community meals, going to house churches . . . there are a lot of ways to express and explore the home as communal center. I have to believe we can stretch beyond the creative boundaries of the potluck. I just have to.

Same Passion

The *SNL* commune is a distant cousin to the creative colony that formed in Montparnasse in early twentieth-century Paris, where artists and ideologues such as James Joyce, Pablo Picasso, Henri Matisse, F. Scott Fitzgerald, Ernest Hemingway, and Amedeo Modigliani incestuously mingled minds and bodies and consequently launched the modernist movement from Gertrude Stein's living room.[8] What *SNL* and Montparnasse share in common— besides a striking resemblance between Gertrude Stein and John Belushi—is that they are secular, godless versions of communal revival.

Revival occurs when God's Spirit stirs in the heart of a community, fanning to flame passion and zeal in a fresh, creative act, the effects of which spread far and wide from the incendiary spark. In the perverse and obscene we still feel the heat from Montparnasse, but what of it? Fires of prayer still burn from the living-room gatherings of the Moravians nearly three centuries ago.

In the early seventeenth century, persecuted believers fleeing from the Protestant wars (particularly Moravian or Bohemian believers) found refuge on the grounds of Nikolaus Zinzendorf's estate. The pious community was pummeled by the Spirit as the modest result of twenty-four men and twenty-four women committing to pray "hourly intercessions" every hour on the hour. The far less modest result was that the prayer meeting lasted for a hundred years.

Not long after the praying began, Zinzendorf met a converted slave from the West Indies. I forget the man's name and don't feel like looking it up, but his firsthand account of the slave trade was so captivating that Zinzendorf brought him back to his estate and his Moravian houseguests. The result was the first organized Protestant mission of the modern era as members of the community headed to St. Thomas to live and preach among the slaves. Missions expanded to Africa, America, and Russia: Before Zinzendorf died there were more than two thousand Moravian missionaries scattered from Greenland to South Africa.

The Moravian influence persists to this day, recently inspiring Pete Greig and the 24-7 Prayer movement. After a visit to Zinzendorf's estate, Greig figured, "Maybe . . . there was something in this Moravian nonstop prayer model that could help us to pray a bit more back home."[9] In September 1999, Greig and his friends began their experiment and found at the end of the month that they couldn't stop praying. They're still praying; thousands of prayer rooms in a hundred-plus countries have been initiated by the 24-7 Prayer movement, inspired by the Moravians.

Out of the small fellowship meeting in Zinzendorf's living room came modern missions, small-group Bible studies, mass printing and distribution of the Bible, and, oh yeah, the conversion of John Wesley, which led to another "revived" community, another living room, and what became the Great Awakening.

The Moravian community is "one-off," as they say. Totally unpredictable, totally unparalleled. But that 1.15 ratio of cities, that higher metabolism, holds true for any Christian community that is experiencing *real* community. And while we're on the subject of metabolism, I think you'll find this interesting . . .

Shared Sickness

Within the walls of a human cell is a remarkable little utopia, and ever since we first viewed it under a microscope, it has been the favored metaphor for dynamic community, whether it's a cell group at church or a terrorist cell.

The cell's citizenry is composed broadly of mitochondria. They work hard, die young (every six or seven days), and unceremoniously drop dead doing whatever it is they were doing. So as you might imagine, the streets of your cells are quite littered with their little bodies. But not to worry—the cell has an industrious sanitation department, and the autophagosomes tirelessly clean the streets, picking up mitochondria and hauling them off to the cell's garbage dumps, the lysosomes.

But something strange happens when we age. The cooperative little community unravels like a failed Marxist state. The autophagosomes stop doing their job, or, more accurately, stop doing it well. With a little shrug of their autophagosome shoulders—*meh*—they walk right past the refuse, and the bodies of dead mitochondria pile up until it looks like the living room of a hoarder. Basically, we die of a garbage strike.[10]

Garbage is always the death of us. Think of all the towns and communities wiped from the earth because their sanitation consisted of an open river running through town. And what is "sin" but garbage and Gehenna but a garbage dump? But it's not really the garbage that kills us; it's the sanitation. It's what we do with the garbage.

When a believing community starts to erode and you don't know why—well, now you know why. Somewhere there's an issue of sanitation—not of sin but its disposal. And what's that disposal? Confession.

In the fall of 1995, a miniature revival broke out on the campuses of some of the larger Christian colleges in the US, one of them being Wheaton College in Illinois. On Sunday, March 19, Wheaton's chapel service started at 7:00 p.m. with about seven hundred students and swelled to more than fifteen hundred as the worship and confession continued into Monday morning. As one participant observed:

> The "beautiful thing" was that when a person would confess sin, 20 to 50 students would gather around the person and pray for him. "There was a real spirit of love and acceptance. . . . You could not point a finger at anyone else," because "all of us there had been stripped bare before the throne of God." . . . Many went back to their rooms and returned with secular music discs, pornography, alcohol, credit cards and other items.[11]

It was labeled "revival," and I think it was, but it wasn't any more than the power of public confession, which is accessible to any community, anytime. In his first epistle, John states that "if we claim to be without sin, we deceive ourselves and the truth is not in us. If we confess our sins, he is faithful and just and will forgive us our sins and purify us from all unrighteousness" (1 John 1:8-9, NIV).

Looking for a way to distinguish true believers from false,

John picks out confession, which is a good pick. Because if you think about it, who else besides us runs around telling God, telling friends, telling anyone who will listen, "I'm sorry I sinned; I'm sorry, I'm sorry I sinned." Confession defines us, and so John distinguishes believer from unbeliever with *confessor* and *nonconfessor*. Christian, confessor; confessor, Christian—one and the same.

There aren't many things each of us can do as individuals to transform a group of Christians into a community, but this is something. I'm not saying we should go around telling other believers our deepest, darkest sins . . . no, wait—yes, I am.

Communal Living

Katie and I were out of town recently, and we called home to check on our son, Will. We wanted to make sure he was okay and hadn't set his hair on fire, or swallowed a crayon, or gotten his head stuck pulling off his sweater. He's nineteen. I asked what he'd been up to and he said, "I got together last night with Mr. Wiedis at Starbucks."

Now, we need to pause here and consider the cosmic improbability of what my son was telling me. Dave (Mr. Wiedis) is a friend of mine. Like us, Dave and his wife, Miho, have older kids, and we enjoy hanging out together. But Dave lives a good twenty minutes away. He doesn't go to our church, doesn't know Will exceedingly well, and it's not like we were in Vietnam together. And yet Dave took it upon himself to call my son for coffee while we were out of town and find out how his life and walk with God were going—a totally unprecedented act of Jesus-ish-ness.

The Greek words for Starbucks and Panera are *anakeimai* and *katakeimai*. Okay, that's a lie, but only sort of. These are New Testament words for *recline*, and you've probably noticed in the Gospels that Jesus and his disciples don't usually sit for their meals. They recline: "A Pharisee invited him to eat with him; so he went in and reclined at the table" (Luke 11:37, NIV). There's a whole Greco-Roman history behind the idiom "to recline at table,"[12] but in short, it entails more than eating in a slouched position. In Israel, "recline" had all the connotations of "hanging out" or "grabbing coffee together."

This "reclining" was characteristic of Jesus' discipleship, which could be described as *intentional, ministry-minded hanging out*. Christians, of course, hang out all the time. But what Dave did was unique. It was intentional—it was whom he hung out with and why. Dave, age fifty-five, invited my nineteen-year-old son to coffee in order to (a) make him feel more included in the Kingdom; (b) help him be more known in the Kingdom; and (c) help him grow and advance in the Kingdom. That's discipleship, and except for the efforts of youth pastors, this building block of community is all but absent in churches.

So last week I met Bob, one of my son's friends, to do this very thing over lunch. We ate, talked about work and college, and somewhere in there I asked him about his walk with God: "So what's God been teaching you?" "What are you reading right now?" "What are two things I can be praying about for you?" I also brought a book along for him to read, which he undoubtedly won't.

It went okay. Not memorable. In meeting with young people, my behavior often horrifies me, as I giggle and fawn like a high school freshman trying to fit in: "Okay, cool, I'll call you, then." My drive home is just one long cringe—*Dude? Sweet? Awesome? Really, Rick? Really?* Even so, something's better than nothing, and that's the attitude you have to have with discipleship because the alternative really is *nothing*.

Initiating with those on the margins of the community, drawing them in: *intentional, ministry-minded hanging out*. A coffee or a breakfast with a younger believer, once or twice a week, is 1.15 additional life for them, for you, for the whole community.

Fellow Soldiers

Even with vaccines and modern medicine, tuberculosis remains one of the world's deadliest viruses. TB spreads through the air and lodges itself in the lungs. At the onset of infection, the body dispatches an army of white blood cells, an army that's quickly overwhelmed by a virus replicating at a phenomenal rate. But before all is lost, the white blood cells mount one last-ditch suicide mission. Andrew Zolli described the gruesome battle in his book *Resilience*:

> In a last, kamikaze-like move, [the white blood cells] engulf an unknown invader, coat it in the cellular equivalent of Saran Wrap, and then, on cue, promptly die, taking the pathogen with them. However, in TB, occasionally just the opposite occurs: TB takes over, . . . preventing them from dying, and turns them into zombie-like incubators for producing more TB bacteria, which slowly replicate inside until they burst their cellular hosts open and spread to others.[13]

The hostile invasion of a virus is the very same methodology employed by terrorist networks, organized crime, cancer, computer viruses, and self-organized evil everywhere. This is how drugs invade a city: Some poor soul gets infected and addicted, and with their will subjugated and soul vacuous, they become a host, selling it to others and spreading and replicating the evil down a chain of distribution. At every level of existence—biological, technological, psychological—evil functions as a highly adaptive network.

In an interview, Dr. John Arquilla, one of the country's leading experts on modern warfare, remarked that "the War on Terror is . . . the first great war in which we're seeing nations at war with networks."[14] He explains that in Afghanistan and Iraq the US military learned that the only way to fight a network was with a network:

The United States . . . initially approached things in very traditional ways: massive deployments, overwhelming force, and shock and awe. . . . Several years into the war . . . we moved our soldiers from huge bases to hundreds of small outposts thirty to fifty soldiers apiece, dramatically expanding the number of nodes in our physical network.[15]

I think this helps us see the way that first-century believers understood their need to pray together. When Paul pleads for prayer, he is most certainly seeking to expand "the number of nodes" in his network of prayer. He is intentionally, strategically fighting a network with a network.

Praying together is fighting together. The deepest bonds of trust and friendship come through shared struggle. Prayer takes on the pain and struggles of the community, and from them it forges a more dynamic community.

Why I Hate Community

These are all very practical things. And where people are doing these things, there's demonstrable vibrancy in the community. With a little initiative, greater wakefulness is within our grasp, so why do we suspect (and rightly so) that this grasping might not happen? The answer probably lies in what I hate about community:

1. It takes me away from getting stuff done, and I value getting stuff done.
2. I struggle with social anxiety, and I get uptight around people. Watching shows like *Downton Abbey* gives me community vicariously—all of the warmth, none of the anxiety.
3. I forget people's names, and I feel horrible about forgetting, feel humiliated to ask, and feel weary of

coming up with phrases that require only personal pronouns.

4. I feel more sinful around other people. Thoughts of comparison or judgment—I hate this about myself, and I hate confronting this about myself, and I don't have to when no one else is around.

5. When I leave a social gathering, I inevitably run through every stupid thing I said (and I'm an extrovert, so there's a lot to run through).

6. I don't like navigating people's personal doctrinal commitments. Should I have mentioned a rapture? It's exhausting dancing around people's toes.

I'll stop there, but I could keep going. These dark and murky ruminations would lead me away from involvement in church or Bible study or any community. But they haven't, and I think it's because I have free will.

Free will is typically understood in terms of the power to act. Do we simply act according to the strongest motive? Do we have the power to act differently than how we have acted? Ignore all that. Far more important than the freedom to act is the freedom *to form the intention to act*.[16] (That sounds more complicated than it is.)

Imagine that you are a recovering alcoholic and someone offers you a drink. Immediately you're barraged with competing desires, memories, beliefs, feelings, and the like. You experience the belief that you could have a drink and be just fine, and you experience the belief that you could not. You remember how fun it was to drink, and you remember how fun it wasn't. What you immediately recognize is that you have a choice—but not about drinking, not yet anyway. The choice is which desire you'll fortify with additional reasons, memories, Scripture, prayer, and so on. Whatever our freedom to act, we surely have the freedom to form intention. We choose which truth to "weight," and Scripture has told us it's this truth here:

> Let us consider how we may spur one another on toward
> love and good deeds, not giving up meeting together,
> as some are in the habit of doing, but encouraging
> one another—and all the more as you see the Day
> approaching.   HEBREWS 10:24-25, NIV

So whatever *your* three, five, or seven reasons are, they'll pop up with every opportunity and invitation to "meet together" with other believers. Can't change that. But you can pay them no heed. Let them dance partner-less around your mind. Give them no audience. Choose instead to believe and obey.

The Tower of David

As I flipped through a *New Yorker* (my wife's—I can barely grasp the cartoons), the words "The Real 'Tower of David'" caught my eye. In the middle of downtown Caracas is a forty-five-story skyscraper, partially erected but never completed. The "David" refers to the Tower's financier, David Brillembourg. When Venezuela's economy crumbled, the building was only 60 percent complete, and that's how it stayed. When contractors moved out, squatters—more than three thousand of them—moved in. With the entire side of the building missing its exterior wall, you can see right into the forty-five-story homeless shelter, each floor looking like a Cuban flotilla bound for Miami. And what's happening in the tower is happening all over Caracas:

> At the end of [2012], there were an estimated hundred
> and fifty-five "invaded" buildings in downtown Caracas—
> including an entire shopping mall. . . . The poverty,
> chronic housing shortage, and government compliance

with many of the *invasiones*, combined with a dramatic breakdown in law enforcement and security, had created a dystopian atmosphere in Caracas—with the Tower of David as the most visible symbol of Venezuela's mess.[17]

Caracas is a monument to what happens when a city falls on the other side of that golden ratio of cities. Systems that operate on principles of momentum don't just fail—they fail with momentum. The opposite of a growing city is a dying city, and there's little in between.

A city's entrapment in a cycle of negative momentum is inevitably because of a lack of economic diversity, as with Detroit and its automobiles. This is what happens with community. Most of us have but a single lifeline to the body of Christ, and when that lifeline is lost because of a move or a falling out, spiritual entropy sets in. Lost is not simply our community but also the drive to find or create new community. If years ago someone had sold Caracas on the idea of "diversify now for the future," the Tower of David feature may have been in *Architectural Digest*. But it didn't happen that way.

I'm ending the chapter on a somewhat somber note because community is serious business. I'm not sure our spiritual lives ever rise above the level of our community, and it's worth any amount of labor to create and maintain these vital connections. A city is either growing or dying, just as we are either asleep or awake. There's not much middle ground.

Creating and seeking community are active roles we play in keeping awake, but we don't always play the initiator. In trials, God instigates wakefulness (1 Peter 1:6-7), and that's where we'll go next.

5

Red Bull

On the Caffeinating Effect of Trials

W. H. AUDEN, one of the great poets of the twentieth century, insightfully observed that "any marriage, happy or unhappy, is infinitely more interesting than any romance, however passionate."[1] But as with most of Auden's insight, it was chemically enhanced: Each day he'd start his writing with a pot of black coffee, move on to Benzedrine, and then wind down for bed with Seconal and vodka. Robert Louis Stevenson wrote *The Strange Case of Dr. Jekyll and Mr. Hyde* on a cocaine binge, and in twenty amphetamine-fueled days, Jack Kerouac wrote *On the Road*, feeding telegraph paper into his typewriter and spitting out a single-spaced, 167-foot manuscript.[2]

Writers, artists, and thinkers of all types have relied on stimulants for their creative output. My middle name is Davy because somewhere in my family is a British inventor named Sir Humphry Davy. Davy discovered several elements on the periodic table, but his invention of nitrous oxide—"laughing gas"—is what made him famous. Wikipedia mentions that my dear relative and namesake, along with "his poet friends," got "addicted" to nitrous oxide, and became the toast of high society by supplying laughing gas to all the parties. Nice.

The reason for dependency is, I think, answered by Jean-Paul Sartre's frank admission: "Amphetamines gave me a quickness of thought and writing that was at least three times my normal rhythm."[3] If your work is "ideas," working harder won't help. You have to think faster.

The brain is a sovereign nation and as such prints its own unique currency: dopamine. Certain thoughts and processes are incentivized with a sudden push on the gas, like the excitement you get in solving a puzzle. What amphetamines do is trick the brain. By raising dopamine levels unnaturally high, amphetamines make mundane thoughts seem revelatory, like you solved a puzzle. It's not "I need to take out the garbage" but "Dude, we're all just intergalactic garbage—we're space junk, dude, space junk."

Caffeine also is a stimulant, but less potent. It, too, hands the brain a forged permission slip, and the brain, gullible as a substitute homeroom teacher, is similarly flummoxed. In order to sedate our thoughts to fall asleep, the brain produces a chemical called adenosine. But caffeine molecules look just like adenosine, and nerve cells can't tell them apart. So they mistakenly bind with the caffeine, causing an immediate rush of stimulation instead of drowsiness. But what's really interesting about caffeine is that our body processes it like poison: With caffeine in your system, there is an increase in neuron firing in the brain. The pituitary gland mistakes this activity for an emergency in the body and releases hormones that alert the adrenal glands. The adrenal glands then produce adrenaline, which dilates pupils, opens breathing tubes, increases heart rate, elevates blood pressure, slows down blood flow to the stomach, and alerts the liver to release sugar into the blood.[4]

Mistaking caffeine for poison, the body switches to a state of hyper-alertness, sweating and speeding itself up in order to flush the toxin. The joy of a strong cup of coffee is the joy of food poisoning. Now, hold that thought as I tell this story.

Last year about this time, my wife Katie and I fell into a crack and disappeared into financial oblivion. There are a number of these cracks in the current economy—tuition costs, cars, gas, medical expenses, unemployment, plummeting home values, and the like. Our crisis aggressively embraced all of them.

As missionaries, we are supported by people who have to have jobs in order to have paychecks in order to support us. So we were receiving partial paychecks. All three of our kids were in college. The cars broke, our house broke, our bodies broke, and we couldn't get an equity loan because, well, what equity? And it all happened at once, out of nowhere—well, I sure didn't see it coming. With thousands of dollars going out the window, our disasters were being paid for by Visa, and if you asked me the difference between Visa and a loan shark, I'd have to say the spelling.

But God always has a plan, some means of deliverance, even if the exit strategy is like getting out of Afghanistan. We prayed unceasingly. We examined our e-mails and screened our phone calls for God's providential leading. We praised God and thanked him, diligently, faithfully, incessantly. We increased our giving as an expression of faith. Whatever we knew to do, we did. We were in a hyper state of spiritual alertness.

As best as we could discern, selling our home was the answer. So, in a matter of days we got our house ready to sell: round-the-clock clean-up, expanding the number of known uses for bathroom caulk, five years of procrastination atoned for in a three-day weekend.

Once the house was ready, our realtor came over for a final walk-through and to have us sign the paperwork. It was Wednesday, and the house would officially go on the market that Friday. But as the realtor was doing the walk-through, our phone rang. Probably a bill collector—I ignored it. Ten minutes later it rang again—probably the collection agency hired by the bill collector. I let it go. The third time it rang, I thought, *Hmmm, maybe this is significant*, so I picked it up.

It was my friend Harold, an elder at our church. "I heard you're selling your house?"

"Yeah," I told him, "our financial state is abysmal; it seems selling is the only option."

"Don't sign anything, Rick," he said.

"Harold, we don't have a choice."

"Just tell the realtor you'll call her tomorrow, and do not sign anything. I want to come over and talk with you guys."

So Harold came over with his wife, Deb. They shared some thoughts, prayed with us, and told us to sit tight as they looked into how the church might help. So we sat tight—and not for long, because in the span of a week, roughly twenty thousand dollars showed up in our mailbox from various members of our church. And that was that: The financial storm died as quickly as it arose.

Now, let me go back and complete my initial thought: Trials are the spiritual equivalent of caffeine. When we are attacked by circumstances that threaten to undo us, our spiritual pulse quickens, the fervor of our prayers begins to rise, and the eyes of our heart start darting around for deliverance and direction. A trial, like caffeine, is a small dose of poison (evil, pain, suffering)—just enough to wake us up. But it is poison, so if not metabolizing properly, it will turn bitter and toxic to the soul.

This is something Jesus discussed with his disciples one day as they rowed across the rich and robust seas of Galilee.

Asleep in a Boat

The story is found in the fourth chapter of Mark's Gospel. As evening sets in, Jesus says to his disciples, "Let us go over to the other side."

A furious squall came up, and the waves broke over the boat, so that it was nearly swamped. Jesus was in the stern, sleeping on a cushion. The disciples woke him and said to him, "Teacher, don't you care if we drown?"

He got up, rebuked the wind and said to the waves, "Quiet! Be still!" Then the wind died down and it was completely calm.

He said to his disciples, "Why are you so afraid? Do you still have no faith?"

They were terrified and asked each other, "Who is this? Even the wind and the waves obey him!"

MARK 4:35, 37-41, NIV

Exhausted after a long day of ministry, Jesus falls asleep in the back of the boat, unaware that a squall threatens to sink the ship. As the boat fills with water, the disciples wake Jesus just in time to save them from drowning. This, at least, is what the text says—but it's not the story.

Sleeping Disciples

The story is an object lesson on trials. The perfect object lesson. As if sailboats and hurricanes existed for this explanatory purpose: to capture the loss of control experienced in a trial and the utter helplessness of facing a force that is magnitudes greater than ourselves. The disciples, for their part, exhibit all the shock, fear, anger, and outrage of someone going through the ordeal. And Jesus—fittingly—plays the part of God, who seems to be asleep, unaware of our crisis and indifferent to our suffering.

The disciples endured considerable trauma for our edification, so what, besides "trust Jesus," can we get out of this story? The answer is "very little"—not until we've acquired some missing background assumed by the text.

Mark uses an organizing theme to structure his Gospel, and that theme is Israel's Exodus. The plagues, the Passover, the parting of the Red Sea . . . these were the seminal events of the nation's birth: the contractions of plagues; the water breaking (or parting); Israel squeezed through the birth canal, spanked upon entry in the world, and screaming like a newborn wanting back in the womb.

Remembrances of the Exodus are a steady refrain in the Old Testament, and no place more so than in the book of Isaiah. But Isaiah uses the Exodus imagery differently: not to call Israel to remember but to call her to look toward her future. Isaiah declares that the coming Messiah will lead a new, reconstituted Israel on a new exodus, not out of Egypt, but out of slavery to sin. In Isaiah 40–60, the prophet develops this "new Exodus" theme, and these chapters serve as the backstory to Mark's Gospel and the story of Jesus calming the sea.[5]

Within these chapters of Isaiah we find a dispute between God and Israel, where Israel accuses God of abandoning them or having fallen asleep:

Awake, awake, arm of the LORD,
    clothe yourself with strength!
Awake, as in days gone by,
    as in generations of old.

ISAIAH 51:9, NIV

God responds to Israel in parody, saying in essence: "I'm not the one who fell asleep, Israel—you did. You need to wake up— not me."

Awake, awake!
    Rise up, Jerusalem.

ISAIAH 51:17, NIV

Awake, awake, Zion,
    clothe yourself with strength!
ISAIAH 52:1, NIV

With that Old Testament backdrop in place, we're looking at a very different scene. This isn't a story about "Jesus asleep in a boat." It's a story about "the disciples asleep in a boat." The raging storm and surging seas won't disturb Jesus in the least, but they will wake the disciples. As in Isaiah, the disciples accuse Jesus of falling asleep when they are the ones unconscious, oblivious to who is in their midst. But coming to the end of the crisis, the disciples, like men waking from a dream, see Jesus for who he really is: "Who is this? Even the wind and the waves obey him!"

Our trials create and re-create this scene. Trials expose our hidden fears, mistrust, and false beliefs, and God's apparent absence exacerbates them. And to be fair, life-disintegrating circumstances do seem to point to God's dereliction of his duties. And sure, "he's sovereign," but that doesn't make me want any less to punch you in the face for saying it.

But as the trial runs its course, our perspective changes. Once we're calmly sitting on the other side, it's pretty clear who was sleeping, uncaring, and detached, pretty clear who needed to wake up. Whatever else we learn through our trials, this shift of perspective and perception—this waking up—is the desired outcome.

Sleeping Jesus

Trials come in a zillion shapes and sizes, but two features remain fairly constant: circumstances that threaten to undo us, and a God who is nowhere to be found. This is the setting we find in Mark's narrative, and whether Jesus is really asleep or not is quite irrelevant because in the midst of a trial, all that's required is that we think he is.

Why the perception of God's absence is so intrinsic to a trial becomes clear if you imagine in Mark's story that instead of sleeping in the stern of the boat, Jesus is awake, standing on the bow, hands outstretched like Leonardo DiCaprio in *Titanic*. A trial just isn't that trialsome when God is clearly present.

So here is the mildly poetic thing: Jesus must "sleep" in order for the disciples to wake up. The disciples need their hearts and minds dragged out of bed, and what's going to rouse them is the fear and terror of a storm—but a storm is only terrifying if Jesus is absent . . . so Jesus sleeps.

Saturday

It was a seemingly normal Saturday until the phone rang. As I've mentioned, a number of teens have lived in our home, and Katie and I love them like our children. Joey is just shy of nineteen and had gone out Friday night, driven into Philadelphia to Kensington and Somerset—a little hellhole called Heroin City—and purchased five or six bags of what the area is proudly named for. He apparently did the drugs in his car and slept at a friend's house. The call on Saturday morning was from the friend, telling us Joey wasn't waking up.

Katie and I jumped in the car and raced over to where he had spent the night, arriving to find the police and ambulance already there. Then came the waves of fear and nausea, and then came the paramedics with Joey on a stretcher, face blue, one of the paramedics shaking his head at us. "He's unresponsive."

For the next two hours he hung between life and death. They couldn't get his heart rate above fourteen beats per minute, he was on a forced breathing tube, and he had a high fever from septic shock. The police said it was the worst case they had ever seen, and no one—not his friends, not us, not the police, not even the doctors—thought he was going to make it.

It was hour to hour, and not until twenty-four hours later was there any confidence Joey was going to pull through. Through the day, my prayers were identical to the cries of the disciples, one moment pleading, the next accusing: "Don't you care if we drown?" Pleading, accusing; pleading, accusing. Jesus didn't just seem to be asleep in the boat—he seemed to have gone overboard.

No two trials are alike. I mean, I don't know that, but I assume it's true. And obviously there are times when God's presence is profound. But speaking generally of trials—and that's what we're doing—a defining characteristic is this hiddenness of God. This is what "tries" our faith: the incongruity of God's loving care and what feels like abandonment.

What I felt that Saturday, sitting in the parking lot outside the emergency room, watching carefree clouds flit across the sky, was "No one cares" and "No one's home." It was convincing. Perfect staging, but it *was* staged, like Jesus sleeping peacefully . . . in a rowboat . . . sinking . . . in the middle of a typhoon.

I never realized the book was this old, but William Golding wrote *Lord of the Flies* back in 1954. The CliffsNotes are newer—the 1960s, I think—and that's all I read in high school. It's a sort of Genesis account of societal depravity, and I assume you remember the setting: a group of young men marooned on an island (surrounded by water), deprived of adult guidance and supervision, left to fend for themselves and grasp for survival. It's in this setting—without the constraint of a moral authority—that all the rebellion in the human heart is witnessed naked and unafraid. It's the stage of Mark 4.

In the Gospels we are drawn to the curious fact that Jesus' absence is as intentional and conspicuous as his healings or miracles. God's perceived (epistemic) distance is a thing. An event in its own right. A planned absence. *Ferris Bueller's Day Off.* The dynamic is essential to God's accomplishment of certain purposes in our life. In *The Elusive God*, Paul Moser gives us a helpful list of some purposes:

Conceivably, God hides on occasion from some people for various perfectly loving divine purposes. At least the following arise: (a) to teach people to yearn for, and thus eventually to value wholeheartedly and above all else, personal volitional fellowship with God, (b) to strengthen grateful trust in God even when times look altogether bleak, (c) to remove human complacency toward God and God's redemptive purposes, (d) to shatter destructively prideful human self-reliance, and (e) to prevent people who aren't ready for fellowship with God from explicitly rejecting God.[6]

Joey did survive that day. And six months later I walked into his room and found him blue in his bed from another overdose; I cried and beat his chest until the ambulance came and, again, Jesus spared both him and me.

I live daily with the trauma of those events (and others), events I'll never get over. There's a self-evident logic to trials, but not always to their severity. That they are measured is assured (1 Peter 1–5), and that they are not a measure of God's anger is assured (Hebrews 12), and I suppose you take your assurances where you can get them. The godless get squat.

In Joey's case, and others I can think of, I imagine the severity is measured to the flesh's obstinacy. The flesh will rationalize and negotiate . . . until it can't. Life-and-death trials don't negotiate. Without Assyrians or Babylonians camped at the border—some brute force that can't be bargained with—certain habits, life-styles, and addictions never surrender.

Asleep on a Cushion

Coming home from the Los Angeles–to–Hawaii sail race, Charles Moore took his boat, the *Alguita*, and its crew on a shortcut back to their home port of Long Beach, California, passing through an untraveled stretch of the Pacific Ocean. Expecting a view of primordial beauty, what Moore found instead was a waterscape as polluted as the New Jersey Meadowlands:

> I often struggle to find words that will communicate the vastness of the Pacific Ocean to people who have never been to sea. Day after day, *Alguita* was the only vehicle on a highway without landmarks, stretching from horizon to horizon. Yet as I gazed from the deck at the surface of what ought to have been a pristine ocean, I was confronted, as far as the eye could see, with the sight of plastic.
>
> It seemed unbelievable, but I never found a clear spot. In the week it took to cross the subtropical high, no matter what time of day I looked, plastic debris was floating everywhere: bottles, bottle caps, wrappers.[7]

This garbage dump, roughly the size of Texas, is found in the North Pacific Central Gyre. A gyre describes the current you'd see in a bowl of soup when you stir it with a spoon. The wind as well as the planet's rotation serve as a spoon on the earth's oceans, a spoon that never stops stirring. But like a tornado, the eye of a gyre is completely calm, and with no wind, current, or waves, it becomes a sewer, collecting refuse like a drain. That eye is the Great Pacific garbage patch, the dump of the Pacific: calm as a bathtub, filthy as a cesspool.

In maritime past, before oceans were polluted, these gyres were simply known by sailors as "the doldrums," immortalized in Samuel Coleridge's "Rime of the Ancient Mariner":

> *Day after day, day after day,*
> *We stuck, nor breath nor motion;*
> *As idle as a painted ship*
> *Upon a painted ocean.*[8]

As you sail into these doldrums, the wind cuts out, water turns to glass, air stagnates, and the sky becomes indistinguishable from the sea, giving the impression of floating in space. Momentum gives way to drift, and the loss of animation in sea, sky, vessel, and crew turns a seascape into a still life.

Left to myself, I'd never see another trial until the day they dropped me in the ground. But if my soul isn't perturbed, and regularly, it stagnates and congeals; it becomes a gyre, a garbage dump—dolphins and tuna cans and milk jugs all stuck in it. Without agitation, without being stirred, the soul languishes: prayer becomes listless, the Spirit is stilled, direction is rudderless, and boredom yearns for indulgence . . . a painted ship upon a painted ocean.

In our text, we read that Jesus was in the stern, "asleep on the cushion." Mark's mention of a cushion is an extravagant detail in an otherwise sparse account, and neither Luke nor Matthew mention it at all. As scenic details are wholly absent in Mark, we should assume the cushion is part of the lesson, a teaching prop in an enacted parable, like Ezekiel laying on his side, or Jeremiah wearing a yoke.

As we've studied the story, we've noted the repeated "it's not me, it's you" pattern, so I'll suggest that just as the disciples were really the ones "sleeping," it's also the disciples who are really "sleeping on a cushion." Hear me out.

A cushion is the buffer between sleep and reality. Think about that. The disciples presumed Jesus to be such a cushion—that is, that he would make their lives softer, plusher, comfier. As members of a royal entourage, they presumed they were exempt from the harsher realities of life outside the palace. Their presumption was wrong *and* dangerous. Disillusioned is not the way you want to enter adversity. Unexpected attacks are unexpected for a reason.

Ultimately, Jesus *does* protect and deliver his disciples from the storm. Royalty (as all disciples are) has its privileges. There is—thank God—a cushion that stands between us and the hostile world. But it's not for sleeping on. It's not for getting us out of hardship or exempting us from painful trials. The degree of shock and resentment roused by adversity is a fair indicator of the type of cushion we think we have in Jesus: one who sovereignly orchestrates our trials and sustains us in them, or one who gets us out of them.

Now Rest

In the story of Jonah, a similar storm threatens the boat as Jonah sleeps belowdecks, and there are undeniable parallels between the two stories. In Jonah 1, the sailors do exactly what the disciples did and what I imagine sailors always do when their ship is sinking: blame and bail.

> But the LORD hurled a great wind upon the sea. . . . And
> they hurled the cargo that was in the ship into the sea
> to lighten it for them. . . . And they said to one another,
> "Come, let us cast lots, that we may know on whose
> account this evil has come upon us."   JONAH 1:4-5, 7

This is the prerequisite response to one's boat sinking or finances sinking or marriage sinking, or I suppose to sinking in general. Blame and bail.

The Doctrine of Blaming

We live near State College, Pennsylvania, where Penn State football is the state's chief natural resource, point of interest, export, and economic indicator. So in the spring of 2012, there wasn't any news in the entire world, according to our TV stations, except for developments in the child-abuse case of Jerry Sandusky, a former football coach for the Nittany Lions. What was strange was, after the first forty-eight hours, no one was interested in Jerry Sandusky. If Sandusky was to blame, then the more pressing question was, who was to blame for Jerry Sandusky?

For several weeks, assistant coach Mike McQueary took the hot seat. Some years prior, McQueary had happened upon Jerry Sandusky with a minor. Surely he could have stopped this, but McQueary had dutifully reported the incident to his superior, none other than head coach Joe Paterno. So it was Paterno—he was to blame.

But Paterno maintained that while he could have done more, he had passed the information on to the athletic director, Tim Curley. So blame passed to Tim Curley, but it was soon discovered that Curley had passed on the information to the president of the university. So investigators continued digging, which led them to the office of President Graham Spanier. Spanier was responsible for Curley, who was responsible for Paterno, who was responsible for McQueary, who was responsible for Sandusky. Spanier was summarily fired, and that, finally, seemed to be that—but not quite.

A grand-jury investigation—involving hundreds of interviews, thousands of e-mails, and millions of dollars—produced a several-hundred-page report finding that Spanier was not the final link in the chain. As it turned out, the Penn State board of directors was well aware of Sandusky's behavior and therefore ultimately to blame. Though Sandusky did it, McQueary saw it, Paterno dismissed it, Curley ignored it, and Spanier hid it, the board of directors did nothing to stop it.

Now, unlike the disciples in the boat, the investigators in the Sandusky case were right to follow this long trail of guilt. But in both cases we see a picture of how blame works: like a lit fuse burning its way to the source, exploding with white-hot indignation. In search of someone to blame, the disciples trace the causal chain back to Jesus. It wasn't the stupid boat, stupid waves, stupid Andrew, it was . . . Jesus. Not that they thought he caused the storm, but they perceived he could have done something about it. And, as the miracle showed, he certainly could have.

There are always primary and secondary causes to a trial, but for the follower of Christ there is no way around the fact that God allowed it, because when you clear away all the caveats—it's a fallen world, we're in a spiritual battle, actions have consequences, humans have freedom—we know that God is powerful enough to have prevented it.

A few years ago, the movie *The Dark Knight Rises* opened in theaters to expectations of being the top-grossing film of all time. Instead it opened to a massacre in Aurora, Colorado. James Holmes, who referred to himself as the Joker, entered the exit door of the Aurora theater and sprayed the audience with gunfire, killing twelve and injuring seventy. Of all the mindless, senseless evil . . . There was apparently no motive for the massacre, and if there were ever a rogue event in the history of the universe, this would certainly be it.

But consider this. One of the victims was a twenty-two-year-old woman named Petra Anderson. Petra is a Christian, and she was hit four times with a shotgun blast. While three shots lodged in her arm, the fourth was in her face: The bullet entered through her nose, traveled through her brain and out the other side, and stopped at the back of her skull. The prognosis was grim, and if she lived, brain damage seemed inevitable, as the bullet had traversed her brain entirely.

But as it so happens, the brain contains a fluid pathway, "like a tiny vein through marble, winding from front to rear." The location of this pathway differs from person to person, and the bullet entered Petra's brain "from the exact point of this channel"—escorting the bullet in, through, and then out the other side. Writer Brad Strait described it this way:

Like a giant BB through a straw created in Petra's brain
before she was born, [the bullet] follows the perfect
route. . . . It's just like the God I follow to plan the route
of a bullet through a brain long before Batman ever rises.
Twenty-two years before.[9]

God, who had shaped Petra's brain into the Holland Tunnel
twenty-two years earlier, isn't blindsided by anything. And this is
why we take our blame and anger courageously to him, because
only here do we ask the right questions: God, what are you doing
in my life? What are your purposes in this? How do you want
me to respond?

To assign *ultimate* blame for our trials to any secondary cause
will, in the end, only increase fear and awe for the power of free
will or Satan or sin or circumstances, and erode our confidence
in the loving sovereignty of God; and any question worthy of
asking will never get asked.

The Doctrine of Bailing

If you've ever bailed out a basement, a boat, or anything at all,
you know the rightness of this metaphor for self-generated effort.
There is the myopia—eyes fixed on the ground in front of you,
the flailing arms, the fruitless effort, physical exertion, frantic
pace, and acute awareness of making no discernible progress.

Bailing is our futile effort to control the uncontrollable. Notice how the disciples seek to secure the aid and cooperation of
Jesus. "Will you rescue us?" is a very different question from the
one the disciples asked, which is, "Don't you care if we drown?"
One is a request, the other a manipulation—something in the
order of "if you really loved me, you'd buy me an Xbox."

As the disciples cannot control (a) the sea or (b) their boat,
they attempt to control (c) Jesus, who can control both (a) and
(b). This is how they'll bail themselves out. It will not be through

Jesus' mercy, compassion, or power that they are delivered, but through their ability to manipulate Jesus' mercy, compassion, and power. Good thinking, boys.

But their manipulation is ill-conceived. To start, Jesus doesn't have to be talked into helping, and as for the accusation of "not caring," Jesus could have responded: "No, if I didn't care, you'd be rowing effortlessly, wind at your back, sea at your command—twelve little buddhas thinking you run the universe." Deeply ingrained in our belief system is the idea that love shelters from hardship and pain, and much of what the New Testament has to say about trials is to directly refute this notion: in fact, "the Lord disciplines the one he loves" (Hebrews 12:6).

Our manipulations reveal the distortions in our understanding of God: that he can be controlled, that he isn't favorably disposed toward us, that we can offer him something not already his. But when we come to the end of all our bargaining and manipulation, there is this liberating realization: We have nothing, we can do nothing, we deserve nothing, and we are nothing. Nothing is what we cling to, nothing is our collateral, and nothing is our alibi. Humbling ourselves before God is giving him the gift of nothing.

My friend Amy is the parent of three mostly grown kids. No one in the family has taken a particularly easy path in life. Her oldest daughter, Tia, has gotten into some serious drug problems, and by serious I mean there are bullet holes in her wall. Issues notwithstanding, Tia loves God.

About a month ago, Tia went missing. She went to West Virginia to visit her grandfather and evaporated on the day she was supposed to come home. Amy filled out a missing-person report, but we heard nothing. One day turned to one week, then two weeks, and then what can you start to think but the worst?

But Amy has some serious faith. If it's a mustard seed, it's one of those Monsanto things, genetically altered to the size of a plum. As the days passed she held relentlessly to God. She prayed without ceasing; in fact, she invited everyone who knew Tia, believers and unbelievers, to an evening of prayer, trusting God to miraculously intervene.

A lot of people came that night, and in a room of hushed praying the ring of Amy's cell was dramatic, like the sound of bowls and vials and trumpets being poured out on the earth. The call showed Tia's cell number, but it wasn't Tia. It was, however, the person who had just bought Tia's phone from her; he felt compelled to call the home number and tell whoever was there that Tia was okay and where to find her. Within two days, Tia was on her way home, and she's now safe and doing well.

Watching Amy walk through the ordeal, I'm convinced that prayer is our God-given means to bail. Put another way, "pray[ing] without ceasing" (1 Thessalonians 5:17) is bailing— same reflex, same manic pace, same need to do something—and we do it again and again until something changes. Bailing by any means other than prayer inevitably ends in an act of the flesh. Prayer is an assertive response to events beyond our control, through appropriately deferential and creaturely means given us by God. We bail by faith, not sight.

Storm inside a Storm

In focusing on the theme of sleep, I realize it would be easy to see it everywhere, even where it's not. But it does seem to me that Jesus puts the sea to sleep like a crying baby—"Quiet! Be still!" (Mark 4:39, NIV)—making an absurd display of power 30 to 40 percent more absurd. But we'll simply note that and move on.

Mark tells us that "the waves were breaking into the boat, so that the boat was already filling" with water (Mark 4:37). The storm *outside* the boat had become the storm *inside* the boat, and that's a good description of the internal chaos (fear, worry, anger) caused by life behaving badly.

So the disciples are in the midst of two storms. But it didn't have to be that way. The storm *outside* didn't have to become a storm *inside*. This is where the disciples failed and, if I might speak frankly for all of us, where we often fail. The disciples' faith could have remained steadfast even in the storm. They didn't have to capitulate to fear. Jesus needed to calm the typhoon; he shouldn't have needed to calm the disciples. So Jesus calms one storm and rebukes the other.

And he awoke and rebuked the wind and said to the sea, "Peace! Be still!" And the wind ceased, and there was a great calm. He said to them, "Why are you so afraid? Have you still no faith?" MARK 4:39-40

The disciples aren't simply rebuked; they are corrected—and the distinction isn't loudness. Through the storm their faith all but disintegrated, only to be reconstituted—stronger, denser, more fibrous from the exercise. Like a muscle, faith is stretched and pulled during God's seeming absence, then tensed and flexed upon deliverance. Only a trial abandoned leaves faith weaker from the exercise.

Coming to the end of a trial seems to call for some kind of evaluation or feedback or consumer survey. You want to know how you did. I'd imagine the disciples felt like failures because, well, Jesus told them they had failed. So that's pretty much that. But lacking such immediate feedback, we tend to grade ourselves, and I doubt that's very helpful. The experience of negative and conflicting thoughts and emotions will always *feel* like failure, so that's no gauge. And then you have all those persecuted believers, singing hymns in boiling tar and wrecking the grading curve for the rest of us. Thanks, suffering saints!

Only God sees and knows all the variables; only God can judge. And he will. In the meantime, the wisest way to process a trial is a dialogue with God that consists of "Where did I pass?" and "Where did I fail?" Assume a P *and* an F, because we never do anything completely right—and rarely completely wrong.

On the Other Side

In the story of Jesus calming the storm, nothing has turned out to be what it appeared—most strikingly Jesus. The structure of the narrative, the constant flipping of perception with reality, reflects the nature of a trial. Just as a parable manifests the characteristic of God's Kingdom in this world—a story alongside a story—the irony of Mark's story is in the text; the text is structured like a trial.

In a trial the world turns upside down, momentarily, so that we'll see it right side up. Spiritual apprehension and wakefulness are the result. That's how our beloved disciples emerge from things: "Who is this? Even the wind and the waves obey him!" (Mark 4:41, NIV). Before the whole storm thing, they weren't aware that their friend ran the universe. They're clear on that now, but they'll forget—and so will we, so the caffeine will just need to keep coming.

Rubber Ducky

It seems as if we should end this chapter on something nautical, so we will.

On January 10, 1992, traveling south of the Aleutian Islands, 44-7°N, 178.1°E to be precise, the container ship known as the *Ever Laurel* encountered the high seas that had made these latitudes maritime legend. En route from Hong Kong to Tacoma, Washington, the ship pitched and rolled, and on one particularly steep roll, two columns of forty-foot-long shipping containers, stacked six high, lunged from the ship into the Pacific.

What was unclear until weeks later was that the treasure traveling in one of the lost containers was 28,800 rubber duckies.

Okay, that's not entirely true—there was an assortment of four different bath toys: a red beaver, a blue turtle, a green frog, and the iconic yellow ducky.

This story didn't become a story for several years, not until the ducks began turning up all over the world. Donovan Hohn, author of *Moby-Duck*, writes:

> In 1995, beachcombers in Washington State found a blue turtle and a sun-bleached duck. Dean and Tyler Orbison, a father-son beachcombing team who annually scour uninhabited islands along the Alaskan coast, added more toys to their growing collection every summer— dozens in 1992, three in 1993, twenty-five in 1994, until, in 1995, they found none. The slump continued in 1996, and the Orbisons assumed they'd seen the last of the plastic animals, but then, in 1997, the toys suddenly returned in large numbers.[10]

Since 1992, the bath toys have bobbed tens of thousands of miles. Some have washed up on the shores of Hawaii, while others have been log-jammed in Arctic ice floes. Nineteen thousand headed for sunnier shores in Australia, Indonesia, and South America. Some traveled to Alaska, then westward to Japan, and then back to Alaska again.

In 2004, what remained of the castaways headed eastward, past Greenland, making landfall on the southwestern shores of the United Kingdom in 2007. And who knows, maybe some are still out there.

What's unfathomable is that these ducks, arriving at destinations all over the world, all left from the same point of origin. The waves of the ocean, blown and tossed by the wind, seem to illustrate the random, unpredictable nature of life's trials. But the waves are only on the surface.

Amazingly, oceanographers—with the help of sophisticated software—were able to discern each leg of the voyage of the rubber duckies because the ocean is governed by currents, not dictated by waves. And the trial you're in or heading into is the same. It will come out of nowhere and seem guided by nothing. You'll thrash around with no sense of bearing. But this is just the surface. There is a current governing the movement. God knows where you are, how you got there, where he's taking you. The waves wake us and move us, but God governs the waves.

Being awake is a matter of perspective and awareness. On the other side of the trial, the disciples saw Jesus differently. For this reason the ultimate action point of any trial is to persevere and to

humble yourselves, therefore, under the mighty hand of God so that at the proper time he may exalt you, casting all your anxieties on him, because he cares for you. Be sober-minded; be watchful.   I PETER 5:6-8

Psychedelic
Altering Spiritual Perception

IN THE MOVIE *Pretty Woman*, Julia Roberts sits down to an intimate breakfast with her client, Richard Gere (which I imagine
is commonplace in the glamorous world of street prostitution),
reaches forward for a croissant—and a moment later seems to be
feeding instead on a pancake. In the movie *Braveheart*, Scottish
clansmen find themselves at a distinct disadvantage as the invading British have apparently conscripted a white Chevy Tahoe
into their fighting ranks. And in the 1961 film *King of Kings*,
our Lord can be spotted wearing tennis shoes and a wristwatch.

These are called continuity errors, and on any movie set,
someone has the dedicated job of preventing them. But they
still happen—a lot, actually. As author Bill Givens explains it:
"They're concentrating on the acting, the lighting, the voice
quality, the pacing of the scene. There's so much they're thinking about when they're cutting the film that sometimes it's kind
of hard to see the trees for the forest."[1]

Givens is right—probably righter than he knows. Beyond the

eye's focal point, we see next to nothing in our broader field of vision. Which is why, even in a normal wakened state, *alert* would hardly be the right word to describe us.

In 1998, on the campus of Harvard University, Daniel Simons and Christopher Chabris thought up an experiment to test visual awareness. Using a vacant floor of the psychology building as a movie set, they made a short video showing two teams of people moving around, passing basketballs back and forth. The video lasted less than a minute, and test subjects viewing the film were asked to count how many times the ball passed between players.

But that was not really the experiment: "Halfway through the video, a female student wearing a full-body gorilla suit walked into the scene, faced the camera, thumped her chest, and then walked off, spending about nine seconds onscreen." After asking the test subjects how many passes they counted, they asked the following questions:

Q: Did you notice anything unusual while you were doing the counting task?
A: No.
Q: Did you notice anything other than the players?
A: Well, there were some elevators, and S's painted on the wall. I don't know what the S's were there for . . .
Q: Did you notice a gorilla?[2]

Roughly half the test subjects never saw the gorilla. Roughly half! This rather odd phenomenon exposing the illusion of attention is called *inattentional blindness*, and it exposes the fiction of attention.

That "fiction," explain Chabris and Simons, is that "we experience far less of our visual world than we think we do. . . . [Our] rich experience inevitably leads to the erroneous belief that we process *all* of the detailed information around us" and "masks a striking mental blindness."[3] Our brains use the world like an enormous library. With limited memory and storage, we leave most of what we see sitting on the library shelf, only thumbing through and occasionally checking out content we find relevant. Go into a room that's familiar and you won't notice anything unless something's been changed. Only then will your brain pull it from the shelf and carefully examine it.

There are general rules that determine things we notice— altered appearance, threat of danger, rapid movement, and so on—but much of what captures our attention is personal: *our* interests, *our* priorities. My wife, Katie, could tell you the pattern of the wallpaper in our friends' homes because that interests her. I couldn't tell you if they had walls. I mean, I've looked at them; I just haven't *seen* them.

So here's a question, and I'll try not to take your answer personally: Did you *see* those last few paragraphs? Did you pull them from the shelf, or did you leave the words sitting on the page? This is perception: truly seeing, evaluating, scanning, probing, measuring, and determining the truth about a person, object, or circumstance. This is what Georgia O'Keeffe meant when she observed, "In a way—nobody sees a flower—really."[4] And I think we'd admit that much of the time we don't see God, not in the details of our day, not *really*.

But God's presence is with us every moment of every day. His Spirit indwells us. As this is an indisputable fact, we have to assume the problem lies with us and our perception—an *inattentional blindness* that impedes our awareness of God. This attentional deficit is the context for Saint Paul's writing in Ephesians 5:7-21, a text composed almost entirely of perceptual metaphors: awake, sleeper, darkness, light, drunk . . .

What's fascinating is that Paul traces the spiritual perception problem back along a causal chain that's straight out of a neurology textbook. Our attention (5:7-16) is altered by our perception

(5:17), which is influenced by our mood (5:18-20); *ergo*, you ran over the guy rollerblading because you weren't looking (attention) and because your windshield was filthy and the radio was blaring (perception), and you were stressed (mood) because you were running late for an appointment. This is exactly how the text flows, beginning with attention.

Attention: Ephesians 5:7-16
One Very Long Metaphor

Last Christmas my son, Will, gave my wife a cute stuffed kangaroo. As Katie opened the box, I remember thinking, *Marsupial. What a great word.* Then I thought, *How strange that some animals have pouches*; then I thought, I *wonder if anyone has ever had cosmetic surgery and attached a pouch directly to their body*; then I thought, *I wonder what it would be like to have a pouch*; then I thought, *I wonder what I would carry in my pouch if I had one—it could be handy for car keys and whatnot.*

Well, "a penny for your thoughts," and those astonishingly vacuous ones are mine. Though it appears random, there is a logic to it—thought moves to related thought—and that's what I want you to notice in Paul's really, really long metaphor in Ephesians 5:7-16:

> Therefore do not become partners with them; for at one time you were darkness, but now you are light in the Lord. Walk as children of light (for the fruit of light is found in all that is good and right and true), and try to discern what is pleasing to the Lord. Take no part in the unfruitful works of darkness, but instead expose them. For it is shameful even to speak of the things that they do in secret. But when anything is exposed by the light, it becomes visible, for anything that becomes visible is light. Therefore it says,

"Awake, O sleeper,
    and arise from the dead,
  and Christ will shine on you."

Look carefully then how you walk, not as unwise but as
wise, making the best use of the time, because the days
are evil.

Here's my best reconstruction of the flow of thought: In
context, Paul is speaking of the lifestyle of the wicked, and he
uses the image of *darkness* to describe it. Simple enough. This
in turn leads to the image of believers walking in *light*. And
speaking of sunlight, *fruit* grows in sunlight, and God's people
ought to be bearing *fruit*. But light also exposes things, things
hidden in *darkness*. Darkness conceals things as *night* conceals
things, and all kinds of *shameful* things, which Paul won't even
mention, are done at night. These things are done in *secret*, and
a secret—if you think about it—is just like *darkness* because it
hides everything.

So the metaphor has migrated from "darkness and light"
to "daytime and night," and this leads to the pairing of "asleep
and awake." The verse "Awake, O sleeper, and arise from the
dead . . ." is found nowhere in Scripture. Perhaps it was a poem
Paul was working on in his spare time, but probably not. Most
scholars think it was a commonly known baptismal creed. That
makes sense, and you can see how it relates to the imagery Paul's
been using: Going under the water in baptism is like sleep and
death and dark and night, while coming up is like daylight and
life and waking up. So that's how that fits.

And finally, we ought to be careful to walk while it's still light,
because the sun is rapidly setting ("because the days are evil").

If you go to the website of Karyn Hollis, a professor at
Villanova University, you'll find her collection of stretched and

strained metaphors compiled from student papers, and by "stretched and strained" I mean, "He was deeply in love. When she spoke, he thought he heard bells as if she were a garbage truck backing up."[5]

Paul's metaphor is stretched but not strained: The imagery is all connected—all meant to *wake* us to spiritual reality, to see the elephant standing in the room. (And I should probably forward this to Karyn Hollis, because I think I just compared God to an elephant.)

But now—this is important—Paul does not simply tell us to pay attention; he tells us what to pay attention to. There are two things, and daily attentiveness to these two things is nothing short of life altering. The world, our world, shifts with this change of focus.

Shifting Attention: Attentive to Jesus' Presence within Us

A couple of years ago I was giving an evangelistic talk on the campus of the University of California, Irvine. This odd little campus has an anteater for its mascot. The unofficial story is that the anteater was chosen as a pacifist statement (though I'm not sure ants would agree), and the campus proudly displays a four-hundred-pound bronzed statue of the rodent. I also remember that among the audience that night were a hundred or so not-so-friendly Muslim students.

The Muslim delegation was polite for the most part, but they weren't there as a show of solidarity or religious tolerance. In fact, two months after my speech, this same Muslim student group was suspended from campus for "disrupting a speech given by the Israeli ambassador."[6]

After a forty-five-minute presentation called "Jesus without Religion," I opened things up for questions and answers, which started off okay but quickly got heated. I could tell that the Muslim students were getting agitated, so in the spirit of the anteater,

I tried to wrap things up peaceably. I told the crowd that anyone with lingering questions could come up and speak with me afterward.

That wasn't a good idea. The Muslim students didn't go anywhere . . . they just circled around me. They were extremely worked up over my mention of the Trinity, a foundational Christian doctrine they considered blasphemous. Well, agitation turned to anger, and I wondered if it would be just a little bit embarrassing to show up in heaven having been martyred in Venice Beach, California—"Well done, *tanned* and faithful servant. "

I had no idea what to say until I remembered something important: The resurrected Christ lives in me.

So I said (not out loud or anything), "Jesus, what do you want me to say?" And then . . . I just knew. I grabbed the young man's finger that was pointed in my face and I gently and lovingly broke it. I'm joking; I gently *held* it and said to him, with all the compassion of God: "It's okay, brother, it's okay, really, it's okay." And everything turned calm and the urgent arguments were dropped and the angry students weren't angry anymore. And a few at a time, they just quietly walked away. In the truest sense, they had seen a Ghost.

The gospel is the death *and* resurrection of Jesus Christ. The significance of the resurrection, we tend to think, is that it proved Jesus rose from the dead. It did that, all right, but its significance is not simply as evidence. It's the other 50 percent of the glorious transaction: Jesus died in place of us, and now *Jesus gets to live his resurrected life through us.* I get his body; he gets mine.

This is why, in the midst of his meandering light-and-dark metaphor, Paul mentions the baptismal creed: "Awake, O sleeper, and arise from the dead." The Christian life is the resurrected life of Christ: Jesus living through me, not me acting like Jesus. It's really him displaying his nailed hands to others through me.

Finding myself going through the motions of my day, I am

immediately brought to life by the reality that the resurrected Christ is in me, looking to do *something*. This awareness opens my eyes, and I start looking, praying, and expecting.

With this awareness my interior monologue turns to a dialogue: "Jesus, what should we do right now?" This is what was so unhelpful about the idea of WWJD (What Would Jesus Do?). If you're thinking about Jesus in the third person, you've already missed the point. The critical shift of attention is in going from WWJD to JWSWD (Jesus, What Should We Do?)—changing our internal narrative from third person to first, from thoughts about God to a conversation with him.

Attentive to Opportunities

When I worked in advertising in the 1980s, our agency counted among its clients the US Army. Creative work on the project was contractually kept secret, which was odd because who's going to steal the Army's ad campaign—the Russians? Be that as it may, a 1981 commercial, hugely successful in rebranding the Army's image, featured the tagline "We do more before 9:00 a.m. than most people do all day." It's a great line—almost made you want to get up at 5:00 a.m. (almost).

The military always has these great slogans that would be perfect for the church: *A global force for good* (US Navy), *That others may live* (Air Force Pararescue), or *Always faithful* (US Marines). (I'm not sure what's up with the Finnish Rapid Deployment Force—according to Wikipedia their slogan is *Look good, do good*.)

Paul's phrase "making the best use of the time" carries a similar ethos, an idea repeated elsewhere in his letters (Colossians 4:5). What is a marine? Always faithful. What is a Christian? Always watchful and attentive for the opportunity to "do good" (Galatians 6:10): the opportunity to encourage, to listen, to serve, to give, to love, to preach, to whatever.

In the 1950s, long before the attentional research done by Simons and Chabris, cognitive psychologists observed the "cocktail party effect." It was labeled as such because in a noisy room—like a 1950s cocktail party—your ears prick up like a German shepherd's at the mere whisper of your name. You hear your name because at some level you're looking to hear it. There's this same sort of effect when a day is spent in search of divine appointments and opportunity.

A few weeks ago I talked to my friend Sean on the phone. He sounded exhausted, so I asked him, "What's wrong? You sound awful," because he did. Apparently Sean and a couple of friends had gone out to minister to the homeless, and one opportunity led to another. Now, here it was three days later, and they were living and sleeping on the street with the homeless, still seizing an onslaught of opportunity.

These opportunities to serve and love and pray had existed since the homeless lost their homes; it's just that no one had gone looking for them.

Sean regularly looks for people in need of prayer and healing. What's odd is that Sean's not very good at healing. I find this endearing about him. His theological reasoning is that in the book of Acts, the disciples went around healing people, and while I know how to refute his reasoning, why would I? He doesn't fake it or make excuses; if the person isn't healed, he humbly embraces the awkwardness.

But now and then God does heal someone and uses Sean in the process. Sean is attentive to God's Spirit in the way I'm trying to be attentive and expectant.

In her book *Rapt*, Winifred Gallagher shared a reflection on the focus of our attention. She wrote:

If you could look backward at your years thus far, you'd see that your life has been fashioned from what you've

paid attention to and what you haven't. You'd observe
that of the myriad sights and sounds, thoughts and
feelings that you *could* have focused on, you selected
a relative few, which became what you've confidently
called "reality." You'd also be struck by the fact that if
you had paid attention to other things, your reality and
your life would be very different. . . . Your life is the sum
total of what you've focused on.[7]

Pay Attention

I watched a quirky movie recently called *The Big Year*, which
was about birdwatching. Apparently birdwatching is a real sport,
which means there are professional birdwatchers and a Super
Bowl for birdwatching. This Super Bowl is called the "Big Year."
It's not a competition with other bird watchers—as riveting as
that might be—but a competition for the record of species spotted between January 1 and December 31.

Each year the American Birding Association (yes, there's one
of those, too) receives around fifty entries: competitors declaring their Big Year intentions. *Dear American Birding Association,
I'm going for it!* Once the year begins, watchers are consumed in
the pursuit of every bird on the planet. Well, that's not really
true. Pharisaic guidelines of the ABA contend that the bird must
be "alive, wild, and unrestrained" and observed somewhere in
Canada or the continental US.[8]

A recent article in *The Atlantic* captures the degree of obsession
that's a part of the Big Year. The article follows John Vanderpoel
during his 2011 bid for the record:

> After an unsuccessful morning of birdwatching this April,
> John Vanderpoel retired to his room at the Travelodge and
> told himself that he was done for the day, his last in Florida.
> To hold himself to this resolution, he threw all of his clothes

into the laundry, save a pair of red gym shorts not fit for wearing in public. Vanderpoel wanted to take a nap. But first—he couldn't help himself—he checked an online "Bird Board" that reports rare sightings in Florida. Immediately, a glimmer of hope: a Fork-tailed Flycatcher—a bird he had never seen before in his life—had been spotted in Fort Lauderdale only an hour and a half before.

The flycatcher represented an opportunity. Normally found year-round between Mexico and Argentina, it is known to wander into the American Eastern Seaboard; on Vanderpoel's self-created scale of sighting probability, the flycatcher scores a 4 out of 6: "possible but unlikely." Vanderpoel threw on a green birding shirt that, luckily, had not made it into the washing machine, and sped to the scene in a car. But he arrived too late, finding only a crowd of dismayed birders.[9]

John Vanderpoel finished his Big Year having spotted a grand total of 744 species. An amazing feat, almost as amazing as spotting 745 species, which was in fact the record at the time. Vanderpoel missed the record by a single bird. What is incomprehensible, besides the fact that he didn't try to cheat, is that Vanderpoel spent every waking minute of an entire year of his life searching for birds.

In *The Message*, Eugene Peterson translates Matthew 6:34 as follows: "Give your entire attention to what God is doing right now." *The Message* makes explicit what's implicit in the text ("Do not be anxious about tomorrow"). The problem, we would say, is that giving God our constant attention is unattainable—an impossible goal. But protests ring hollow because, point of fact, we all birdwatch—we all give inordinate attention to very trivial pursuits. Why not God? Why not a Big Year for God? That would be interesting.

Our choice of attention has enormous implications for awareness, but it's not everything. As evidenced by the roughly 300,000 people injured in drunk driving accidents each year,[10] attention is drastically altered, aided, or impaired by our perception.

Perception Altering: Ephesians 5:18

The watch stander on the *Valdez* telephoned the Coast Guard's commander. . . . "I've got the *Exxon Valdez* hard aground Bligh Reef."

"Are you serious?"

"I'm serious as a heart attack."[11]

At just past midnight on March 24, 1989, while sailing over the sharp reefs off Bligh Island, the voluminous oil tanker known as the *Exxon Valdez* popped like a balloon, deflating 1,264,155 gallons of thick, black, Alaskan crude oil into Prince William Sound. The damage took more than three years and 2 billion dollars to clean up, and the toll on Alaska's wildlife was apocalyptic. Numbered among the casualties: 2,800 sea otters; 250 bald eagles; 250,000 seabirds; and 22 killer whales.[12]

The ship's captain, Joseph Hazelwood, had twenty-one years of experience with Exxon Corporation and an IQ of 138,[13] and he had been awake and alert in the ship's wheelhouse, as several crewmen later testified. While there were a million unanswered questions, one point was clear from the investigation: The source of the shipwreck was floating in Hazelwood's bloodstream, not the Prince William Sound. The captain admitted to drinking three glasses of vodka before the *Valdez* left dock. Still, had the Coast Guard warned the *Valdez*, the collision could have been averted, but that wasn't going to happen because the two men on duty that night both tested positive for alcohol and marijuana. What sunk the *Valdez* was not a lack of attention but a lack of perception.

Ken Johnson, art critic and author of *Are You Experienced?*

How Psychedelic Consciousness Transformed Modern Art, describes what I imagine we already knew about the 1960s: Cultural perceptions changed radically, and drugs played no small part in the revolution. In an interview, Johnson said,

> I think the main thing is the idea that in psychedelic experience, people start thinking about their own perceptions.
>
> They don't take their perceptions for granted, but they start thinking about how our perceptions work and how interesting it is the way we think about the world. . . .
>
> It's common to take note of [this change] in pop music . . . Bob Dylan's music changed in the mid-60s and the Beatles changed, and many of them have publicly acknowledged that they were changed by sampling marijuana and LSD. . . .
>
> I think psychedelic experience makes you think that there are multiple realities, that there isn't just this one normal real world to which we're supposed to conform, but that the reality changes depending on the state of consciousness that we're in when we're experiencing it.[14]

But with or without drugs, perceptions would have changed in the 1960s, and that's because ideas, philosophies, politics, media, and culture also influence perception. Alcohol and drugs are simply the most obvious, most pained examples of perceptual influence, which is why Paul uses alcohol to talk of perception, shifting his metaphor from dark versus light to drunk versus sober: "And do not get drunk with wine, for that is debauchery, but be filled with the Spirit" (Ephesians 5:18).

Guy Walks into a Bar
Interestingly enough, Ephesians 5:18 is not the first time that alcohol and the Holy Spirit are contrasted in the New Testament.

In Acts 2, when believers filled with the Spirit are accused of being drunk, the church is faced with a public relations crisis, which Peter averts with a swift, public rebuttal: "Men of Judea . . . these people are not drunk, as you suppose" (Acts 2:14-15).

But whenever two things are contrasted, there has to be some baseline of comparison. You wouldn't say, "Never wear a sombrero, but instead be filled with the Spirit." The basis for comparison between alcohol and the Holy Spirit is the idea of influence, and how they both affect and alter perception—God's Spirit leading to ever-increasing knowledge of God and apprehension of the truth, and alcohol leading to greater impairment and delusion.

Like a DVD of *Ironing Man* or *Lets Miserable* on the streets of Shanghai, alcohol is the cheap knock-off of Spirit-filled transformation, though there are surface similarities between the two. Drunkenness, for example, progresses in degrees, as does the influence of the Spirit. Affection, joy, empathy—inebriation can momentarily create such sensations. There is also confidence and courage that comes from the Spirit, which we see in the disciples as they boldly proclaim the gospel. A similar loosening of the tongue is evidenced in someone intoxicated.

So that all makes sense, but here's what's odd: the strict either/or choice, as if there were only two possibilities in the world—being drunk or being filled with the Spirit. I mean, can't you simply *not* be under the influence of anything?

No, you really can't. There is no such thing as a "blank slate" (*tabula rasa*) of perception. Our perception is deluded from the get-go, already distorted through sin, the flesh, evil, and an endless string of other influences (greed, lust, ambition, jealousy, pride, anger, etc.). Delusion is our natural state.

And what this means is that being drunk with alcohol is paradigmatic; that is, you could substitute "Do not be drunk with greed" for "Do not be drunk with pride." The point is, you're going to be deluded by something. No one is sober apart from the regenerating work of the Holy Spirit. You don't get to choose whether your perception is influenced but only what influences it. That's the madness of living in a *fallen* state, in a *fallen* world. So, how do we know if we are under the Spirit's influence—or under the influence of something else?

Toxicology

Sitting in our closet is an enormous box of drug tests. In light of the many "users" who hang around our home, we finally bought in bulk. Twenty years ago, if you had magically transported me to today to see this box sitting in my closet, I don't know what I would have thought. What I do think is, it's a good thing life happens in degrees.

The tests are simple enough: Fill the cup, and five minutes later you get a color-coded toxicology report. Unfortunately, the Internet spreads precious knowledge that once upon a time you learned only from your cellmate. And so there are websites devoted to mentoring nascent drug users in the chemistry of test manipulation, showing them how to use a drop of Visine or Clorox to get a false negative. It doesn't matter; in the end, the most reliable indicator is not the test but the response to the request for a sample. "Dude, I just went" or "Dude, I can't seem to go right now" doesn't bode well. (Really, any statement that begins with "dude" doesn't bode well.)

I'd like it if there were something similar in the spiritual realm. Maybe greed or anger or discontent or anxiety is affecting the way I see the world, the way I see God, and what I'm writing. Jesus did give us a gauge of sorts, and we should look at it.

Salt Water

When Jesus spoke of the Holy Spirit's influence within the heart of a believer, he also placed it in contrast, though not with alcohol:

Jesus stood up and cried out, "If anyone thirsts, let him come to me and drink. Whoever believes in me, as the Scripture has said, 'Out of his heart will flow rivers of living water.'" Now this he said about the Spirit, whom those who believed in him were to receive.   JOHN 7:37-39

The phrase *living water* sounds magical, but it's not meant to be taken that way. *Living water* was a common designation for *fresh water* in ancient times. The Arabian Peninsula is a seashore of sand and ocean, and that makes fresh water living water because it grows crops, keeps living animals living, and broadly sustains life. The power of the analogy is that the alternative to living water is not dead or stagnant water—it's salt water. And if there's a better metaphor for sin than salt water, I can't imagine what it is.

Here's something nearly identical to fresh water, except drinking it makes you thirstier; drinking it actually *de*-hydrates you. Think about that. Salt water plays the same sick joke that sin plays on us: promising to satisfy our thirst, only to increase it. You could float atop an entire ocean of salt water and still die of thirst, just as you could possess the whole world and lose your soul. So where *do* we go to satisfy our thirst? *Thirst* is the clue.

Throughout the day we experience pangs of thirst. If you aren't conscious of it—and most people aren't—just watch a smoker. Whenever they feel a need (thirst), they light up. If they feel lonely, they light up. If they're nervous, they light up. If they need confidence or motivation, if they're bored or dissatisfied, need clarity or concentration . . . they light up. That's not to single out smokers. Smoking is paradigmatic the way alcohol is paradigmatic: You can do the same thing with music, texting, Facebook, energy drinks, E*TRADE, or anything else. The point is, we experience incessant thirst—for comfort, wisdom, strength, encouragement, direction, companionship, stimulation, motivation, and so on—and all day long we're sipping from some canteen to meet that thirst.

So here are some grotesquely personal questions we should ask ourselves:

- When you feel the thirst of loneliness, do you turn to God and the things of God (prayer, community)? Or do you turn to Netflix or Facebook or food to fill the loneliness? Where do you go for water?
- When you feel the thirst of insecurity, do you turn to God and the things of God, or do you shop or flirt or work out or put others down? Do you look for approval, pretend to be someone you're not, or perform for praise? Do you self-talk, self-soothe, self-analyze, self-medicate, or self-indulge?
- When you feel bored, dissatisfied, or depressed, do you fill the vacuum with iTunes or sleep or stimulants or fantasy or video games or pornography or ESPN or travel or news? Where do you go with your thirst?

It's not that iPhones and Facebook are evil. The point is to get at what's really influencing us, not to become Amish. All day long we're drinking something that's "filling us," and what's filling us is either increasing perception or distorting it.

To be filled with the Spirit is to be sipping-drawing-drinking-inhaling God's presence throughout the day. Incessantly breathing the air of the New Jerusalem. The question of *how* causally leads back to mood, or ambience.

Mood Altering: Ephesians 5:19-21

If your car ran out of gas or you needed some emergency assistance, statistically speaking, I'd be more inclined to help if I were downwind of a Pizza Hut or Krispy Kreme—so says a recent study on altruistic behavior. Researchers approached a random sampling of shoppers in a mall and asked them for change for a dollar. Standing in front of Cinnabon or Mrs. Fields, 60 percent of responders dug into their pockets, but that percentage dropped below 20 percent when approached in front of mundane clothing retailers—Shoe Tree, Pants World, that kind of thing.[15]

A corollary study found romantic inclinations heightened by death-defying heights that blurred in the mind the "rush" of love with the "rush" of I'm-about-to-fall-ten-thousand-feet-to-my-death,[16] and such is the power of atmosphere or ambience upon the heart and mind. You can better visualize the perceptual relationships if you think of it like driving: Keeping your eyes darting up ahead on the road is an act of *attention*; *perception* is equivalent to the car's windshield aiding or distorting the view; and what's going on inside the car (blaring music, crying babies), and inside your head (anxiety, frustration) is the *atmosphere* or *mood*.

If you ever attended a college party or a seedy bar, you've experienced the negative effects of ambience. The room is dark, the music's pulsing, clothes and conversation are sexually suggestive, and alcohol impairs judgment and erodes inhibitions. Spiritually speaking, an atmosphere's been created that's conducive to sin: No one is forced to drink or lust or gossip; but basking in the mood, the music, and the low lighting, you drift there on your own. This is how sin, as well as righteousness, is influenced by atmosphere.

So in his exposition on spiritual awareness, Paul now turns to "atmosphere" or "ambience," completing the causal chain.

But be filled with the Spirit, addressing one another in psalms and hymns and spiritual songs, singing and making melody to the Lord with your heart, giving thanks always and for everything to God the Father in the name of our Lord Jesus Christ, submitting to one another out of reverence for Christ. EPHESIANS 5:18-21

Like any living space, the heart has an ambience all its own, and what Paul describes here is an atmosphere of the heart that fosters the greatest perceptual influence of the Spirit. He gives the same instructions, nearly verbatim, to the church in Colossae:

> Let the word of Christ dwell in you richly, teaching
> and admonishing one another in all wisdom, singing
> psalms and hymns and spiritual songs, with thankfulness
> in your hearts to God. And whatever you do, in word
> or deed, do everything in the name of the Lord Jesus,
> giving thanks to God the Father through him.
> COLOSSIANS 3:16-17

Do you know what's *not* enticing and has *no* appeal whatsoever to the flesh? That same seedy bar or same seedy party . . . at 8:00 the next morning. Same place, no ambience. No ambience, no influence.

What we want is the experiential reality of the Kingdom of God living and laughing in our hearts, but it's an atmosphere that must be created, a party we have to throw.

Throw a Party

> I saw more clearly than ever, that the first great and
> primary business to which I ought to attend every day
> was, to get my soul to be happy in the Lord. . . .
> How different, when the soul is refreshed and made
> happy early in the morning.[17]

This quote is from George Müller, a spiritual giant of the nineteenth century whose life of prayer and faith has inspired Christians for centuries. Müller's great revelation was to begin his day in Scripture instead of prayer, and from his meditation on Scripture would flow prayer, worship, and thanksgiving.

The result of this is, that there is always a good deal of confession, thanksgiving, supplication, or intercession mingled with my meditation, and that my inner man almost invariably is even sensibly nourished and strengthened, and that by breakfast time, with rare exceptions, I am in a peaceful if not happy state of heart.[18]

Notice his emphasis on a happy soul and happy state of heart. Müller was a leathery Prussian missionary. He used the language purposefully, not colorfully, to call attention to the ambience or atmosphere of the heart. This atmosphere is what he saw as crucial, and he believed Scripture was essential to creating it.

I wake up each day as spiritually sensitive as a lizard. That's simply a given. Müller must have too, which is why he knew that this is "the first great and primary business to which [we] ought to attend every day." This is how we participate, partner, and cooperate with the Spirit: by throwing the party. And once the party is going, our job is to keep it going: keep the music playing, the food from running out, and the conversation from dropping off. And isn't that exactly what Paul is describing in Ephesians 5:18-21?

Mood influences perception, and perception influences attention; and what we attend to circles back around to affect our mood. It all hangs together.

Notes on Throwing a Party

There are many theologies of spiritual growth, many ways people answer the question "How does God grow and mature us?"

An easy way to discover someone's view is to notice how they address difficult and habitual problems of sin. Do they think the answer is to believe more, repent more, fast more, take more authority over evil, go to a healing service, reckon themselves dead to sin, see a counselor, join a small group, or memorize

Scripture verses? And yes, *none of these things are bad in and of themselves.* That's not the point.

The point is that everyone operates from some model of sanctification. My good friend believes that the secret is fasting and spiritual disciplines, but how can that be? It's never commanded in any epistle or given as a spiritual prescription to any believer or any church for any reason in the entire New Testament. Not to be dismissive, but I suppose that was. It's just super important to understand that spiritual growth resides not in holding funerals for the flesh but in throwing parties for the Spirit.

The vehicles of spiritual transformation—praising, thanking, worshiping, singing, fellowshiping—are the elements of a party. This party plays host to the presence of God, filling us with his Spirit, and the Spirit's filling is what transforms us.

Deep Breath

When we take our dog, Joey, on a trip, like most dogs he likes to stick his head out the window. Actually, he likes to whine until we wish we didn't have a dog, and then we let him stick his head out. I always thought dogs did this because they wanted a better view of the scenery, and in a way that's right—though not quite.

A dog's sense of smell is about a thousand times more powerful than a human's, and that's how a dog sees the sights: with his nose. The added benefit of sniffing the air from a moving car is the forced airflow funnels scent to the back of the nostrils, where the olfactory receptors are located. This is as close as a dog will ever get to the sensation of standing on top of a mountain.

We do the same thing when we sniff the air. Breathing regularly, only about 5–10 percent of our fragrant surroundings reaches the smell receptors at the roof of the nasal cavity.[19] So to smell, to truly intoxicate ourselves in scent, takes a concerted effort—a deep drawn-in breath through the nose.

Unlike sight or sound, smell isn't processed consciously but instead goes right to the memory and emotion centers of the brain. The result is a mood or ambience: a sense of Christmas past or your grandfather's closet. If you breathe deep on a crisp fall morning you can feel the jitters of those first days of school.

I'm not very fond of clichés, and I've never liked this one: "Take time to smell the roses." And yet I cannot deny that something quite profound is observed. There is that deliberate choice to redirect attention, to regard what typically goes unnoticed, the awareness of another sphere of reality, the intoxication of senses, the inversion of priorities and values, and the brightening of mood and overflow of gratitude for the least of things. This, I think, captures the essence of Paul's teaching on the Spirit: the idea that we can be awake to God moment by moment, aware of his movements within our day.

7

Perks
Driven by Reward

ABOUT FIFTEEN YEARS AGO, I was in Shanghai attempting to set up a summer missions trip for college students. It's the only time I've been someplace where it's illegal to be a Christian, unless you count Berkeley, California. My two traveling companions, Ron and Phil, and I were invited to attend a social gathering at one of the universities.

We were warned by an in-country missionary not to talk about Jesus at the event because the room would be filled with Communist Party members. He assessed us as a liability and was assuredly right in doing so; there's little doubt that within ten minutes of an interrogation I'd be wearing one of those little Chairman Mao caps and drawing maps to the underground churches.

So anyway, Ron, Phil, and I went to the party. People were friendly, and all seemed to be going well until I saw a crowd gathered at the far end of the room. There in the center of the melee was my friend Phil, and as I looked over at him I heard him shouting, "Well, what about the evidence for the resurrection . . ." Phil had gone rogue. He later claimed he had been goaded into it, but it's difficult to imagine how one is provoked into proclaiming the gospel by a room full of Communists. Thankfully, no damage was done, and we weren't personally responsible for ending the growth of the church in China.

The day before going home, we went, like all tourists, to see the Great Wall. It's quite a sight. As we walked along the top of the wall, I saw a government worker down below picking up trash at the base of the wall. What captured my attention was the speed, or lack thereof, at which he worked. It was like a child picking up his room in a state of protest, one dirty sock at a time.

A few hundred yards from there was a shopping bazaar selling souvenir Great Walls and battery-operated pandas and that sort of stuff. What was interesting about this, though, was that the bazaar operated on the free market: The people selling souvenirs got to keep any of the extra profit, and there, in contrast to Mr. State Rubbish Collector, I beheld a motivated work force. As I walked past a market booth, a woman actually grabbed me by the coat and pulled me into her stall, which is why I own one of those battery-operated pandas.

A contrast between the two workers would make a good argument for a free-market economy: The state employee was going to make the same wage no matter how many McDonald's wrappers he rescued, so why try?

But politics is not our interest. What's disturbing about my free-market theodicy is that it seems to capture the motivational inertia affecting many believers, including myself. A steady diet of eternal security, perseverance of the saints, and other salvation-affirming doctrines—and the neglect of Scripture's warning and promise of loss and reward—has instilled in modern believers the mind-set of a Communist worker. Put bluntly, most Christians see little benefit in exerting themselves for a salvation that's theirs no matter what kind of performance they turn in.

In contrast to this Soviet sensibility is, for lack of a better word, a *free-market* mentality that animates the New Testament. A motivation driven by the prospect of future reward, the potential for devastating loss, and the stern accountability for every investment made.

> And the fire will test the quality of each person's work.
> If what has been built survives, the builder will receive a
> reward. If it is burned up, the builder will suffer loss but yet
> will be saved—even though only as one escaping through
> the flames.   1 CORINTHIANS 3:13-15, NIV

I don't think this way, do you? I think about going to heaven and being with Jesus. I mean, sure, I'd like to hear, "Well done, good and faithful servant" (Matthew 25:21), but I could live with a pat on the rear and a "Nice try, James, we'll get 'em next year." Clearly I'm missing something. It's like seeing those long lines of people camped out overnight for the newest iSomething—I'm just not sure what drives that level of devotion.

T. S. Eliot once remarked, "I had far rather walk, as I do, in daily terror of eternity, than feel that this was only a children's game in which all the contestants would get equally worthless prizes in the end."[1] Maybe it's a little overstated, but it's a lot closer to the biblical perspective than my own, and so I have to wonder, where's the disconnect? What were the apostles envisioning in these rewards and this judgment that created in them such alertness and attentiveness? I'm honestly not sure, but I intend to spend this chapter chasing it down in hopes of reclaiming some missing motivation, as much for myself as for anyone else. I imagine the best way forward is to backtrack: to try to figure out how we got into this motivational quagmire to begin with.

Thinking about Heaven
Bad Analogies

In an old *Twilight Zone* episode, the opening zooms in on the debauched life of a second-rate gangster named Rocky Valentine. Having robbed a pawnshop, Rocky is shot by the police, and as his dreadful little life comes to an end, he awakens in the afterlife. There he's greeted by a portly man in a white suit who introduces himself as Pip. Pip is something of a celestial butler whose job, apparently, is to tend to Rocky's every whim. Whatever he wants, he has only to ask, and so he asks: women, cars, alcohol, money . . . everything his wretched heart wants, it gets.

But then guilt and confusion start to nag at Rocky: "I must have done something good that made up for all the other stuff. But what? What did I ever do that was good?" So he visits the great Hall of Records in search of his file, but when he finds it, he's even more confused. Apparently there's no mistake; he's exactly where he's supposed to be. Later Rocky pleads with Pip for an answer: "I don't belong in heaven, see? I want to go to the other place." Pip, now appearing more sinister, looks at Rocky in disgust and says, "This *is* the other place."[2]

This is where our problems begin. We come to the subject of eternal rewards with distorted ideas about eternal life, maybe more in keeping with "the other place." When we think about the life to come we think analogically, extrapolating from a world we know to a world we don't, and any faulty thinking along the way gets monstrously magnified because we're multiplying everything by infinity—*In heaven we'll eat ice cream* (oh fun!) . . . *forever* (oh noooo!).

In pondering our eternal state, our analogical thinking can fail us on three fronts, and it most certainly has.

The first error of analogy is to think of heavenly existence as so wholly different from anything we know that we try *not* to conceive of it at all. But minds must conceive, so we end up conceptualizing in negative terms: what heaven is *not* and what we *won't* be doing there. C. S. Lewis speaks to this theology by negation:

> Our present outlook might be like that of a small boy who, on being told that the sexual act was the highest bodily pleasure should immediately ask whether you ate chocolates at the same time. On receiving the answer "No," he might regard absence of chocolates as the chief characteristic of sexuality. . . . The boy knows chocolate: he does not know the positive thing that excludes it.[3]

Thinking of future existence as merely timeless, painless, sinless, or sexless only calls to mind the notion of sleep or sitting in a rocking chair—our only referents for actively doing nothing.

An example of the second error is my *Twilight Zone* illustration, a view of eternity so earthly and carnal it amounts to little more than a beer commercial—a worldly fantasy of the good life. This is what identifies the heaven of many beliefs as works of human fiction and fantasy, and typically *male* fantasies at that.

It's astonishing to compare the concept of heaven found in other religions with Jesus' description in John 17:3: "Now this is eternal life: that they know you, the only true God, and Jesus Christ, whom you have sent" (NIV). Who says this kind of thing? "Let search be made in the . . . archives" (if I might steal a line from Ezra 5:17) and you will find no equivalent. In envisioning heaven, human minds don't invent John 17:3; they invent Mardi Gras.

The third error of analogy is to conceptualize our future home in terms of the symbols the Bible uses to describe it. Biblical symbols are like the symbols they use at the Olympics— androgynous stick-people biking and swimming and making merry. They're quite adorable, actually. But if aliens came to Earth and actually looked like those icons? I'd forfeit Earth and live underground. A slain lamb sitting on a throne, multitudes clothed in garments dripping with lamb's blood . . . taken as *symbols* of power and glory, the imagery is awesome. Taken as literal *description*? I don't know—a Quentin Tarantino film?

The result of this gruesome pastiche is a scarred mind and stunted imagination. Heaven is our hope and our home, but honestly? I'm scared to go home. I'm scared "home" is going be an Albrecht Dürer woodcut. And theologians, for their part, have only added to my nightmare . . .

Hate What You've Done with the Place

Aesthetics is an odd duck. Like, try defining the color green without use of examples. You can't do it. Beauty has properties all its own and operates by principles other than logic. The disciplines of theology and aesthetics were, once upon a time, tightly braided, but they've been drifting apart for centuries. Aesthetics philosopher Paul Guyer contends that after Kant the "analysis of . . . beauty and sublimity" disappeared and the field of aesthetics was winnowed down to the mere "philosophy of art."[4]

What that means, as far as we're concerned, is that theologians now theologize without aesthetic reflection, which is no great loss *except* when it comes to subjects like heaven, hell, and the world to come. As Thomas Aquinas put it, an aesthetic point of view determines whether you see a proud stag as an object of beauty or an object of dinner.[5]

Picture, for example, those tinny doors you see in new house construction—the ones with the imitation lathed panels, faux wood grain, and hollowed-out interiors. To the aesthetic maxim of "truth in materials" these doors are impostors; they are not what they seem. But theologians don't typically ponder aluminum doors or notice planters made out of tractor tires. And that's quite all right—but not when handling the theology of heaven.

This is where a theologian needs a copy of *Dwell* magazine on their nightstand, not just a Bible.

See, if I were to decorate a room, I would decorate it to death. If the room had a country theme, I'd cram it with roosters and weather vanes and pig pillows and doorknobs fashioned like cow udders. I can't help myself; I simply don't know when to stop—when to *continue* a theme and when to *contrast* it. This is the acumen of artists, the aesthetic intelligence required of heavenly theoretics: postulating what will remain consistent with our earthly life and what will be in contrast. This is our great hope, and I have to say that apart from C. S. Lewis, theologians have generally described it with all the warmth and charm of Denny's.

Well, it's atop our foundational understanding of heaven that we construct our ideas about future reward. And as in a game of Jenga, building upward from a foundation already askew does not bode well for the upper stories.

And More Baggage
When we speak of heavenly reward, we are referring to those promises of Scripture for faithfulness and obedience that exceed the eternal life freely given us in Christ. For example, 1 Corinthians 3:13-15 tells us:

> Each one's work will become manifest, for the [Judgment] Day will disclose it, because it will be revealed by fire, and the fire will test what sort of work each one has done. If the work that anyone has built on the foundation survives, he will receive a reward. If anyone's work is burned up, he will suffer loss, though he himself will be saved, but only as through fire.

The text is clear: Our labor in Christ will be judged, and some will receive, in addition to salvation, some kind of reward. This is supposed to be motivating—it certainly drove Paul—and I'm sure it would motivate us, too . . . if it didn't fly in the face of certain beliefs we hold about heaven.

Eternal life, we know, is an undeserved gift, but rewards seem to smack of a meritocracy. Heaven, we imagine, will be a place of perfect happiness, but it sounds like some will be happier than others. We also would assume that everything done for Christ would be out of gratitude, so why the promise of compensation? How do we harmonize these apparently conflicting notions? Not very well, I'm afraid, and usually not on a conscious level.

More commonly we ignore the topic as well as the conflicts. We know we're going to heaven and, hey, that's good enough, right? But good enough for what? To motivate a very middle-of-the-road, mediocre kind of faith? Yeah, it's perfectly sufficient for that. But the problem with "Who knows?" is that it's just inches from "Who cares?" and I suspect that it's apathy, not humility, behind the "Who knows?"

Another solution is to separate heaven from rewards (or lost reward) sequentially: one long stern day of accountability and judgment followed by an eternity of egalitarian grace. But who can't live with a fifteen-minute sit-down for a bad report card? Judgment and reward lasting merely the duration of the reward ceremony, as a motivational fuel, is about as unleaded as it gets, so this can't be right.

Or we marginalize the rewards—thinking of them in terms of commemorative crowns because, let's be honest, it wouldn't be catastrophic not to wear a crown. I mean, who looks at a royal crown and thinks, *Man, if only I had one of those things sitting on my head*? But even in this life, the significance of a crown is the position, honor, privilege, and power it represents, not the crown itself. So we cannot lessen these crowns to something merely commemorative, like a trophy or a retirement watch.

These ways of integrating the notion of reward and loss into our concept of heaven don't really solve much, nor do they retain any motivational force, so where does this leave us? Honestly, it leaves us right where we are: completely unmotivated by eternal rewards. Ah yes, but at least now we know how we got here. And as that conceptual building has just toppled, we are now set to build another, starting with square one . . .

What Is Heaven?

Using the tools of language, Scripture provides a sketch of the life to come. But a sketch is not a photograph and most certainly not reality. The beauty of a sketch is its *lack* of detail—the capture of significant features, the omission of others, and the mere suggestion of what is unseen.

Filling in the details of a sketch turns it into something less real. Instead of imagining what *could be*, we stare at what *isn't*. But a sketch, viewed as a sketch, points to something greater, something uncontainable . . . something *more*. And this is all Scripture really has to say about heaven, that it will be more: "I have come that they may have life, and that they may have it *more* abundantly" (John 10:10, NKJV, emphasis added). Eternal life will be more logical, more beautiful, more personal, more relational, more fulfilling, more joyful, more interesting . . . more.

Going back to that aesthetic balance, it will not be so wholly different from life here that we have no reference. All that is good and right and God-given about earthly life points to its reality, yet the reality will be *more* in ways that exhaust the imagination: Time will not give way to time*less*ness but to time*full*ness.

The Right Place

Something very basic to Scripture, and for the most part simply assumed, is that the coming Kingdom—our ultimate destination and eternal home—will be *here*: a newly constituted heaven and earth (Revelation 21:1). We are uniquely spiritual/physical beings made for here. *Here* is our home. Randy Alcorn nicely summarizes it in his book *Heaven*:

> *When we die, believers in Christ will not go to the Heaven where we'll live forever.* Instead, we'll go to an intermediate Heaven. In the intermediate Heaven, we'll await the time of Christ's return to the earth, our bodily resurrection, the final judgment, and the creation of the new heavens and New Earth. If we fail to grasp this truth, we will fail to understand the biblical doctrine of Heaven.[6]

So much of the unhelpful imagery that erodes our hope comes from this confusion: seeing our intermediate state of affairs as our eternal state of affairs. Those dying before Christ's return—everyone so far—are immediately united with him and no doubt with other believers. But as our physical body is no more, and our resurrected body is yet to come, it seems that we will be in a spiritual, un-embodied state during this time. This is the intermediate state.

How would we live without a body? The most obvious answer is that demonic spirits pull it off quite nicely. (Presumably they are disembodied, unlike angels, as they are always out shopping for a home—see Matthew 12:43-45.)

That we experience the world through our body and senses is plain enough. But if you consider John's vision in Revelation, the mind is clearly able to see without eyes, speak without talking, hear without ears, and even taste without eating: "Take and eat it; it will make your stomach bitter, but in your mouth it will be sweet as honey" (Revelation 10:9). The senses of the mind (spirit) interface with the senses of the body, but function in their absence.

The Right Mind

Whatever the "new heavens and new earth" will be like, we will experience it with new minds. A psychological outlook undamaged by the Fall. This is important because boredom, dissatisfaction, depression, anxiety, and isolation are primarily states of mind, and it's better to imagine a renewed mind immune to such corruption than to creatively speculate on a heaven that might satisfy them. Not that we'll sit around watching grass grow, but I imagine that even a blade of grass could hold the fascination of a redeemed mind for quite some time.

While a lot more could be said about heaven, it's neither the focus of this chapter nor the focus of Scripture. Actually, that's interesting—that it isn't the focus of Scripture. There's a good bit of talk about the future judgment but not much about our future life, and I assume that's because we need to know that we will be judged and held accountable (we really do), and we don't need to know what we'll be eating and wearing in the world to come (we really don't).

Rewards

> The year was 2081, and everybody was finally equal. They weren't only equal before God and the law. They were equal every which way. Nobody was smarter than anybody else. Nobody was better looking than anybody else. Nobody was stronger or quicker than anybody else. All this equality was due to the 211th, 212th, and 213th Amendments to the Constitution, and to the unceasing vigilance of agents of the United States Handicapper General.[7]

This is the setting for Kurt Vonnegut's dystopian short story "Harrison Bergeron." In 2081, ballerinas are "burdened with sash-weights and bags of birdshot, and their faces [are] masked, so that no one, seeing a free and graceful gesture or a pretty face" will feel bad about themselves.[8]

George, the main character, has above-average intelligence, so he is forced by law to wear a mental-handicap radio that scrambles his thoughts every twenty seconds through a sharp burst of sound, keeping "people like George from taking unfair advantage of their brains."[9]

Vonnegut explores the idea of a modern utopia, where all are happy because all are equal. But this version of utopia is not God's. In the coming judgment, reward will be given with disparity, to the extent that not even a "cup of water" given in Jesus' name will fail to be recognized or "lose [its] reward" (Mark 9:41).

I struggle picturing this judgment; I struggle picturing any end-time event. How do people in twenty-four different time zones see Jesus coming with the clouds? These things bother me. It's true and I believe it; I simply cannot conceive of it. But one event, related to our future judgment, has already taken place, and this I picture well enough. Between AD 30 and AD 33, Jesus took upon himself the judgment for our sin. Having believed and placed our faith in Christ, we were given eternal life:

> Truly, truly, I say to you, whoever hears my word and believes him who sent me has eternal life. He does not come into judgment, but has passed from death to life.
> JOHN 5:24

But there is a second event, a future judgment, not *for* eternal life but for our experience of it. At the judgment for reward we will stand accountable for everything "done in the body, whether good or evil" (2 Corinthians 5:10). It will not be a ceremonial exercise, but it will decide our inheritance and allotment: what we will be, how we will appear, our capacities, our gifts, our freedoms, our abilities, our privileges, our responsibilities, and our glory. Everything about our *experience* of eternal life will be decided then and there.

While not exhaustive, here—broadly speaking—are the characteristics (not descriptions) of future reward found in Scripture, followed by commentary, which we'll place squarely in the theological genre of "biblically informed guesswork."

Promises

To the one who conquers I will give some of the hidden manna. REVELATION 2:17

To the one who conquers I will grant to eat of the tree of life. REVELATION 2:7

Looking at these promises of reward in Revelation, let us make a bold and courageous observation: They're not very motivating. I don't mean not motivating to me; I mean not motivating to anyone. How can you be motivated by a tree you've never eaten from or by food you've never tasted? You can't. Would you like to taste those things? You wouldn't know.

Such an observation would lead to the conclusion that there's a deeper meaning to the imagery, that what's being offered is greater intimacy with Christ in the life to come. But again, like the taste of manna, I have no concept of this. How does this differ from or improve upon eternal life? I mean, I already assume I'm going to be hanging out with Jesus a lot, so how is this an upgrade?

What I'm getting at is that Scripture does not disclose the actual reward but rather the *promise of reward*, and that's a big difference. The motivation of a *promised* reward is faith; the motivation of an actual reward is the reward itself.

By not telling us what's really being offered, all of the comfort and encouragement of the promise is derived by faith—faith that

God knows, sees, and cares, that obedience matters, and so on. However intimate, however trusting we've grown in our relationship with Christ, well, that's exactly how motivating this promise of reward will be. No more, no less. This is why reward-based obedience is not works-based obedience.

Organic

In 1949, Harry Harlow, a psychology professor at the University of Wisconsin–Madison, enrolled eight rhesus monkeys in a thought experiment. As "Russian cosmonaut" was the only other job opening at the time, the monkeys eagerly engaged in the task, which involved solving puzzles.

Without outside coercion or lure of bananas, the monkeys solved the puzzles. In fact, they seemed to enjoy themselves. What stumped Harlow was the reigning theory at the time, which explained all animal and human behavior in terms of two drives: a biological drive like thirst or hunger and an environmental drive fueled by reward and punishment. But this fit neither category, so Harlow proposed that it was a third, previously undiscovered drive: intrinsic motivation. "The performance of the task," wrote Harlow, "provided intrinsic reward."[10]

What I think is more impressive than Harlow's discovery is that several years earlier, C. S. Lewis wrote this about the nature of heavenly reward:

> There is the reward which has no natural connection with
> the things you do to earn it. . . . Money is not the natural
> reward of love; that is why we call a man mercenary
> if he marries a woman for the sake of her money. But
> marriage is the proper reward for a real lover, and he is not
> mercenary for desiring it. . . . The proper rewards are not
> simply tacked on to the activity for which they are given,
> but are the activity itself in consummation.[11]

Yeah, that's intrinsic motivation, and Lewis didn't need monkeys to discover it, just a Bible: "For what is our hope, our joy, or the crown in which we will glory in the presence of our Lord Jesus when he comes? Is it not you?" (1 Thessalonians 2:19, NIV). Notice that the reward Paul speaks of in this passage is one *intrinsic* to his ministry. It's what Lewis described as "the activity itself in consummation." Referring to the Thessalonians as "the crown in which [he] will glory in the presence of our Lord Jesus," Paul sees as his reward, at least in part, the worship of Thessalonians, presented to Christ, unceasingly, through all eternity.

In a way, the passage is proof of unique, personal, eternal reward, tied to earthly faithfulness. In the worship of the Thessalonians, Paul will uniquely enjoy something, eternally, that you and I won't. I'm happy for him.

Privilege

Then James and John, the sons of Zebedee, came to him. "Teacher," they said, "we want you to do for us whatever we ask."

"What do you want me to do for you?" he asked.

They replied, "Let one of us sit at your right and the other at your left in your glory."

"You don't know what you are asking," Jesus said. "Can you drink the cup I drink or be baptized with the baptism I am baptized with? . . . [T]o sit at my right or left is not for me to grant. These places belong to those for whom they have been prepared." MARK 10:35-40, NIV

Do you know what I want to do when I get to heaven? I want to plop down in a chair right next to Jesus. But guess what: I don't get to do that, because that place has been reserved for someone, and that someone's not me. There may be many privileges not ours for the asking; maybe people will be able to fly in the world to come, but it doesn't mean I will.

I think what James and John learned from Jesus is that the eternal Kingdom is a real place where not *everyone* gets to do *everything*, and where privilege is tied to reward and reward tied to faithfulness ("Can you drink the cup I drink?"). Surely part of our failure to see the significance of eternal reward is that we think that all of heaven's privileges are already ours. That we will be happy, whole, and holy in heaven, of that we can be sure—just that. Everything else is privilege, and privilege ties to faithfulness.

Embodied

Dear friends, now we are children of God, and what we will be has not yet been made known. But we know that when Christ appears, we shall be like him, for we shall see him as he is.   1 JOHN 3:2, NIV

Iron, magnesium, hydrogen, helium . . . there are ninety-two elements in nature. The additional twenty-six elements found on the periodic table are called synthetic elements, or, to those who failed chemistry, "the purple-y squares." If you've ever pondered the periodic table, you would probably assume, as most scientists did, that they were simply part of the universe from its beginning. In fact no one thought any differently until 1957, when astrophysicist Fredrick Hoyle published a paper on stellar nucleosynthesis—or, in less technical terms, "how a star burns out."

Hoyle proposed that only two elements, hydrogen and helium, existed at the beginning of the universe, and that these two elements coalesced into stars. Extreme gravity inside the star causes the hydrogen to fuse with helium, and this process is what "lights" the star and turns it into a massive fireball.

Eventually, after a couple billion years, a star burns through its fuel supply of hydrogen and helium, and as it does it produces the next few elements on the periodic table: lithium, boron, beryllium, and carbon. This brings us to six elements in the universe.

But the star, like some crazed pyro intent on incinerating itself, proceeds to burn through those elements and creates six more in the process, all the way up to magnesium on the periodic table. But these, too, must go—everything must burn. In fact, as the star burns itself down, it creates the first twenty-six elements of the periodic table, all the way to iron. But that's where the fire dies: "Iron is the final peal of a star's natural life."[12]

So where do the rest of the elements in the universe—elements twenty-seven through ninety-two (cobalt through uranium)—come from? Well, when a star finally burns itself down to a cold iron core, it dies. But, oh, what a death, described here by Sam Kean in his book *The Disappearing Spoon*:

> Suddenly lacking the energy to . . . keep their full volume,
> burned-out stars implode under their own immense
> gravity, collapsing thousands of miles in just seconds.
> . . . Then, rebounding from this collapse, they explode
> outward. . . . For one glorious month, a supernova
> stretches millions of miles and shines brighter than a
> billion stars. And during a supernova, so many gazillions
> of particles with so much momentum collide so many
> times per second that they high-jump over the normal
> energy barriers. . . . Every natural combination of element
> and isotope spews forth from this particle blizzard.[13]

So here is the awaited analogy—and thank you for your patience. In the worldly furnace of trials and temptation, certain *elements* of godliness are produced in our lives: patience, kindness, self-control, and so on. These *elements* could only be forged in the crucible of earthly sanctification. But when Christ appears, sanctification will be subsumed in a glorious supernova of resurrection power, taking "our weak mortal bodies" and transforming them "into glorious bodies like [Christ's]" (Philippians 3:21, NLT); "we will all be changed—in a flash" (1 Corinthians 15:51-52, NIV); and we shall "shine like the brightness of the heavens" (Daniel 12:3, NIV) with a whole new array of *elemental* gifts and capacities.

The doctrine of rewards would lead us to understand that at the moment of our transformation, what we are formed into will have everything to do with what we are formed from (1 Corinthians 15). The raw material of that supernova will be us: our choices, thoughts, actions, attitudes, character, and our entire lives and what has been made of them. Each unique, individual life will be magnified, glorified, and transformed—and our reward will be in the resulting likeness: in our radiance, however bright; in our capacities, however gifted; in our being, however glorious; and in our magnitude, however attractive. Our reward will not simply be upon us; it will be us.

Unfairly, it would seem, talent, beauty, intellect, education, wealth, and opportunity are meted out in this world without regard to personal merit. Brad Pitt does not deserve to look like Brad Pitt. He should look like me. Rewards flip this right-side up—our life *here* determining what will be innate to us *there*.

Worship

The twenty-four elders fall down before him who sits on the throne and worship him who lives for ever and ever. They lay their crowns before the throne and say:

"You are worthy, our Lord and God,
    to receive glory and honor and power."
REVELATION 4:10-11, NIV

While not speaking directly to rewards, this symbolic vision of the elders in Revelation illustrates the end which they serve. In these crowns is something of irreplaceable value with which to worship God. It's an instrumental value. And yet again, only the sincere Christ follower perceives the value of what's being offered. Only people who have struggled with the impurity of their motives, the coldness of their prayers, or the fickleness of their affections will be encouraged by such a prospect.

Vindication

> Friends, comrades, and fellow South Africans . . . On this day of my release, I extend my sincere and warmest gratitude to the millions of my compatriots and those in every corner of the globe who have campaigned tirelessly for my release.[14]

These were the first public words spoken by Nelson Mandela after his twenty-seven-year imprisonment by the apartheid government in South Africa. I think most sinful creatures would have wanted to start that talk with "How do you like me now?" But his election as president of South Africa, a Nobel Peace Prize, and a couple hundred honorary degrees have done a better job of saying it. Every award has been a public vindication of what he believed and fought for. And so it will be with our reward—an ultimate vindication:

> Now there is in store for me the crown of righteousness, which the Lord, the righteous Judge, will award to me on that day—and not only to me, but also to all who have longed for his appearing.   2 TIMOTHY 4:8, NIV

At the Judgment, nothing will be so clear as how *right* we were to believe, love, serve, and suffer for him. We will be like Noah as the rain finally began to fall, like Mandela giving his inaugural "I told you so."

Reigning

In *Drive: The Surprising Truth about What Motivates Us*, evolutionary biologist Daniel Pink summarizes current research in the study of human motivation. What drives personal fulfillment and happiness, states Pink, is the "deep-seated desire to direct our own lives, to extend and expand our abilities, and to make a contribution."[15]

The three things cited by Pink are (1) autonomy (the personal freedom to take ownership of a task and creatively manage the process—think "entrepreneur"), (2) mastery (the skills and capacity to carry out a task with excellence—think "army ranger"), and (3) purpose (performing a task that is meaningful and serves some greater purpose—think "philanthropist").[16] And really, Adam in the Garden was all three. In exploring what drives human motivation, Pink has unwittingly tripped over work as God created it.

It is the absence of these—autonomy, mastery, and purpose—that is responsible for much of the "meaninglessness" of the human condition. And I think it's the promise of these we find in the reward of reigning with Christ (2 Timothy 2:12): the offer of purpose-filled service, of responsibility that commands honor and respect, and of the skills and capacities to administrate this God-given authority. But it is a reward, which means we get not the responsibility we choose but the one we earn.

Surprised by Reward

To summarize this biblical montage, a helpful analogy comes to my mind (though I feel a little stupid telling you what it is): *Willy Wonka and the Chocolate Factory*.

In the movie, candy mogul Willy Wonka announces that hidden inside some of his Wonka Bars are five golden tickets, and that the finders of the tickets will receive a free tour of his factory as well as a lifetime supply of chocolate.

Charlie, who supports his impoverished family by delivering

newspapers, is one of the lucky winners, and he and his grandfather go for the tour of Wonka's factory. Somewhere along the way, however, they are tempted to steal one of Wonka's new confections: the Everlasting Gobstopper. But before leaving the factory, Charlie returns the Gobstopper, becoming the only ticket winner to pass what turns out to have been a test. It's then, and only then, that Charlie finds out the real reward, and it's not chocolate: it's the entire factory and everything in it. Wonka, it turns out, was looking for an heir.

As in this story, God's reward will be beyond our imagining, comically out of proportion to our faithfulness—and once it's revealed, the opportunity to acquire it will have passed.

In the 1950s, political scientist Robert Dahl did his landmark studies on the coercive use of power. Dahl defined coercive power (military, economic, etc.) as the use of threat or *reward* to get someone to act against his or her preference.[17] The definition reflects something remarkable about God's promise of reward. It's motivation free of coercion. For those striving to be faithful, God's promises are an added incentive, motivating only the degree of one's faith. To the apathetic, God's promises offer nothing viscerally appealing that would cause them to choose "against their preference."

Everything Matters

On a missions Sunday when I was speaking at a church about our ministry, a woman came up to me and said, "I can't imagine all the rewards that you've stored up." It was a nice thing to say—I hope it's true—but I think she was imagining eternal rewards given out in a few standard categories like the Oscars: number of conversions, hours logged in prayer, and the like.

But there's no reason to think that the metrics of ministry are the metrics of reward. Jesus' teaching on reward centers on stewardship: In his parables of the sower, of the talents, of the faithful steward, and of the moneylender, stewardship of his teaching is primarily in view. In other words, the question asked in the parable of the talents is not "What did you do with your talent for calligraphy or gardening?" but "What did you do with Jesus—his Word, his commands, his mission, his grace, his suffering, his love, his forgiveness, his guidance, his gifts . . . ?"

This is what stewardship is about, and I think it answers the question "On what will we be judged?"

Get Rich or Die Trying

I purposefully did something a while back that I'm pretty sure is theologically outside of orthodoxy. Before my mother died I dedicated a book to her, and I asked God that any fruit from the book might be credited to her life. I'm pretty sure such things are nontransferable, and God's Spirit gently affirmed to me, "You can't do that, moron," but I'll let you know for sure when we're dead.

While encouraging the Philippians to support him in ministry, the apostle Paul says something very surprising: essentially, *I don't need your help. I'm not looking for a reward from you. I'm actually trying to help you get your full reward from the Lord* (Philippians 4:17).

Whatever was theologically wrong with my reward-laundering scheme—and there is much—this was at the heart of it. I wanted to see my mom rewarded fully, and this seems to be the heart of God in Scripture's teaching on reward.

Reward, warning, and accountability have a very natural link to Jesus' wakefulness teachings on sin and hypocrisy, and that's the serious subject we'll turn to next.

8

The Sin You
Never Saw Coming
Invisible Sins

So LAST YEAR, my dear, precious Katie got breast cancer, requiring a double mastectomy. She found the lump in June, and it was confirmed with a biopsy. That began a process and a journey that went on for months. The experience of cancer (and all that entails), then a double mastectomy (and all that entails), then breast reconstruction (and all that entails), and then hormone therapy (and all that goes with that) are what make that pink breast-cancer ribbon a medal of honor. Being the husband of a medal-of-honor winner has its challenges, one of which is knowing you have no right to whine about anything, not with all your wife is going through.

I accompanied my Katie to the doctor at a facility I like to imagine was called the Grand Medical Institute of Womanly Things and Magical Thinking, but I think it was called Labcorp. As we walked in, the receptionist greeted Katie, and no doubt me as well, with a warm smile, but I imagined a glance that said, "Thanks for prying yourself from the sports bar long enough to escort your deathly-ill wife to the doctor. We'll see if we can't squeeze her in during half-time and get you back to the game." My imagination comes from some kind of free-floating generational hysterectomy guilt husbands have to deal with: angst that some male descendant committed their wife to an asylum for menstrual cramps. We checked in and walked over to the waiting room, which I think was postered with Georgia O'Keeffe prints or maybe real flowers or perhaps just a chart of female reproductive organs. I grabbed a *People* magazine from the coffee table and it sprang open to a photo of Kate Upton and her larger-than-life chest. *Is this a joke? Am I being filmed? What sort of Philistine sits with his wife in a breast cancer ward, thumbing through pics of over-endowed women? Turn the page, Rick, turn the page.* I turned the page, and Kim Kardashian came spilling out all over. *This really looks bad.* I had to will Katie to look in the opposite direction while I flipped to some G-rated pages. *An article on Caitlyn Jenner, perfect. Woah, breast implants, not perfect, keep turning.* And then a nurse came out and called us back, so as far as I know the affair remained secret.

After a short wait, the doctor came in and spoke with us. She answered a few questions and explained a few procedures, then turned to Katie to examine her.

"Should I stay?" I asked.

"It's up to you," said the doctor.

It's a test. If I go to the waiting room she'll label me Mr. Hysterectomy. So I said, "Sure, I'll stay." I'd played this game before, years ago, during childbirth: "The baby's crowning. Would you like to look?" *Sure.* "Want to cut the umbilical cord?" *Sure.* "Want to touch the placenta?" *Sure.* "Want to see a foot after it's stepped on a land mine?" *Sure.* I can go all day. All day, my friend. No one is going to label me Mr. Hysterectomy.

Alas, the conversation turns to mastectomy. The concept is conveyed to the man in a language he understands: "This is the operation Angelina Jolie had. She had both removed." Ah, yes, the day the music died. Now I understand. Now I know what you mean. Now I get *mastectomy*. What those blackguards did to Angelina, they're gonna do that to you. Got it. I said, "Oh," because it seemed safe and ambiguous, like, "Who is the Angelina Jolie of which you speak?" They got nothing out of me. Angelina Jolie, Angela Merkel, all the same to me. I'm as blind as justice.

So somewhere in the cancer conversation come the mastectomy conversation and the implant conversation. A world within a world within a world. After a couple of minutes talking, Katie and the doctor look at me for my input. And what in the world am I supposed to say? "Small. Small is the new big. Small is how I like them. Smaller the better. Yessir, I like my women like I like my celery—just a straight fibrous stalk." They have protocols for everything dealing with cancer. They ought to have one for that question so no one gets hurt.

So, appointment over, land mines cleared, trip wires evaded, just the walk to the car and I'm home free. Just two hundred feet without saying something stupid or insensitive. *Whatever you do, don't try to fix it: no action points, no aphorisms. Almost there, buddy; bring it in for a landing.* And opening the car door . . . annnnd we're out. Nice work, everybody. That's a wrap.

I was on my best behavior—but *behaving* was precisely the problem. I was playing the angles, gaming it out, and anticipating the obstacles, and it was utterly exhausting. It would have been a whole lot better if my heart had been in a better place. If I had been consumed with Katie, consumed with compassion or empathy, consumed with anything other than appearances. That's always the choice: Obsess about everything, or get your heart in the right place. I don't think this is a spoiler, but I think what we'll find in this chapter is that sin isn't the unforeseen obstacle—that which must be navigated or circumvented—the heart is.

Flowing through the middle of Luke's Gospel is a glorious

river of lucidity, where the progression of thought is unseasonably clear. First we observe the disciples at recess, out on the playground behaving like Pharisees. Four stories of bad behavior, one after another, point this out to us: their inability to rid a boy of an evil spirit, their argument over status and position (who should be first?), their competitive attitude toward those outside the inner circle, and their exclusionary attitude toward little children. It's hypocrisy beginning to bud and flower in the disciples.

Then, in Luke 11, Jesus launches into the Pharisees for their sin and hypocrisy while the disciples watch and listen, and it is a butt-kicking of biblical proportions. Finally, in Luke 12, come the slew of urgent warnings—*watch, watch out, beware, be awake*—as Jesus warns the disciples not to become like the Pharisees:

> Beware of the yeast of the Pharisees, that is, their hypocrisy. LUKE 12:1, NRSV

> Take care, and be on your guard against all covetousness, for one's life does not consist in the abundance of his possessions. LUKE 12:15

> Blessed are those servants whom the master finds awake when he comes. LUKE 12:37

It's a wake-up call. *Don't let this happen to you.* But you'll notice something ironic in these calls to wakefulness: Jesus, in essence, says, "Be on the lookout for sins you'll never see coming." But if they are invisible, how are we supposed to watch for them? The implied answer is that what needs watching is our heart: "Therefore be careful lest the light in you be darkness" (Luke 11:35).

If we're asked where sin came from, the traditional answer is free will. God gave us choice, we chose to sin, and that's certainly how it happened. But why did we want to? Why do *I* want to? John Feinberg suggests that the more fundamental cause of sin is desire. We want stuff we shouldn't want, or we want it more than we should want it, or we want it because someone else wants it, or we don't want it as much as we ought to want it. Sure, it's difficult to say no to a second piece of cake, but more disturbing is my desire to eat the entire cake when I'm not even hungry. What's up with that? What's wrong with my desires? As Feinberg explains,

> Morally evil acts, then, ultimately begin with our desires. Desires alone are not evil, but when they are drawn away and enticed to the point of bringing us to choose to disobey God's prescribed moral norms, we have sinned. Desires aren't the only culprit, for will, reason, and emotion, for example, enter into the process. But James says that individual acts of sin ultimately stem from desires that go astray.[1]

James, too, envisions desire as the primary mechanism of sin: "Each person is tempted when they are dragged away by their own evil desire and enticed. Then, after desire has conceived, it gives birth to sin" (James 1:14-15, NIV). This brings us back to *watch* and *watch out*. As we go through Jesus' calls to wakefulness, remember, we're not looking *out there*, we're looking *in here*—to our hearts, our desires, what we crave, and what we long for.

Yeast of the Pharisees

> Beware of the leaven of the Pharisees, which is hypocrisy. Nothing is covered up that will not be revealed, or hidden that will not be known.   LUKE 12:1-2

At the Institute of Food Research in Norwich, England, are housed some four thousand different samples of yeast. Should a global jihad wipe out America's microbreweries, it's from here that we would rebuild civilization. Particular beers require particular yeasts, and the NCYC (National Collection of Yeast Cultures) is where a brewing company can store back-up copies should there be some sort of natural yeast disaster.

Besides a repository, this is also where you'd get your hands on precious yeasts of the past, used in beers and breads they don't make any more.[2] In the online store, I can buy Fleischmann baker's yeast (*Saccharomyces cerevisiae*) from 1942, and for only $242, which is totally worth it.[3]

Jesus calls hypocrisy the yeast of the Pharisees. Hypocrisy, like yeast, comes in strains, and the Pharisees are spokesmen for the religious kind. This is the worst possible hypocrisy because of who's being deceived, who's putting on the show, and whose reputation is getting dragged through the mud.

Our family Bible growing up, with all the births and anniversaries written inside it, had a special illustrated section in the New Testament called "Stations of the Cross." Here's some of what it said:

> The faithful who perform this pious exercise, may gain
> a plenary indulgence as often as they perform it. If they
> receive Holy Communion and have made the Stations
> of the Cross ten times, receive an indulgence of ten years
> per station. For those sick in prison or living in a pagan
> country, if they hold a crucifix in their hand, blessed for
> this purpose by a priest and recite twenty times, Our
> Father, Hail Mary, and Glory Be to the Father, they are
> entitled a partial indulgence.[4]

The New Catholic Version was printed in 1950 (though it sounds like 1550), and since we were Catholic it was our Bible. New York (where I grew up) and Boston have two of the largest

Catholic populations in the US, and the Catholic Church carries considerable heft in both cities. That stuff about the Stations of the Cross—I believed that stuff. I mean, I wouldn't have died for it, but I had no reason to think it wasn't true.

We also believed in our priests, yet at the same time we were also suspicious. When I was a teenager, a priest asked me if I wanted to go jogging with him, and my dear wise mother said, "That's wonderful, Rick. Be careful, if you know what I mean." And I did know what she meant; thirty years before the child-abuse scandal in Boston's parishes, everyone knew. I passed on the jog and maybe saved myself thirty years of therapy.

This all does strange things to your view of God, and down-right horrific things if you were one of the abused. One of the most disturbing aspects of the child-abuse scandal involving priests in Boston was hearing from the victims what it had done to their faith. The movie *Spotlight* dramatized the famous investigation by the *Boston Globe*, and one of the scenes captures that disturbing link between Pharisee and God:

> When you're a poor kid from a poor family . . . when a priest pays attention to you, it's a big deal. . . . How do you say no to God? . . . What child, who is yearning for attention, would turn down love from God?[5]

Recently interviewed after the movie won an Oscar, the *Boston Globe*'s editor Walter Robinson (played by Michael Keaton in the film) shared this depressing reflection about his own faith:

> We were stunned to find out that these unspeakable crimes had been going on and had been enabled and condoned and perpetuated, then covered up for decades while thousands of children were abused by priests. . . . I was a lapsed Catholic at the time, and I'm super lapsed now.[6]

Michael Rezendes, the reporter who first broke the story, was affected similarly:

> Even though I was a lapsed Catholic, I still considered myself a Catholic and thought that possibly, some day, I would go back to being a practicing Catholic. But after this experience, I found it impossible to do that—or even think about doing that. . . . What we discovered was just too shattering.[7]

There's no question about it: These priests were the Pharisees, black robes and all. Given Jesus' warnings, it's unimaginable how we wound up here. And Protestants have their own tales. The egregious can always be a distraction for more serious and subtle dangers, such as not seeing *ourselves* in the Pharisees.

Jesus says of them, "They do all their deeds to be seen by others. . . . They love the place of honor at feasts and the best seats in the synagogues and greetings in the marketplaces and being called rabbi by others" (Matthew 23:5-7). It could be you—or me. I'm a people pleaser; I like to be liked. What was magnified in the Pharisees was incipient in the disciples. All of them. They already showed signs of infection, as do we.

I was speaking at a university recently on the evidence for God. As you might imagine, a lot of Christians came to the talk, but it was a campus-wide outreach, so a lot of nonbelievers came as well. After the talk I did an open forum, and questions from students ranged from provocative to petulant. For my part, I was magnificent. A peacock of many colors. I had answers and more answers. Wit and articulation. And when everyone was duly enlightened and impressed, I sat down—but not so fast.

Walking away from the podium, I felt a wave of shame for the moral and spiritual tragedy that had just occurred. My hypocrisy was vulgar. When the wave passed, I felt I was supposed to go back on stage, and I did. To the mixed audience of believers and unbelievers I apologized "for trying to appear smarter than I am. For using words to make myself sound more intelligent. For thinking more about my thoughts than yours."

Not a sound from the audience. Everyone just sat registering what they heard. From the nonbelievers I interacted with after the talk, it was the most significant thing I had said all night. As measures go, it was drastic, but it kind of had to be. Hypocrisy is usually in view whenever Jesus' prescription is to *rip it out, tear it off, sell it,* or *throw it away.* When hypocrisy is the problem, self-immolation is the solution.

I'm sort of kidding, but sort of not. The flesh is always planning its next big comeback, and corrective measures are required regularly and violently. If I notice I've been keeping up appearances, it's an immediate reminder to haul some of my garbage out to the curb.

Now, if I may put in a good word for the both of us, *not* keeping up appearances and *not* managing our image is nearly impossible. People always whine about hypocrisy in the church, but it is, technically, a "holiness convention," and how else are you supposed to act? Like it's a casino? A saloon? There are all kinds of social currents at play in a churchy context, and Jesus surely understands, so long as we're aware, engaged, and transparent. Within the family of religious yeast, far more serious than "image management" is judging the impressions we have of others.

I cannot think of anything more terrifying in the Gospels than the reaction of the wealthy moneylender when he finds out the guy he just let off the hook is shaking down others: "In anger his master handed him over to the jailers to be tortured" (Matthew 18:34, NIV). Whatever "tortured" is a metaphor for, I really don't want to know.

Because *hypocrite* is now a label instead of a word, hypocrisy is better pictured as the quality of doubleness. This is almost all

James talks about in his epistle: bifurcation of the mind (double-mindedness), vacillation of the will, faith separated from works, hearing from doing, rich from poor (partiality and prejudice), double-talk of the tongue (blessings and curses), divided motives, jealous ambition, and warring desires. The answer to which is integrity, wisdom, and wholeness:

> But the wisdom that comes from heaven is first of
> all pure; then peace-loving, considerate, submissive,
> full of mercy and good fruit, impartial and sincere.
> Peacemakers who sow in peace reap a harvest of
> righteousness.   JAMES 3:17-18, NIV

And finally, before turning from hypocrisy, I did want to let you know that *Saccharomyces cerevisiae*, yeast of 1922 ginger beer, is currently half price.

All Kinds of Greed

> Watch out! Be on your guard against all kinds of greed;
> life does not consist in an abundance of possessions.
> LUKE 12:15, NIV

In May 1980, two California school teachers, Ed Drummond and Stephen Rutherford, decided they needed media attention for their protest of the imprisonment of Black Panther Geronimo Pratt. And when one needs media attention and needs it fast, the clear solution is to strap on suction cups, climb up the Statue of Liberty, and unfurl a banner declaring your demands: "Free Geronimo Pratt." So that's what they did. The plan was to scale the back of the statue and spend a week, or however long it took to get Geronimo out of prison, holed up inside Lady Liberty's ear, which in light of her size is quite a cave.

The plan, however, never got further than the back of Liberty's knee cap, because their suction cups wouldn't adhere to the statue. Lady Liberty's green skin had millions of little puckers, because, point of fact, Lady Liberty was rusting out like a 1980 Civic. A survey of the damage revealed that "one-third of the statue's twelve thousand framing rivets were loose, damaged, or missing, and more or less half of the frame had corroded."[8]

Rust, if you're interested, is the corrosion of iron. Corrosion is, broadly, the oxidation of any metal, and all metals corrode, except for "noble" metals like gold or platinum. What makes an average metal average, and not noble, is its relationship with air. The bonding of air and average metal is very destructive to the metal.

What happened to Lady Liberty was *galvanic* corrosion. When you galvanize iron or steel, you coat it with a less corrosive metal. Galvanizing or rust-proofing your car, for example, is dipping the undercarriage in zinc.

But we like our statues big and we like them green, so Lady Liberty was dipped in copper. Out in the open air you need a buffer between the two metals, but the buffer between Liberty's copper skin and iron superstructure had disintegrated. The metals were touching—and that's not good because it creates a battery. Liberty had become the world's largest battery, and she'd been left on for half a century.

This is galvanic corrosion. Once a battery is created, electrons migrate from the weaker metal to the stronger. The bronze skin of the statue was sucking out all the iron; there were iron beams in Lady Liberty's chassis that weighed half of what an iron beam should weigh—like driftwood. It was a miracle the statue hadn't collapsed.

Restoring metallurgic integrity to Liberty took six full years and cost $162 million. According to author Jonathan Waldman, "Rust is costlier than all other natural disasters combined, amounting to 3 percent of GDP, or $437 billion annually, more than the GDP of Sweden. That averages out to about $1,500 per person every year."[9]

Admittedly, corrosion won't sell movie tickets, but what makes it fascinating is that when Jesus thought of wealth's power, the corrosion of metal is what came to his mind: "Do not lay up for yourselves treasures on earth, where moth and rust destroy and where thieves break in and steal, but lay up for yourselves treasures in heaven. . . . For where your treasure is, there your heart will be also" (Matthew 6:19-21).

The point of Jesus' analogy is not that worldly treasure is temporal and disintegrates over time. The point is that our hearts can disintegrate. Greed nibbles away at the heart like a moth at a sweater or rust at iron. This is what we don't see. Can't see. Think of all those tourists looking up at Lady Liberty, admiring the massive monument to honor, integrity, and freedom—and all the while she was rotting from the inside out.

Unchecked, this is what wealth can do, but so can a lot of other things. Jesus said, "Be on your guard against all kinds of greed; life does not consist in an abundance of possessions" (Luke 12:15, NIV). Greed is the desire for more, to acquire without reference to need. Jesus defines greed as finding life in abundance, which is why he says "all kinds of greed." So defined, lust and drunkenness and excess of any kind fall into this bizarre dynamic of sin: pleasure derived not from possession but from saturation. Contrast that with the saturation of worship. Greed and other sin is saturation leading to death. Worship is life-yielding saturation, reveling in God's person and presence.

Getting to the heart of greed, we see it's more about our attitude than the wealth, but we need to be watchful here, too. One could say, "I have a billion dollars, but I don't worship it, I don't rely on it, and I'm not saturated in it." And while that may be true, how do you know? How can you separate your attitude about money from what you do with it? I think this is what lurks behind Jesus' instruction to give it away freely. There seems no reason that God should take our word for it when it's easy enough to show him it doesn't own us.

Election Season

In the 2016 presidential election season, a lot of odd things happened, none odder than Donald Trump. The cover of the July 27, 2015, *New Yorker* was a cartoon of Republican candidates crowded into a swimming pool, with Donald in mid–belly flop, heading for the fray. That pretty much summed it up. But it wasn't simply that he was a DC outsider or had made his fortune in casinos or had a reality TV show—no, he was something altogether different. What he said, how he said it, and what he got away with defied logic.

He said Muslims should be banned from entering the country. He ridiculed Marco Rubio's ears.[10] He made fun of Carly Fiorina's face.[11] When asked a tough question by a female reporter, he joked about her menstrual cycle.[12] And yet with every new outrage, his poll numbers rose. Trump said, "I could stand in the middle of 5th Avenue and shoot somebody and I wouldn't lose voters,"[13] and he was probably right.

No one could figure it out. Trump had captured something, and even the news media called it a "movement." One theory was that he gave voice to the frustration experienced by many Americans, and that was clearly part of it. People were sick and tired of Washington. But Matthew MacWilliams had another theory, and it was pretty provocative.

MacWilliams, a doctoral student at the University of Massachusetts, conducted a poll of Trump voters. He asked respondents to identify which traits they believed were more important in children: independence or respect for their elders; curiosity or good manners; self-reliance or obedience; being considerate or being well-behaved. The test is well known among political scientists, who have used these questions since the early 1990s because of their accuracy in predicting authoritarian behavior.[14]

Of the 1,800 people MacWilliams polled, he found that only authoritarian attitudes and fear of terrorism—not income, age, education, or even race—predicted with statistical significance whether someone would support Trump. MacWilliams writes,

> While its causes are still debated, the political behavior
> of authoritarians is not. Authoritarians obey. They
> rally to and follow strong leaders. And they respond
> aggressively to outsiders, especially when they feel
> threatened. From pledging to "make America great
> again" by building a wall on the border . . . Trump is
> playing directly to authoritarian inclinations.[15]

Now, I'm about to transition to the point of all this, and please hear me say that the point ultimately has nothing to do with Donald Trump. But MacWilliams captured two important dynamics of leaders and those who follow them. The first is that given certain social conditions (fear, insecurity, frustration, disillusionment), a sizable population will support and follow charismatic authority.

The second is that the people we listen to, the people we invest with authority and allow to influence us, manifest our beliefs, preferences, hopes, fears, and aspirations. We want to believe them because we want what they're saying to be true.

When Jesus says, "Beware of false prophets, who come to you in sheep's clothing but inwardly are ravenous wolves" (Matthew 7:15), the danger is not identifying them, but identifying *with* them. It's a heart susceptible or inclined to their message, means, and motivations.

For Christians, these are shaped by our expectations of the

Christian life, and our expectations should be carefully defined and controlled by what the New Testament declares to be the normative Christian experience. If not defined by Scripture, our expectations will be defined by a range of things, but most dangerously by what we want to hear:

> For the time is coming when people will not endure
> sound teaching, but having itching ears they will
> accumulate for themselves teachers to suit their own
> passions, and will turn away from listening to the truth.
> 2 TIMOTHY 4:3-4

So what do we want to hear? A tomorrow better than today, a happy and harmonious family, safety from harm and from evil in the world, complete equality, the end of cancer and deadly diseases, financial help, wealth and prosperity, moral freedom to live any way we want, destruction of our enemies, long life, comfortable retirement?

If you watch much religious programming, or notice what's popular in many Christian books, then you're aware that these things are sometimes promised in sermons, not just campaign speeches. The question is, do we as Christians have a right to expect these things from God? Some of them? Any of them? None of them? What should be a present expectation, and what should be a future hope?

A single verse will not provide an answer. Our sense of rights and privileges is notoriously conditioned by our culture. Messengers prospering from our support are suspect on grounds of a conflict of interest. Only deep immersion in Scripture can be trusted to set the footings and shape the form of expectations.

Personally, I hedge on the side of safety. When the apostle Paul planted a church or visited for a short time before being called away, I think this question of "expectation" was the most critical in his mind. Would the experience of trials or persecution or sin lead to disillusionment? Well, it would do that only if their expectation was for something different, better. So notice how he "strengthened the soul," managed expectations, and guarded against disillusionment:

> When they had preached the gospel to that city and had made many disciples, they returned to Lystra and to Iconium and to Antioch, strengthening the souls of the disciples, encouraging them to continue in the faith, and saying that through many tribulations we must enter the kingdom of God. ACTS 14:21-22

It's the same thing Jesus said before he left town: "I have said these things to you, that in me you may have peace. In the world you will have tribulation. But take heart; I have overcome the world" (John 16:33).

None of us gets the same sorts of trials, hardships, blessings, or gifts, which means there is no uniform, universal set of expectations for "the Christian life." Mileage will vary. But passages that address general expectations, like the ones above, are always, always sobering. Sober expectations protect the heart from the allure of false teachers.

Different World

In 2011, David Ricci and his friends were walking through the slums of Calcutta on the way to an orphanage. They were in India on a mission trip, working with children infected by AIDS and HIV. Having spent four months in training at a Youth with a Mission base in Colorado, they were now out on the mission field, in one of the planet's filthier corners.

Passing by a small train station, they took a shortcut across the tracks. In order to navigate the land mines of refuse and human waste, David Ricci was staring at the ground, and so he never saw the train coming. It whizzed past at fifty miles per hour and snagged his shirt, wrenching him under the train and dragging him for more than one hundred yards. They rushed him to a local clinic, and all Ricci remembers—before blacking out—was the doctor unpacking a leather bundle of metal tools and pulling from it a machete. Ricci woke with his right leg amputated.

The problem with Calcutta medical clinics is that they're all in Calcutta, and that meant David's ordeal wasn't close to being over. As the days passed, his condition slowly worsened; he was transferred to another Indian hospital, and for several weeks doctors tested and tried everything but without effect. He was still getting worse. Now, three weeks after the amputation, there was finally a medical consensus on his condition: David was going to die, and soon, and there was nothing anyone could do about it. With no other options, David's family flew him from India to the trauma unit at Harborview Medical Center in Seattle.

Back in Seattle, Ricci's lab reports turned up something unexpected and horrifying. He had contracted the NDM-1 bacterium, most likely from the clinic in Calcutta. NDM-1 belongs to a family of bacteria known as gram-negatives, which, loosely defined, means the bacteria has adapted and mutated to the point of immunity to all known antibiotics—the stuff of dystopian science fiction.

Of all the gram-negative bacteria, there is something uniquely terrifying about NDM-1 because you don't get sick from the bacteria. Instead, NDM-1 infects normal, treatable bacteria with a gene that makes them resilient to antibiotics.

This particular bacterium was bred in the squalor of New Delhi (the ND of NDM-1), and the most comforting fact is that it had stayed there. But David Ricci had it, and he was now in Seattle, which meant NDM-1 was in Seattle. The hospital went on red alert, Ricci was quarantined, and infectious disease experts were brought in. Even if Ricci couldn't be saved, NDM-1 could not be allowed to leave the hospital.

As the bacteria couldn't be treated, the only option was to remove every shred of infected tissue in Ricci's body, which they did, or thought they did, anyway. A month after his release from the hospital, it was back again. Then another operation, another discharge, and then back again. As a last-ditch effort to save Ricci's life, they tried a new antibiotic, which in fact was an old antibiotic. The drug colistin hadn't been used in sixty years, and so maybe, just maybe, NDM-1 had not developed a resistance. But there was a reason colistin hadn't been used in sixty years. Ricci remembers:

> I began a course of strong antibiotics, including an
> antibiotic of last-resort called colistin, which is rarely
> used because it's so toxic. I felt my body shutting down
> from the toxicity of the treatment. My immune system,
> kidneys, and liver were failing, and I could feel my body
> giving up.[16]

Ricci survived the treatment and, for now, seems to be doing well, but this, too, may be temporary, so David continues to walk by faith:

> Now, eight months after my accident, my wounds are
> closed, but my worries are not over. My life consists of
> watchful waiting and praying that the infection, like
> some awful type of cancer, does not return.[17]

Since Ricci's diagnosis in 2011, there have been sixteen cases of NDM-1 reported in the United States. The Centers for Disease Control and Prevention (CDC), generally the opposite of reactionary, issued a public health warning regarding gram-negatives, calling them "nightmare bacteria." Dr. Arjun Srinivasan, associate director of the CDC, has stated the situation more bluntly than anyone has wanted to hear: "We're running out of antibiotics."[18]

Sin is this bacteria. If you get it, only God can get rid of it. Extreme resilience, potency, and adaptability have made it invincible and us terribly vulnerable. It's a new world, more dangerous than the old. Evil has mutated, and sin has adapted. While we encounter the same types of sin, the same types of temptation, and the same types of evil that have always existed, they are now in forms that are magnitudes more potent, resilient, addictive, and deadly.

What culture hasn't had its illicit substances? Marijuana, alcohol, or something like it has been around as long as time. But heroin is the new marijuana, and the new heroin is fentanyl (synthetic heroin one hundred times more potent than morphine). You don't outgrow these drugs; you don't live to outgrow them. Like NDM-1, treatments have proved futile against this plague of pharmaceuticals.

The same could be said of pornography. There's nothing new under the sun, but there's a whole new sun. Pornography has adapted and mutated, and the percentage of people addicted is staggering. Once you start looking, it's nearly impossible to look away.

Sexuality, like other things we grow into, has some elasticity, but gender and sexuality have been so contorted we no longer recognize their shape.

The music, the art, the entertainment: all digitally enhanced, aesthetically nuanced, creatively layered, and endlessly streaming. Lies have never felt truer.

The point is that spiritual mediocrity is no longer tenable. Not that it was ever desirable, but there really was a time when even wrong paths didn't stray far from the road. Sometime quite recently we entered a stark age where it's quite observable that

those not with Christ are against him (see Matthew 12:30)—
where there is no longer dabbling in sin, only addiction to it.

> For you are all children of light, children of the day. We
> are not of the night or of the darkness. So then let us not
> sleep, as others do, but let us keep awake and be sober.
> For those who sleep, sleep at night, and those who get
> drunk, are drunk at night. But since we belong to the
> day, let us be sober.   I THESSALONIANS 5:5-8

9

The Coming Clouds
Anticipation of Christ's Return

IN THE LATE 1950S, Belgium renounced its colonial claim on Zaire, granting them independence. And so was born the Democratic Republic of the Congo.

The transition of power was marked by King Mobutu's transition from the name Joseph-Désiré Mobutu to Mobutu Sese Seko Kuku Ngbendu Wa Za Banga, roughly translated as "Warrior who knows no defeat because of his endurance and inflexible will and is all-powerful, leaving fire in his wake as he goes from conquest to conquest."[1] So, that name's taken.

The Congo is where you'll find Shinkolobwe, if you were looking for it, and why you'd be looking for it is if you were planning to build a nuclear bomb. Shinkolobwe is where we excavated the uranium used in the bombs dropped on Hiroshima and Nagasaki. And, as a token of gratitude for that uranium, we sold the Congo its very own nuclear reactor, which was up and operational by the fall of 1959.

As the Congo's economy has deteriorated, so has its reactor.

It's still functional, but the cooling water is sewage, and the power is only turned on once a week for maintenance. A visiting journalist, Michela Wrong, recently described the facility:

> No carefully monitored perimeter fences, guard dogs, or electric warning systems. Only a small sign—one of those electrons-buzzing-around-an-atomic-core logos that once looked so modern and now look so dated—alerts you to the presence of radioactive material.[2]

It gets worse: In its current state of neglect, two uranium rods have been stolen. One turned up in Rome in the possession of a mafia family trying to sell it to Middle Eastern buyers, and the other . . . only God knows—perhaps glowing inside the fish tank of some Saudi prince.

The mine at Shinkolobwe was officially closed in 2004, and whatever "officially closed" might mean, mining still goes on there. Following the routes of the illegal-drug trade, cases of uranium, known as "Congo caviar," are smuggled out of the Congo each year, funded by traffickers in India, China, Lebanon, and probably Iran.

In the fable of Pandora's box, Pandora is lured by forbidden knowledge: By opening "the box" she empties all the minions of hell and inadvertently imprisons hope. Forbidden knowledge is forbidden for the very reason that it can't be unlearned—one is damned or doomed for simply knowing the contents. This is how Oppenheimer, father of the atomic bomb, viewed this nuclear age. While the first mushroom cloud bloomed on the horizon, Oppenheimer famously quoted the *Bhagavad Gita*: "I am become Death, the Shatterer of Worlds!"[3] The list of countries that have nuclear weapons is now nine.

The reactor in the Congo, the nuclear programs of Iran and North Korea—there are a hundred real-life stories I could have started this chapter with, all making the same point that really has to be made before we engage the subject of Christ's return. And that is this: The fanatical Christian worldview of a rapidly approaching doomsday is neither fanatical nor Christian.

Secular Doomsday

It was not, in fact, evangelicals who started the world buzzing about the end of days. The modern world has been buzzing since 1914, when H. G. Wells, seeking to avert World War I, published his anti-war novella *The World Set Free*. At the center of the story is a fictitious element called Carolinum (an atom whose nucleus was so unstable that it was continuously casting off pieces of itself), and an atomic bomb (a term invented by Wells) that war-mongering scientists were trying to make from Carolinum.[4] This was 1914!

Decades before the atom was split, Wells captured the public imagination with doomsday, and it was his novella that circulated among the scientists of the Manhattan Project, not books on Bible prophecy. Soon would come Hiroshima and Nagasaki, then the Cold War and Cuban Missile Crisis with a popular culture that fed on the frenzy: fallout shelters, "atomic" car washes, "neutron" diners, and a million monster movies about something "colossal" and radioactive. The apocalyptic mind-set of postwar America is accurately captured in William Faulkner's 1950 acceptance speech for the Nobel Prize: "There are no longer problems of the spirit. There is only the question: When will I be blown up?"[5]

Secular historian Tom Zoellner recently observed, "Whether it stems from a genuine divine source or a neurological twinge (or both), the suspicion that the earth is ticking away its final hours . . . exists on a grand collective scale."[6]

Christians, particularly second-generation evangelicals, seem unaware of this broader history, assuming end-time angst to be the whole-cloth creation of evangelicals. And while zealots have been predicting Armageddon since the turn of the *first* millennium, the atomic weapon of AD 1000 was a hammer, so feasibility clearly awaited another age. Since that age has arrived, it's been the secular writers and scholars blubbering that "the end is nigh." There is now a shared global awareness that civilization could end with that same push-button action you use to get a Snickers bar from a vending machine.

In the face of current technological, economic, and political realities, to assume the world's perpetuity (apart from God's providence) beyond this next century is denial, gross optimism, or naiveté. That's not overstatement. The variables necessary for a global collapse are relatively few (a financial market crash could do it), while exigencies required for a harmonious twenty-second century (decisions made by Iran, militant Islam, Russia, China, North Korea . . .) are astronomical.

Looking at doomsday from a broader secular perspective brings out the peculiar irony of our day: Nonbelievers set their watches by Mayan calendars and fritter about as though the sky were falling, while Christians stand on street corners with placards that read, "Relax. We've made the same mistake ourselves."

It's just sort of ridiculous to look around and wonder—somewhat agnostically—if current circumstances might actually mean something. God is sovereign over history; how exactly could the technology to implode or explode the planet with the push of a button *not* mean something?

Already Not Yet

As I mention in chapter 1, attentional studies have identified two distinct processes of human awareness: "top-down" and "bottom-up" attention.[7] By way of a quick review, *bottom-up* attention is our awareness of the immediate environment. Let's say you're walking along the sidewalk, and out of the million things you could look at, your attention is drawn to a hazardous banana peel (perhaps left by Laurel and Hardy) lying on the ground: This is bottom-up attention. *Top-down* attention is conceptual, big-picture awareness, concerned with things like: What are my goals? Where is my career headed? Should I join a gym? Both types of attention are critical, and successful navigation of life requires an exquisite balance between the two.

This same balance of attention regulates our spiritual lives, or should anyway. Theologically speaking, the Kingdom of which Jesus spoke is already here . . . but not quite. Wherever Christians are living for Christ, we see God's Kingdom, yet the full manifestation of this Kingdom is still to come, ushered in when Christ returns. In theological terms, the Kingdom is "already but not yet."

Kingdom-already attention (the equivalent of bottom-up attention) is focused on urgent issues confronting the church: justice, gender, culture, education, poverty, and so on. *Kingdom-to-come* attention (the equivalent of top-down attention) is forward-looking, focused on the eternal horizon, and concerned with teachings such as heaven, hell, evangelism, and missions. As in the physical world, wisdom lies in the "tricky push and pull"[8] between the two foci.

Christ's return is the cardinal doctrine given to the church to secure its top-down, Kingdom-to-come attention. Without it, we become nearsighted, focused only on the here and now.

To be spiritually nearsighted is to view Jesus as merely a guy without an agenda, led solely by forces like compassion and the needs of others. It's to sneer at doctrines like heaven and hell and the return of Christ because they divert us from the practical needs of loving others, and it's to understand "preaching the gospel" solely in terms of engaging the social issues of the day.

Maybe you've been there, are there, or are headed there. I've been there. I've also swung in the other direction. It's that elusive Quidditch ball of balance, and without an abiding awareness of Christ's return tent-staked in the mind, we'll always drift to the left—a perspective formulated from the shifting landscape in front of us, and not the horizon. And speaking of balance . . .

Satan the Great

In his book *Fooling Houdini*, Alex Stone gives an insider's tour of the magic subculture: the world of magicians, scam artists, and illusionists. Reading the book, this quote caught my attention:

> At magic shows . . . you can sometimes tell the magicians [in the audience] from the laypeople based solely on when they clap. Laypeople applaud the effects, while magicians clap during the seemingly uneventful moments, when the secret moves occur.[9]

Stone tells of a card shark who made his living from back-room poker games. He'd play his cards straight all night until the end of the evening, and then he'd dramatically point to the clock on the wall and yell, "Look at the time! This has gotta be the last one, guys." When everyone turned to look at the clock, he'd switch out the cards for his own marked deck.[10]

Satan's deception of Eve was essentially a magic trick. Diverting Eve's attention to the wrong object—what she couldn't have rather than what she could—meant paradise disappeared. This is the magician's particular genius, the ability to misdirect attention: While you focus on the waving wand, a white tiger is escorted past you. Misdirection is why the magician's assistant is a woman in spandex and not a plumber in overalls.

I think you see this misdirection in the controversies that always surround the teaching of Christ's coming, controversies that go back to the beginning of the church:

> We ask you, brothers and sisters, not to become easily
> unsettled or alarmed by the teaching allegedly from
> us—whether by a prophecy or by word of mouth or by
> letter—asserting that the day of the Lord has already
> come. 2 THESSALONIANS 2:1-2, NIV

If wisdom lies in the balance between Kingdom-now and Kingdom-come attention, then the goal of the magician is to tip the balance: to focus attention on one at the expense of the other. The misdirection is accomplished through some unsettling (2 Thessalonians 2:2) predictions, and there have been many. Harold Camping's 2011 date for the Rapture is a recent example, and a *New York Times* article shows just how "unsettling" such predictions can be:

> Thousands of people around the country have spent
> the last few days taking to the streets and saying final
> goodbyes before Saturday, Judgment Day, when they
> expect to be absorbed into heaven in a process known
> as the rapture. Nonbelievers, they hold, will be left
> behind to perish along with the world over the next five
> months.[11]

Featured in the article was the Haddad family of Middleton, Maryland. The mother, Abby, left her job as a nurse to "sound the trumpet," as she and her husband devoted all their time to evangelism. Work, planning, saving—everything was dropped as the days counted down. Joseph, their fourteen-year-old son, told the *Times*, "I don't really have any motivation to try to figure out what I want to do anymore . . . because my main support line, my parents, don't care." Grace, one of their daughters, would respond to her mother's chores with, "Mom, it doesn't matter, if the world's going to end!"[12]

But that's simply the first act—the second is when the end doesn't come, and you and I try to distance ourselves from anything to do with the end times, so as not to be implicated in all the nonsense. That's the real trick . . .

The Real Trick

I was on the phone with a Christian woman when the conversation turned to the chaotic state of the world: nuclear centrifuges, jihadist governments, human trafficking, seismic earthquakes . . . Netflix. And I said, "It's sounding more and more like the end of the world, isn't it?" But before the cement of that statement could harden, I blurted out, "Unless the Lord tarries."

After the conversation, I reflected on my use of the phrase "unless the Lord tarries." The first and most obvious observation is that no one has seriously used the word *tarry* since the Hoover administration. So why was I using it? I concluded the phrase was code, communicating some or all of the following: *I'm not one of those fanatical John-the-Baptizers on the fringe of Christendom, claiming that if you take the batting average of Derek Jeter, divide it by the number of pages in the King James Bible, and multiply it by the price of a Whopper, it will yield a return date for the coming of Christ.*

I had attached the phrase because I didn't want her to associate me with the whole end-of-the-world circus. But what my reputation gained, it stole from vigilance. To see exactly what was lost, consider the following statement: "Young man, you are going to be in serious trouble when your father gets home."

Ominous, right? Now consider this version: "Young man, you are going to be in serious trouble when your father gets home . . . whenever that is." Attaching the qualifier "whenever that is" postpones the event, even calls it into question.

It is to maintain urgency and vigilance from generation to

generation that the Scriptures declare, free of any qualifiers, that the Lord's return is "at hand" (James 5:8), "ready to be revealed" (1 Peter 1:5), undelayed (Hebrews 10:37), and "coming soon" (Revelation 3:11). You'll search the New Testament in vain for any of-course-it-could-be-another-thousand-years equivocation.

Even if we're not qualifying our statements, we can qualify the disciples'—dismissing their eschatology as a naive misunderstanding that the Lord would return in their lifetime. What this insinuates is that the disciples' teaching on the Second Coming was inspired, but their sense of urgency was not. Whatever the disciples personally believed about Jesus' return, God chose to preserve their urgent and hurried mind-set in Scripture—a mind-set that could have easily been tempered by a simple "it may be a while" from Jesus.

Sadly, whatever distance we create between ourselves and this teaching is how far we are removed from the *reality* of his coming.

As I've been hopping around quite a bit, you could have been wondering, *When is he getting to the point?* But we've already gotten to the point, at least one of them. What would you have said if I had asked at the outset, "How much of your hope in the future is derived from Jesus' return"? It's difficult to assess, isn't it? But I think through all of this preamble you have some sense of whether this teaching is keeping you awake, as Jesus intended it, or whether you've distanced yourself from it. That accomplished, we can push forward.

Well, here's a fun fact: The sight in my right eye is 20/30; the sight in my left is 20/100. I assumed I needed glasses, but apparently I should be wearing an eye patch. My sight has probably been this way for years, but I wouldn't know; I didn't check it until recently. So here's an idea: Why don't we go back and see what Scripture actually says about Jesus' return—sort of recheck our sight and see if we're remembering things rightly?

Hang In There

Riots in the streets, blockaded airports, the teeth of storefronts kicked in, the smell of burning cars, tires, and tear gas in the air: In the fall of 2010, France "appeared" to be on the brink of collapse. As one displaced citizen assessed the chaos, "It's Baghdad here."[13] At the center of the storm was not a military coup or civil war, though both seemed imminent, but rather the raising of the retirement age from sixty to sixty-two. The sentiment of the French people concerning this new law was abundantly clear: Don't mess with naptime.

The finish line of any difficult or painful situation is the focal point of motivation and hope, and in the mind of the French working class, the government had moved that finish line. The additional distance was only two years, but that's 1,051,200 minutes when you hate what you do or who you work for. The reaction of the French reflected the hope and motivation that was lost.

The return of Christ is the finish line of the Christian life. And right now your mind is telling you that you already know this, but I assure you, your mind is lying: It will continue to think, plan, and dream as if the finish line were not the *return of Christ*, but rather the *day you die*. And your mind, as optimistic as a schoolgirl with a crush, believes that to be sometime in your nineties.

I often speak to college audiences, so maybe I see the distance between these finish lines a little clearer. Imagine being me and speaking to a room full of college students: a room packed with young men and women in the spring of their attractiveness and sexual drive, a room reeking of Axe body spray. Now, imagine calling these students to live a life of sexual purity: "Listen, all God is asking is for you to remain pure for the next *seventy years*." At a heart level, you could assume a reaction similar to that of the French working class.

But instead, what if you said to these students, "Hold tight to your purity; the Lord is coming very soon, and you'll be so happy you waited." Do you see the difference? One finish line is right around the bend; the other, right around the twenty-second century. The motivational difference between the two is enormous.

This is the genius of God in the doctrine of Christ's return: The finish line is ever before us. And this is precisely how the apostle Peter uses the teaching when he states, "Set your hope fully on the grace that will be brought to you *at the revelation of Jesus Christ*" (1 Peter 1:13, emphasis added).

Notice the delivery date of grace: It's right around the corner, "when Jesus Christ is revealed" (NIV). Like me addressing teens on sexual purity, Peter is concerned for the holiness of this community. He's not deluded about Christ's return; he's making use of its flexible location to encourage and impart hope.

To borrow a metaphor from Scripture, the Christian life is a race—a marathon. If we are living with the notion that the finish line is fifty to sixty years from now, we will probably plan water breaks (dipping back into old habits of sin). What's more, we'll probably run the race at a more relaxed and comfortable pace.

Keep Pace

I'm writing this chapter in my living room, a room filled with boxes. We're planning to move in a month, and I had always envisioned us as lean, travel-light missionaries. We're not. We're hoarders. I have a metal statuette of an ant—why? I'll tell you why: When you picture yourself hanging around for another century, you don't want to throw stuff away . . . you might need it.

Like that illusion of water on a highway off in the distance, the horizon of life plays with the mind. If deep down we believe we'll be running this race another fifty years, we'll try to make the running as pleasant as possible: slow the pace, buy expensive running shoes, plug into an iPod—heck, why run at all, why not scoot around on one of those motorized Segways like a mall cop?

So it isn't just sin but worldliness that's restrained by the nearness of Christ's coming. When his protégé Timothy was getting entangled in worldly controversies and civilian affairs, Paul saw an opportunity to move up the finish line, encouraging Timothy to "keep this command without spot or blame *until the appearing of our Lord Jesus Christ*" (1 Timothy 6:14, NIV, emphasis added).

Do you see how this doctrine is being used by Scripture? The main point of the teaching is to provide a finish line . . . right around the corner . . . for the entire church age. People in past generations who wrongly believed Jesus would return in their lifetime, in a way, weren't wrong at all. This is exactly how God wanted them to live, and this is what the doctrine produces: watchfulness and expectation. In fact, the expansion of the Kingdom is most indebted to those most wrong about the timing, because they were most right about the teaching and how to live in light of it. If the disciples really did think Jesus was going to return in their life . . . thank God.

This is where those who make predictions about specific dates—years, hours, months—have missed the point. The point of the doctrine is primarily inspirational, not informational. To know the exact day would subvert the evergreen nature of its motivation.

Leaning In

There is one more crucial way that the return of Christ is meant to animate an eternal perspective, and it's found in Hebrews:

> Let us . . . not [give] up meeting together, as some are in the habit of doing, but [encourage] one another—and all the more as you see the Day approaching.
> HEBREWS 10:24-25, NIV

I like watching the NBA playoffs: the greatest players in the world competing for the championship of professional basketball.

In the first three quarters, by all appearances, the players are trying their hardest. But in the final quarter, the players tap into some reserve of energy: Every in-bounds pass is contested, everyone's glancing at the clock, every dribble of the ball is an opportunity to steal possession. No matter how motivated or financially compensated, it's clear that no one plays their heart out until the final minutes.

And this is the idea behind the phrase "all the more as you see the Day approaching." That "Day" is the return of Christ, and as we see it approach, as we get down to the final minutes, our pace—our labor—in Christ should instinctively quicken. But notice that the "all the more" effort is predicated on watchfulness, on seeing that Day approach. No watchfulness, no "all the more" effort.

So the question staring at us is, how will we know when "the Day [is] approaching"? It's a good question, and we know that because it's the same one asked by the disciples: "The disciples came to [Jesus] privately. 'Tell us,' they said, 'when will this happen, and what will be the sign of your coming and of the end of the age?'"(Matthew 24:3, NIV).

Jesus lived at a time like ours, where eschatological expectations fueled messianic claims, rumors, and predictions. So what Jesus *doesn't* say in response to his disciples is as surprising as what he does. He doesn't say, "Don't look for signs," or "Avoid speculation," or "Concentrate on the Kingdom here, not the Kingdom to come." Rather, he gives them very specific signs and encourages them to be on the lookout. Odd, isn't it?

This idea, that believers should have a general awareness of the Day's approach, is implied in the very giving of signs by Jesus, and statements like Paul's to the Thessalonians: "You . . . are not in darkness so that this day should surprise you like a thief" (1 Thessalonians 5:4, NIV). I'd imagine the onset of the final days will be a lot like Jesus' first coming: a vague but discernible horizon, viewed clearly in hindsight. According to Jesus, his first coming was, generally speaking, foreseeable—and likewise his return. "You know how to interpret the appearance of the earth and the sky. How is it that you don't know how to interpret this present time?" (Luke 12:56, NIV).

A friend of mine thinks that the reemergence of Russia as a political power is a clear indication that the end is beginning. I think it's a clear indication I'm going to have to pay more for gas. As annoying as it may be when Christians see everything from an ATM to an iPhone as signs of the apocalypse, the best we can hope for is better sign reading—because it was Jesus who told us to be looking for signs.

Are We There Yet?

Most honest discussions about the end times, regardless of the theological heights at which they began, wind down to this simple and subjective question: How close are we? My evasive but honest answer is that we are always close, and that, in fact, is the genius and intent of the teaching. We can also say that we're getting closer because history moves in a line, not a circle. And while history does not repeat itself, it does echo: Familiar themes and events reoccur throughout biblical history because history is a story whose author reveals his presence and plot through foreshadowing.

For those within the story, stuck inside its pages, it's impossible to know with surety when the convergence of events and signs indicates yet another instance of foreshadowing or the actual climax of the story. Those *in* history, who have mistaken the two, should be forgiven for their understandable lack of omniscience.

And here we are going to have to be careful ourselves, because we're also inside the story, and anticipation can fork toward either fanaticism or cynicism, viewing potential signposts with either doe-eyed gullibility or a rolling of the eyes.

The signs given by Scripture lead quite naturally to the end, by which I mean they are organic to the story of redemption: all of its major themes and threads coming to a climax. There have been many antichrists, but the field will narrow to one; creation has been groaning but will finally vomit its bellyache; the gospel mailed by Jesus at the start of the age will arrive to all recipients; and wars will escalate into one great conflagration—end of story. There have been echoes or iterations of these signs all along; what we are watching for is their culmination and convergence— whatever that looks like.

Wars and Rumors about Them

> *Till armageddon no shalam, no shalom*
> *Then the father hen will call his chickens home*
> *The wise man will bow down before the throne*
> *And at his feet they'll cast their golden crowns*
> *When the man comes around*

JOHNNY CASH, "THE MAN COMES AROUND"

In 2009 and 2010, the cyber security experts at Symantec were watching their monitors with the intensity of World Cup soccer spectators. Analysts had discovered a computer worm so massive, so ingenious, that it would earn the title of the world's first "cyberweapon." It had been loosed into the cyber stream nearly a year earlier like blood in the water, and all analysts could do was watch and wait, as no one knew how to stop it or what its intended target was. Then came the report that one thousand uranium centrifuges at the Natanz nuclear facility in Iran had inexplicably spun out of control. Stuxnet, the name given the cyberweapon, had found its target, smashing the centrifuges like a sledge hammer while avoiding the unpleasant side effect of starting World War III.

At the time, the brain trust behind Stuxnet chose to remain

anonymous . . . sort of. As experts pored over the encyclopedia of code, they discovered a six-letter clue—the word *Esther*, the Jewish heroine who had saved Israel from annihilation by her enemies. The cyber attack, the Obama administration later confessed, was a partnership between Israel and the US.[14]

According to Jesus, "wars and rumors of wars" (Matthew 24:6) would be one of the signposts at the end of the road. Stuxnet is the newest, latest iteration of war, the weaponizing of ones and zeros. There have always been wars, and I suppose rumors about them. The end will be the climax of this story line first introduced through Cain and Abel—murder, war, brother against brother, nation against nation.

What makes the time in which we live significant, and distinct from the rest of history, is the technological capability to make a bonfire of humanity. As I mentioned earlier, the secular world's fascination with Armageddon is directly correspondent to the never-before-in-the-history-of-mankind capacity for global destruction. Unlike past culminations of "war and rumors of war," such as WWI and WWII, a global conflagration at this point in history would in all likelihood not hint, echo, or point to some greater cataclysm, some worse ending. It would *be* the ending.

Coke Zero

These are the days of miracle and wonder
This is the long-distance call
The way the camera follows us in slo-mo
The way we look to us all
The way we look to a distant constellation
That's dying in a corner of the sky
These are the days of miracle and wonder
And don't cry baby, don't cry
PAUL SIMON, "THE BOY IN THE BUBBLE"

In Jesus' statement "You know how to interpret the appearance of the earth and the sky. How is it that you don't know how to interpret this present time?" (Luke 12:56, NIV), we have something of a template for how to look at the signs given in Scripture. A forecast is a general projection from weather patterns that are unfathomably complex and—as any weatherperson will admit—extremely fallible. But this doesn't mean meteorologists and weather channels are useless; I'm glad someone's watching the skies.

This age will end, said Jesus, with the completion of its intent and the mandate that launched it: God's glory proclaimed to all creation, the gospel of Jesus Christ preached to the nations.

> And this gospel of the kingdom will be preached in the whole world as a testimony to all nations, and then the end will come. MATTHEW 24:14, NIV

The world has yet to be preached to. That's a fact. So we should note that this sign, if taken seriously, would have eliminated every half-cocked prediction of Christ's coming to date. Score one for sign watchers.

When the Great Commission will be fulfilled is impossible to say, and defining its fulfillment will be like defining the moment you fell asleep. That said, dramatic shifts and movements in globalization, travel, and technology would infer that the global spread of the gospel is not far on the horizon. The world we now live in dictates the same answer to any question of globalization, whether it's *How long until everyone has the Internet?* or *a can of Coke?* or *a Walmart?* or *the gospel?* The answer is ridiculously and unimaginably soon.

It's hard to imagine that in the coming decades Google will not be preached to every tribe and tongue, so we should assume as much for the gospel. Surely this isn't something to take lightly—that of every generation since the inception of the church, we alone may observe this signpost.

Now, you could shrug and say that Jesus' words don't indicate his immediate return following the fulfillment of this sign, and of course you would be right. But you have to ask yourself if shrugging your shoulders is what Jesus was hoping to elicit in giving this sign to us. The very definition of a *sign* is that it is significant.

Seizing Seismology

> *I see the bad moon arising*
> *I see trouble on the way*
> *I see earthquakes and lightnin'*
> *I see those bad times today*
> CREEDENCE CLEARWATER REVIVAL, "BAD MOON RISING"

Just outside of New York City is a scenic overlook, a mountain from which you can see twenty miles in any direction.[15] It is the highest geographic land feature on the entire East Coast: the Fresh Kills landfill located on Staten Island. It's literally a mountain of garbage.

Cursed as a result of Adam's sin, nature now reflects our own moral and spiritual deterioration. The Fall brought acrimony between man and woman and at the same time joined us to nature in a marriage just as antagonistic and exploitive. If global warming didn't exist, something just like it would. No matter what environmental laws may be passed, the pollution in the world will keep in step with the pollution in our souls. We are bound up with our world.

Tsunamis, famines, earthquakes, floods: These are nature's nauseous reactions to our outrageous behavior, not God's judgment upon it (see Romans 1). To use the words of Leviticus, it is "the land vomit[ing] out its inhabitants" (Leviticus 18:25, NIV).

And so as humanity disintegrates so does our world, and that means that any natural disaster carries an eschatological warning, and the increase and severity of these warnings are, *according to Jesus*, important signs: "Nation will rise against nation, and kingdom against kingdom. There will be famines and earthquakes in various places" (Matthew 24:7, NIV).

So the oil spill in the Gulf of Mexico: Did God cause this to happen? Of course he didn't. Does it point to man's failure as steward of the planet? Yes. Does it illustrate our alienation from nature caused by the Fall? Yes. Does it point forward to a final "falling out" between nature and us? Yes. Does it raise in us a longing for the new heaven and earth that will precede judgment? Yes. So how is this not a sign? To say it was a specific sign *caused* by God, well, that's presumptuous; but to say it means nothing, well, that's just as presumptuous.

As I was walking past a newsstand in the airport, the cover of a *Newsweek* magazine grabbed my attention. In bold type was the headline "Apocalypse Now." The subhead read:

Tsunamis. Earthquakes. Nuclear Meltdowns. Revolutions. Economies on the Brink. What the #@%! Is Next?[16]

As man goes, so goes nature. And what this means is that mankind's final slide into moral and spiritual oblivion should be as obvious on the Weather Channel as it is on CNN.

All Israel
The eastern world it is exploding
Violence flarin', bullets loadin'
You're old enough to kill, but not for votin'
You don't believe in war, but what's that gun you're totin'
And even the Jordan River has bodies floatin'
But you tell me

Over and over and over again my friend
Ah, you don't believe
We're on the eve of destruction

BARRY MCGUIRE, "EVE OF DESTRUCTION"

On January 28, 2006, all of Israel was in mourning for its most elder spiritual leader. Regarded as a Torah prodigy from the time he was a teen, Rabbi Yitzhak Kaduri was estimated to be 108 when he died, bringing to an end one entire century of Torah study. Some 200,000 Israeli mourners turned out the day of Kaduri's funeral, the day the controversy began.

Prior to his death, Kaduri claimed to have had conversations with Israel's messiah. Kaduri told his many followers that he would disclose the messiah's identity in a letter to be opened one year after his death. A year later the letter was opened, and to the shock of Israel and humiliation of his family, Kaduri had written the name "Yehoshua," which is effectively the name "Yeshua," which is effectively the name "Jesus."[17]

The editor of *Israel Today*, Aviel Schneider, found himself in a moral dilemma as to whether to run the story. There was an onslaught of e-mails and phone calls, not least of which was from the family of Kaduri, claiming the letter was a forgery.

As *Israel Today* journalists investigated Kaduri's writings to determine if this was in fact a forgery, they found evidence to the contrary. Schneider noted that in the margins of his journal, Kaduri had drawn what looked like crosses, and as Schneider observed, "In the Jewish tradition, you don't use crosses. You don't even use plus signs because they might be mistaken for crosses."[18] In the end, *Israel Today* ran the story, declaring the words contained in the envelope to be authentic.

Now I have no idea of the specific relevance of Kaduri or this event, but Scripture does indicate that the Jewish people turning to the gospel is significant, a sign:

> I do not want you to be ignorant of this mystery,
> brothers and sisters, so that you may not be conceited:
> Israel has experienced a hardening in part until the full
> number of the Gentiles has come in, and in this way all
> Israel will be saved. ROMANS 11:25-26, NIV

In Romans, Paul declares that in the last days "all Israel will be saved." Given the context of chapters 9–11, New Testament scholar Douglas Moo provides—I think—the most satisfying explanation of this verse. Moo states:

> Paul here predicts the salvation of a significant number
> of Jews at the time of Christ's return in glory. The
> present "remnant" of Israel will be expanded to include
> a much larger number of Jews who will enter the eternal
> kingdom along with converted Gentiles.[19]

It's quite possible to see God's ingathering of the Jews as biblical, whether or not you think the nation-state of Israel has end-time significance. An appreciation of this Jewish ingathering does not require belief in a rapture or literal millennium; rather it is simply taking Romans 11:26 at face value: The last days will be characterized by an overflow of God's grace back to the Jews.

From a literary perspective, this adds a pleasing symmetry to the story of redemption. Salvation was supposed to be "to the Jew first," and from Israel it was to surge out to the nations. But Israel rejected her Messiah. And so salvation flowed first to the nations, and then, as Paul prophetically states, once "the full number of Gentiles" have responded, God's grace will ebb back to the Jews, fulfilling Jesus' axiom "The last will be first, and the first last" (Matthew 20:16).

According to *Christianity Today*, "In 1967, before the Jewish people regained control of Jerusalem, there was not a single

Messianic Jewish congregation in the world, and only several thousand Messianic Jews worldwide."[20] As of 2007, there were over four hundred Messianic congregations in the US,[21] and in 2012 some 350,000 Messianic Jews worldwide.[22] In fact, right now, there are approximately 263 Messianic organizations . . . in Israel.[23]

So let me understate this with all possible restraint: *Something*, it would *seem*, *might* be happening among the Jewish people.

Sum of the Parts

None of this, of course, *proves* anything—nor was *proving* anything the point. Rather the point is that there is ample reason for us to be awake and alert. But even if the future looked as bright as *The Jetsons*, we should still be alert, because Jesus told us to be. And it would be sad, perhaps tragic, if a few crazy predictions or a few crazy people caused us to knee-jerk away from this glorious hope, and from "encouraging one another—and all the more as [we] see the Day approaching" (Hebrews 10:25, NIV).

If Christ's return is irrelevant to your outlook on the future, if you have no sense of expectation, no eschatological interest in world events, or no desire to reexamine the prophetic books of Scripture, you are not looking at the future the way the disciples did, the way the New Testament does. You could be missing biblical motivation and anticipation, but that certainly doesn't need to be the case.

My own thinking regarding how end-time events will unfold has changed a lot over the years and will probably change again. And I suspect events will play out differently than I imagine them, however I imagine them. That's okay, because I worry that being locked into certain events and chronologies could cause the church to be *unprepared*. I'd be thrilled if there was a Rapture, but what if there wasn't? I imagine this would be confusing and disheartening for many: not a great mind-set for entering into a time of unimagined stress and sorrow. It's better to be awake, ready for whatever, than to be sure and caught off guard. Jesus didn't instruct us to be pre-wrath, or pre-millennialist, but he did instruct us to be awake—and that's what I'm aiming for.

10

Metanarrative
The Power of Plot

FROM THE AGE OF TWO until she was twelve, Hope was abused by her grandfather. The abuse ended with her grandfather's death, but too late: The trauma had already set Hope's life in motion on a trajectory definitively down. To survive the filth and the fury, Hope began drinking, and by the time she was fifteen, she needed Jack Daniels just to make it through a school day.

She met Ben at a party while she was still a junior in high school. They both were young and liked to drink, and that's more than enough to sustain a high-school romance or at least to get pregnant, which is what happened.

Raised in Christian homes, they were pressured into marriage to hide the shame (their parents') of an out-of-wedlock pregnancy. Hope was now married to a guy she barely knew and didn't love, a guy who was abusive when he drank, which was much of the time. Daily there were bruises and welts, and that's pretty unimaginable if you know Hope—you'd take her over Joan Jett in a bar fight. Friends and family ignored the cuts and abrasions, treating them like they were normal, like watching a "Wile E. Coyote and the Road Runner" cartoon.

By the time Hope was twenty-two, she had four children. Ben was now a full-blown drug addict. He would disappear for weeks at a time, come home, fight, abuse, and traumatize the family, and head back off to wherever. With no alternatives, Hope courageously ended the cycle: She grabbed the kids, pawned her wedding ring, moved into an apartment, and took on three jobs to support her family.

The story might have ended here—not a happy ending, but not a bad one considering her life to this point. But life keeps going, so the story must.

As a single mother holding down three jobs, Hope's workweek left little time to spend with her kids. There aren't *many* jobs where you can support a family working only a few hours a day, but there is one. Hope took a job at a strip club: great hours, great tips, more time at home . . . a lucky break if you can imagine a life where this is your lucky break.

She felt an emptiness inside, a spiritual void she couldn't fill, but proceeded to take it to the wrong god. Hope became a witch. Giving in to the darkness that had courted her since childhood, Hope began practicing witchcraft, and within a few years that had turned into Satanism. She began to traffic drugs at the club where she worked, selling to high-paying, high-profile clients, and by the fall of 2006, she had moved herself and her children into a $3.2 million estate. Satan had blessed Hope beyond her wildest dreams—except Satan doesn't do that, so it was all about to go away.

Hope quickly became hooked on the cocaine she was selling. To finance her habit, she and her kids left the large house and moved to a smaller one, and then to a smaller one, and then finally into an apartment. That didn't last, either, and when they were forced out of the apartment, the kids were parceled out to friends and family while Hope lived in cars, in hotels, or on the street.

In 2008, Hope made her final drug run. At 10:36 at night, driving through Philadelphia with a car full of drugs and money, she had the misfortune of being pulled over for making a wrong turn. For some reason, the policeman asked to search her car, and Hope went to jail on seventy-eight counts of possession and seventy-eight counts of intent to sell.

Sitting in her jail cell with despair and hopelessness sinking in, Hope asked for a Bible:

> I didn't open it at first. I just placed it on the desk and stared at it for hours. My first night in jail: It was time for lights-out, and there I was alone with my thoughts, my pain, my guilt, my shame, and a Bible.

Hope wasn't just a dabbler in witchcraft, one of those harmless Wiccans born too late for Woodstock. She was long and far into the world of Satan, and you can imagine the sort of war that went on in her soul:

> I felt the love of God, and it was unbearable. I cried out to God. I cried out for him to stop, because I knew he was loving me and I didn't want it, I didn't deserve it. But he wouldn't stop. He was relentless.
>
> When I awoke in the morning, my whole body ached, like I had physically gone through a war. All I could say were three words: "Jesus loves me." I felt perfect love, perfect peace. I came out of my cell that morning, and I looked at all the broken people around me, and I *loved* them. I had never loved anybody in my whole life.

On the day of her sentencing, Hope stood before the judge. After reading her charges, the judge asked if she had anything to say on her behalf. This, word for word, is what Hope told the judge:

Every charge you have read, sir, is true, and I'm guilty
for everything and guilty of many things you haven't
read. Your Honor, Jesus found me in my cell, broken
and scarred and hopeless, and he has given me new life.
I am ready to serve this sentence and pay for my crimes.
If this is where God wants me, he will use me in the next
years to tell of his glorious love and power of forgiveness.
And sir, I will be back to this very jail, but not as a
criminal but as a testimony for my Lord and Savior.

The words were met by complete silence in the courtroom.
Even the court recorder stopped her tapping. Hope's lawyer
started to sob, and then the judge spoke:

Ms. Wallace, I have never heard anyone speak with
such truth and sincerity, and if you do all that you say
then you are going to be successful. Ms. Wallace, I am
changing my judgment against you. Today you are a free
woman. And today you will be released.

It was Good Friday, 2008, and Hope walked out a free woman.

Good Story

Hope has been a good friend and an important part of the
Christian community Katie and I have here in West Chester,
Pennsylvania. I wanted to start the chapter with her story because
I knew you'd like a story and Hope has a good one. Furthermore,
if I hadn't included a story, I'm sure the editor would have suggested one, because she knows you like stories and probably
wouldn't buy a book without any.

And it's not simply that we *like* stories or find them
entertaining—it's much bigger than that. We see, think, dream,
and comprehend our world through stories. If you know someone

with autism, then you have some sense of what life is like without a metaphoric/narrative framework. In such a world, "I'm no Einstein" means only that I am not Albert Einstein: nothing more, nothing else, no attending meanings or associations.

In *The Redemptive Self: Stories Americans Live By*, psychologist Dan McAdams explores the redemptive narrative deeply ingrained in the American psyche: the story of something bad turned something good. His research shows that when Americans are asked to tell their story, most describe it in chapters, following a redemptive outline similar to Paul's conversion on the road to Damascus. What's fascinating about that is McAdams's book isn't a Christian book or study. "We find," says McAdams, "that these narratives guide behavior in every moment, and frame not only how we see the past but how we see ourselves in the future."[1]

Exploring the depth of our narrative framework was the goal of experiments conducted at Yale's Perception and Cognition Lab. As part of the experiments, short films of basic geometric shapes were shown to test subjects. One film showed two squares, A and B, situated side by side. In the film, Square A moves closer to Square B, but as Square A nears, Square B moves away, back to their original distance apart.

Asked to describe what they saw, observers described a chase scene: Square A chasing after Square B. Others saw a romance: Square A in pursuit of the sexy but not-so-curvaceous Square B. It goes without saying that the squares were neither "chasing" nor "dating" each other, but this is how instinctive it is for you and me to create stories and use them to interpret our experiences.

Since we see life as a story, it's the plot of life (far more than the events) that gives life its interest, engages us, and gives us that sense of forward movement. It's the story of our lives that keeps us moving ahead, hopeful that the story will get better, or at least that the next chapter will. Finding our days dull, our jobs boring, our lives going nowhere, and our careers at a dead end has everything to do with a perceived lack of plot.

This is the connection with wakefulness in the New Testament, and it's not a specific verse, but the book as a whole. We are entering into a story that is moving, and if we engage with it, it moves us.

The Battle for Plot

While we probably know what we mean by "plot," we should give it a proper definition. *Plot* is a series of causally related events, involving some sort of conflict or tension, leading to a climax and resolution. Plot is what gives meaning and purpose to the events, actions, and characters of a story. Plot is the cattle rancher; people, places, and events are the cattle.

In the presidential election of 2012, polling numbers became a bigger story than the candidates themselves. In an interview with CNN, Cornel West, Princeton scholar and adviser to the Obama campaign, accused the media of allowing the polls to drive the national narrative, and what he feared, he feared for good reason. As story-writing machines, we need only a few points of data to start constructing a plot. West didn't want the polls to start people writing the underdog story: the one where the unlikely candidate, against all odds, takes on the establishment, comes from behind, and beats Goliath. That one. Because once we anticipate a particular story line, we can't see the story ending any other way, so it doesn't. It's self-fulfilling.

Our narrative understanding of the world makes us vulnerable to just this kind of manipulation, which is why there's always a battle to control the narrative. And this struggle for narrative control exists in every realm, every field of study, wherever ideas influence—even in our minds, where we choose daily between the gospel and competing narratives like *I'll never amount to anything* or *I need to be successful to be loved.*

But battles are not the war, and that war is for the meta-narrative, the story about the stories, the truth of where we came from and why we exist. The explanatory power of this story wields enormous influence over people's thoughts, actions, motivations, and lives. Naturalism is a metanarrative, and so is Buddhism, Marxism, determinism, existentialism, hedonism . . . "isms" don't get very far unless they're driven by a metanarrative. And dictators don't get very far unless they can co-opt and control it.

But regardless of the metanarrative and who conceived of it, behind all the worldly "isms," agendas, philosophies, lyrics, ads, movies, and news, it's really Satan who's driving the narrative, and where it drives is unimportant as long as it's far away from God.

What God has given to us is the story as it really is. I hope you see the immeasurable value of possessing such truth. Scripture is the metanarrative from God's perspective—the story of how we came to be, the meaning of life, the purpose of history, the designs of evil—and all without slant or spin. What could possibly be more energizing than to know the plot of life?

Well, point of fact, there's a boatload of believers sleeping through their Christian lives, wandering aimlessly without purpose or motivation. And as these are the hallmarks of a missing plot, something must be wrong someplace. I think it's someplace between purpose and plot.

Purpose versus Plot

In the final pages of C. S. Lewis's *The Voyage of the Dawn Treader*, Aslan tells the children they need to return to this world. "There," says Aslan, "I have another name. You must learn to know me by that name. This was the very reason why you were brought to Narnia, that by knowing me here for a little, you may know me better there."[2] In these sentences, we can see Lewis's reason and purpose for writing the Chronicles of Narnia. That people would come to know Christ. But purpose is not the same as plot.

Using our working definition, the *plot* of the Chronicles of Narnia would be something like the forces of good seeking to rescue Narnia from the evil enchantment of the White Witch. But conversely, the plot is not the same as Lewis's purpose in writing it.

Here's where I'm going with this: I think we've gotten terribly confused between the purpose of the Christian life and the plot of the Christian life. To see the difference, imagine a new TV series based on the successful drama *Lost*—a Christian version airing on TBN and starring Kirk Cameron. In the show a plane crashes, and survivors are stranded on a mysterious island. The *purpose* of the Christians on the island is the same as the *purpose* of Christians everywhere: to glorify God.

So they cook to the glory of God, sing to the glory of God, fish to the glory of God, turn coconuts into iPads for the glory of God, and so on and so forth. On the whole it's a purposeful little community but as boring as *Teletubbies* to watch, and that's because there's no plot. Purpose, but not plot. Now, if we introduce to the story that the castaways must find a way off the island and safely evacuate an indigenous tribe of headhunters who live on it before a hurricane swallows up the island—well then, I just might be able to sell the story to TBN.

We were created to glorify God, to love and serve him in everything we do. This is the purpose for which we were made, but this is not the plot for which we were made. And it is not until we engage in the plot that we experience a driving, motivating, eye-opening context for living on this planet.

So what is the plot? The plot of the Christian life is precisely the same—maybe to keep us from getting confused—as the plot of Scripture. Yes, the Bible has a plot.

In *Kingdom through Covenant*, biblical scholars Peter Gentry and Stephen Wellum underscore this often-overlooked fact: that though the Bible has many books, authors, and genres, it must be understood *canonically*—as a single text with one overarching literary plot.[3] While the themes of Scripture are inexhaustible, there is but a single plot or story line, one axis around which rotate conflict, tension, climax, and resolution.

This plot has been stated a variety of ways in a spate of recent biblical theologies. For example, Christopher Wright, in his book *The Mission of God*, summarizes the plot this way: "The God of Israel, whose declared mission was to make himself known to the nations through Israel, now wills to be known to the nations through the Messiah."[4]

Mike Bullmore would describe the Bible's plot as a four-act play (creation, fall, redemption, restoration),[5] as would James Hamilton in *God's Glory in Salvation through Judgment,*[6] while G. K. Beale, in his *New Testament Biblical Theology*, gives us this extremely nuanced synopsis:

> [Scripture] is the story of God, who progressively reestablishes his eschatological new-creational kingdom out of chaos over a sinful people by his word and Spirit through promise, covenant, and redemption, resulting in worldwide commission to the faithful to advance this kingdom and judgment (defeat or exile) for the unfaithful, unto his glory.[7]

However it's stated, there is broad consensus on the Bible's story line, and for simplicity's sake, let's work with this plot summary: *the expansion of the Kingdom of God in this world, over and against the powers of sin, death, and Satan that oppose the purposes, plans, and reign of God.*

One reason we miss the plot of Scripture is that we read the Bible piecemeal, not as we would a novel. But seeing as the plot of the Bible is also the plot of our lives, it would be helpful to trace that story line, in some abridged fashion, and allow the divine narrative—as written by God—to have its full and intended effect.

The Mission of God

In most books the opening pages introduce the major elements of the plot, and in this sense—although it feels a bit heretical to say—the Bible is like any other book. In the account of Adam and Eve, we are introduced to the crown of God's creation, made in his image, entrusted with the administration and expansion of God's Kingdom in this world.

Being made in God's image carried with it a freedom of mind and will that allowed for the unthinkable—not just the freedom to choose among alternatives, but to choose an alternative to God. The stage is set, then, and all the story needs is for the antagonist to slither in.

Satan appears without a back story. What we know of Satan is no more or less than what we need to know: There is a spiritual dimension beyond our world, and in the temptation of Adam and Eve that world bleeds into ours. Evil begins here but doesn't start here. Adam and Eve are the first corrupted, not the first to corrupt. There is a cosmic struggle that is played out in the Garden, and in this struggle we chose the side of evil.

Yet, even as Adam and Eve conspire to betrayal, God intervenes to preserve and protect creation and rescue the administration of his Kingdom in this world.

Salvage Operations

While the first couple fell, hope springs to life in their godly off-spring, Abel. But hope doesn't live long, and neither does Abel. By merely the sixth page of Genesis, we are reading a requiem for the human race: "The Lord saw how great the wickedness of the human race had become on the earth, and that every inclination of the thoughts of the human heart was only evil all the time. The Lord regretted that he had made human beings" (Genesis 6:5-6, NIV).

Sin, spreading so rapidly through the human populace, leaves a lamentable option: Preserve the healthiest moral specimen, and amputate the gangrenous remains. And so a righteous man is found by the name of Noah. He and his family are preserved from the flood of judgment—godly seed artificially inseminated into a postdiluvian world.

Though the immediate threat is destroyed, evil survives the flood because man survives the flood.

In Genesis 11, we see the self-organizing properties of sin as it swarms and builds a hive for itself in Babel. A tower is built in defiance of God, a siege work for making a run on heaven. God surveys the threat and mounted rebellion and declares that "if as one people speaking the same language they have begun to do this, then nothing they plan to do will be impossible for them" (Genesis 11:6, NIV). Remediation is swift: God splinters the human language at Babel, and while sin will continue to spread, this merciful intervention will serve as a quarantine to keep it from multiplying.

Like the opening sequence of a James Bond film, these first chapters of Genesis are a sudden, shocking immersion into the story line and plot, but in Genesis 12 the pace slows. The plot continues—the expansion of God's Kingdom in this world over and against the forces of evil—but at a slower pace, spread out over seasons, like *Downton Abbey*.

In Genesis 12, we are introduced to Israel, which will be the means through which God's Kingdom will be administered and expanded in the world. Israel will occupy the leading role in the drama for the rest of the Old Testament. As goes Israel, so goes the plot.

Israel

On a map, Israel resides on the shared love handle of two obese landmasses (Africa and Eurasia). And this is because God created Israel to be "a city set on a hill" (Matthew 5:14), the only tourist attraction along the only turnpike between continents, a place where any son of Adam could pass through and marvel at God's reign and rule, clearly on display.

When Babel shattered, shards of humanity were flung every which way. Drawing the ever-sprawling nations back to God required a beacon with sufficient illumination: a godly nation whose renown would spread to the corners of Creation. As no such nation existed, God would create one from scratch, starting with a godly man named Abram. In Genesis 12, God tells Abram to leave his home in Babylon and head to the land of Canaan:

> The LORD had said to Abram, "Go from your country, your
>   people and your father's household to the land I will
>   show you.
> "I will make you into a great nation
>   and I will bless you;
> I will make your name great,
>   and you will be a blessing.
> I will bless those who bless you,
>   and whoever curses you I will curse;
> and all peoples on earth
>   will be blessed through you."
>
> GENESIS 12:1-3, NIV

Over the next eighteen hundred years and thirty-eight books of the Bible, the plot will drag, stall, and sputter as Israel falls into idolatry and disobedience again and again and again. Yet hope for the mission endures, a hope fixed on the coming Messiah:

> Behold my servant, whom I uphold,
>   my chosen, in whom my soul delights;
> I have put my Spirit upon him;
>   he will bring forth justice to the nations.
>
> ISAIAH 42:1

Jesus' Mission

Owing to a ponderous string of moral and spiritual failures, plot development in Israel grinds to a near halt prior to Christ's coming. However, as Jesus begins his public ministry, the pace quickens, and over the next three years the tension and conflict will build until erupting in the climactic death and resurrection of the Son of God. Dying for the sins of the world, Jesus accomplishes redemption for all of mankind—for all who would be saved.

But the story's not over, though it seems like it should be. That's what's interesting about being in the middle of a story— you don't know when a sharp rise in the plot is actually the story's climax. If you're in a movie theater, all you can do is stare at the screen and wait to see if the story resumes, resolves, or rolls the credits. This is essentially where the disciples find themselves after Jesus' resurrection: What will happen to the plot now? Was that the climax? Is the story over? "So when they had come together, they asked him, 'Lord, will you at this time restore the kingdom to Israel?'" (Acts 1:6).

To a first-century Jew, Israel's rejection of the Messiah was an entirely unanticipated turn in the story. In hindsight, clues can be found in the Old Testament, and certainly in the words of Jesus. But foreshadowing never gives the surprise away, so the disciples were . . . surprised. They had no idea where the story was going next, but it was important they find out. They were, after all, starring in it.

And this is the significance of Jesus' Great Commission discourse. After his death and resurrection Jesus gives these final instructions, and it is both a summary and explanation of how the story line of history will proceed, climax, and ultimately resolve.

> Jesus came and said to them, "All authority in heaven
> and on earth has been given to me. Go therefore and
> make disciples of all nations, baptizing them in the name

of the Father and of the Son and of the Holy Spirit,
teaching them to observe all that I have commanded
you. And behold, I am with you always, to the end of
the age." MATTHEW 28:18-20

Great Commission

If the Bible is a unified story driven by a singular plot, then we
might imagine the closing words of Part One (the Old Testament)
would in some way set the stage for Part Two. Not necessarily,
but it's worth looking into.

In the Hebrew Scriptures (the Bible of Jesus' day) it is
2 Chronicles, and not Malachi, that serves as the bookend to
the Old Testament. Second Chronicles 36 is the final chapter,
and verses 22 and 23 are the closing verses of the Hebrew Bible.
Here's how Part One ends:

> The LORD stirred up the spirit of Cyrus king of Persia,
> so that he made a proclamation throughout all his
> kingdom and also put it in writing: "Thus says Cyrus
> king of Persia, 'The LORD, the God of heaven, has given
> me all the kingdoms of the earth, and he has charged
> me to build him a house at Jerusalem, which is in Judah.
> Whoever is among you of all his people, may the LORD
> his God be with him. Let him go up.'"

In the final scene of *Batman Begins*, the first movie in a recent
Batman trilogy, Commissioner Gordon warns Batman of a socio-
path on the loose with a "taste for the theatrical": a criminal
mastermind who has left Batman his "calling card." Turning over
the playing card, a Joker is revealed, and this informs the audience that this is only the end of *part one*, and that the story will
continue. This is precisely how 2 Chronicles 36:22-23 functions
in the redemptive story.

The Old Testament ends by bringing the reader back to the plot. The Jews had been exiled from their land, and God used their captor, Cyrus, king of Persia, to recommission them and call them back to the plot. That plot, once again, was the expansion of God's Kingdom, which centered on Israel as a lighthouse to the nations. They were told to "go" and rebuild that lighthouse (Jerusalem), knowing that God would be "with" them in the mission. And Cyrus makes this declaration on the basis that "all the kingdoms of the earth"—all authority—had been given to him.

Now look again at the great commission of Matthew 28:18-20. Notice the connections Jesus makes with the closing lines of the Old Testament. Jesus tells his disciples to "go," that his presence would be "with" them, and that "all authority" was given to him. These are all concepts lifted directly from 2 Chronicles. Jesus is picking up the Old Testament story line and threading it into the New.

There will, however, be changes, and chief among them is the lead role in God's redemption story. That part will now be played by the church, not ethnic Israel. Here are other twists in the plot:

- His disciples are to "go out" to the nations, not "go up" to Jerusalem. (Israel, geographically, was no longer central to God's plan.)
- Kingdom expansion is now the responsibility of the church, not geopolitical Israel.
- The church will manifest the Kingdom of God on earth as a spiritual kingdom, not a geopolitical one like Israel.
- This Kingdom will be comprised of people from every nation, not just one, as was the case with ethnic Israel.
- The king of God's Kingdom, unnamed in the Old Testament, is Jesus.

Though the plot has thickened, it hasn't changed. God's people are to expand God's Kingdom to the world, spreading the knowledge of Christ to every nation.

When Jesus is asked by his disciples when this age will come to an end, his response is, quite naturally, "when the plot resolves": "And this gospel of the kingdom will be proclaimed throughout the whole world as a testimony to all nations, and then the end will come" (Matthew 24:14).

One of the wonders of the Bible is that its divine author is able to traipse through time. And so in the book of Revelation, we see the end of the story, well before the story's end. And what John sees in his revelation is this:

And they sang a new song, saying,

"Worthy are you to take the scroll
    and to open its seals,
for you were slain, and by your blood you ransomed people
        for God
    from every tribe and language and people and nation."

REVELATION 5:9

End of story.

Embrace Plot to Get Plot

The day following her miraculous jail-cell conversion, Hope felt overwhelming compassion for the other women in the jail: women as hopeless as she had been just the day before. She prayed, asking God to use her to reach these women with the love of Christ. She knew next to nothing of the Bible, but no matter, she knew as much as the woman at the well, and what more is there to say than "Come, see a man who told me all that I ever did. Can this be the Christ?" (John 4:29).

Nearly every day for the two months leading up to the trial, Hope had a new cellmate. She'd listen to the woman's story, share her own story with her, pray with her, pray for her, and the next day the woman would be gone, replaced by someone new in a bright orange jumpsuit. Hope recalls some fifty different women who came and went in just those two months. Demonstrated in Hope's life is something totally *unremarkable* in the New Testament, but it's something of an anomaly today: For Hope, conversion led immediately to participation in the plot. And why wouldn't it?

In the Great Commission, Jesus invites his followers into the plot of history. What he doesn't mention—what we find out by experience—is that when we embrace this plot, our life suddenly gets plot. All of a sudden we experience drama, purpose, conflict, tension, sorrow, joy, victory, redemption . . . all the ingredients of a great story. When we embrace *the* plot, we get plot. Think of all the chase scenes, sleepless nights, heart-wrenching relationships, harrowing adventures, and dramatic rescues that accompanied the apostle Paul, all because of engagement in the mission (the plot). If life resembles more the grind of Saul the Pharisee than Paul the apostle, it's probably plot that's missing.

Hope doesn't just have an exciting conversion story—rather, her conversion has led to an exciting story, and it will stay exciting as long as there's plot. To borrow some obnoxious phrases from the covers of current bestsellers: Our Christian lives are not the "exhilarating," "pulse-pounding" "thrill ride" "shot through with adrenaline" that they could be, and much of that is owing to disengagement from the plot.

Seeking, desiring, and instigating the expansion of God's Kingdom in the world is what precipitates persecution, spiritual battle, the need for deliverance and divine enablement, a sense of mission and purpose, an invigorated prayer life, and the deepest community with fellow laborers. In lieu of plot, what Christians will experience is "drama" in that adolescent-Facebook sense of the word—self-absorbed melodrama. When expansive, forward-moving energy for the plot is suppressed, it comes out sideways in criticalness, discontent, cynicism, boredom, gossip, depression . . . *drama*. Plot or "drama"— you'll get one or the other.

Publisher's Clearinghouse

No one knows better than the publishing world what makes for a compelling story, since their survival hinges on it. Here are some sobering realities:

Roughly four out of five people in the literate world believe they have "a book in them"—that their life, if put to paper, would make fascinating reading. While most people never get that far, there are at the moment somewhere between 6 and 8 million unpublished manuscripts floating around out there.

Publishers drastically reduce that number by reviewing only those manuscripts represented by agents. It's left to the agents, then, to comb through the refuse, and literary agencies receive upward of ten thousand queries a month. From this mountain of proposals they'll select only a handful to represent to publishers. Of the books they represent, not all will get published. Of those that *are* published only 5 percent will make a profit; and of books purchased, the average reader reads only the first eighteen pages.

The lesson hard-learned by the literary community is this: *Just because you have a story doesn't mean it's a good one.* Most stories are contrived and formulaic, flat characters inhabiting unconvincing worlds, meandering plots, crude dialogue, pointless subplots, and climaxes that, well, don't.

But as life is also a narrative, that description could be applied to a lot of lives, don't you think? Using the grandiose language of narrative—"life is a journey," "I'm starting a new chapter"—can make life sound epic, but that doesn't make it so. Just because our life is a story doesn't mean it's a good one. And being a Christian only ensures that one chapter will be worth reading—the one where we came to Christ.

Yet someday we'll give an account of our story before God, and a determining factor—that which will separate a mediocre story from a great one—will be the plot: the degree to which we engaged in the expansion of God's Kingdom and proclaimed its King.

Strangling Subplots

Imagine walking into a high school, having no idea what a high school is. You mill around with the students, hang out after school, read their texts, stalk their Facebook pages, and go to their parties. And then imagine, after all your research, I ask you, "What is high school all about, Chaz?" (I've named you Chaz for my scenario.)

How long do you think I'd have to wait before you gave me any semblance of an answer such as *knowledge* or *education* or *ethical wisdom* or *college preparation*? Probably a long time, probably forever, and that's because the subplots of high school (dating, sports, popularity, friends, sex, etc.) have risen to the level of the main plot.

I think this happens with our mission in the world. No one sets out to turn the church's new building project—the new annex or narthex or whatever—into the mission of their life or the church, but it happens like that. It's always happened like that.

Throughout the Old Testament there was always a building project to test the faith and obedience of God's people: an ark to build, land to clear, a wall to assemble. But it's the ongoing construction of the Jerusalem Temple that has the most direct correspondence to the mission of the church.

In a sense, Jesus' commission to disciple all nations is the New Testament continuation of that Temple building project, or as G. K. Beale puts it: The great commission is really a commission to build a bigger Temple,[8] one that fills the entire earth. And so it's suggestive to see what delayed and derailed construction of the Temple in Jerusalem. Listen to these words from the prophet Haggai, addressing Israel's ambivalence to rebuilding the Temple:

> Is it a time for you yourselves to dwell in your paneled houses, while this house lies in ruins? . . . Thus says the LORD of hosts: Consider your ways. . . . You looked for much, and behold, it came to little. And when you brought it home, I blew it away. Why? declares the LORD of hosts. Because of my house that lies in ruins, while each of you busies himself with his own house.
>
> HAGGAI 1:4, 7, 9

Essentially there was a housing bubble in Jerusalem, and people were pouring all their time and money into their homes and neglecting construction of God's Temple. Maybe they weren't completely apathetic; maybe they threw something into the collection plate earmarked "Temple Construction." But whatever money they made, the Lord simply "blew it away": pensions, profit sharing . . . gone. With a few liberties, this is what Haggai recounts.

Considering God had just rescued the Israelites from Babylon, it seems a little heartless of them to ignore the Temple. But remember, the whole city of Jerusalem needed rebuilding, and wasn't Jerusalem *also* God's dwelling place? And what kind of witness would it be for God's children to be living in squalor, and . . . well, you see how easy it is to rationalize, and make our house, home, and family our only mission in the world.

Sure, I'd like my kids to come down at night singing, "So long, farewell, *auf Wiedersehen*, good night," even if they are in their twenties. It's a compelling mission, but it's not everything. And yet it certainly can become everything: all of our time, energy, creativity, finances, and prayer, focused solely on the well-being of our family. And once it becomes our sole mission in life—once the subplot has become the plot—it's difficult to turn attention elsewhere. Because when do you ever have enough saved for the future? When aren't there engulfing domestic issues? When wouldn't a better job be a better fix?

Competing subplots are manifold. Personal wholeness, for example. The mission to right all wrongs, heal all hurts, rehabilitate minds and memories, break spiritual bondage, eradicate negative emotions, assert boundaries, and live the life we always wanted. Even now, armies of counselors and therapists are being trained and mobilized for the mission. (Sorry, that came across more cynical than I intended, but you see the point.) And it's a mission that never ends because when do we ever get over ourselves? When do we ever feel like, "Good, that's fixed"?

But here's the thing, I'm speaking to missions not so much in the broader fly-a-Piper-Cub-into-Zimbabwe sense but in the personal sense. What I notice in my own life is that no matter what Christian stuff I'm doing, no matter what I give to the work of missions, if there aren't people in my life that I'm personally praying for, trying to drag to church, getting involved in a Bible study, discipling, or building relationships with, something is missing—and what's missing is plot. My life has great meaning and purpose but not always great plot. Plot is forward momentum, an invisible surge. Only God and momentum deserve the title "game changer."

If NFL football has any lasting redemptive value, it's in its graphic display of this invisible dynamic. No one's performance, not even Tom Brady's, affects a game's outcome like momentum: when it's gained, who controls it, and when it's lost. Momentum decides football games and presidential elections and careers and anything with a narrative flow to it. We cannot escape it; the very fabric of the universe is the forward direction of time and the narrative nature of consciousness.

Momentum's power and influence is what places it at the strategic center of spiritual battle. Satan targets momentum and the perception of progress, seeding in its place determinism and the perception of cyclical failure and setback. Poverty is negative momentum. Addiction is negative momentum. But say no to temptation a few times running, and forward momentum is established. You feel your story progressing, a turning point in the narrative, an anticipation of the next chapter. Once established, momentum is hard to stop. If it is to be sabotaged, it cannot be allowed to get off the ground. It is attacked at the joints, at the start of an undertaking, right before midway, and when you're near the end but know it. Just watch football, or just watch evil at work in your life—you'll see.

Our narrative is tied to God's narrative, the spread of his Kingdom in this world, and our involvement in that narrative, or lack of, determines our sense of progress, our sense of plot. We need momentum to finish the race, a personal mission to get to the finish.

Speak Now
Making the Most of Opportunity

WE LIVE IN THE QUAINT BOROUGH of West Chester, Pennsylvania, on a street lined with postwar houses—all different shapes and sizes. It's really Pleasantville, except for the maze of power lines and cable wires that intersect over our backyard. We are not on the grid; we are exactly under it.

In a recent breeze, our TV cable ripped from the house and lay on the backyard, uncapped, spilling hundreds of broadcasting hours into the environment. So I called Verizon to come out and clean up the spill—mop up all the *Everybody Loves Raymond* episodes seeping into the water table and destroying the wetlands.

The cable guy arrived at the house—a young guy in his late twenties. I invited him in and explained the problem, and he astutely deduced from my fear of being electrocuted by the TV cable that I was a member of the privileged gentry who live in ignorance of how stuff works. Over the next hour we got to know each other, as my charm and everyman brand of humor wore down whatever prejudice I imagined he held for men who were no longer "handy." I really liked him. And as we stood there talking, I felt a strong desire to talk with him about Jesus. But how?

A good transition to the gospel is like a good transition to breaking off an engagement. What are you supposed to say to a cable guy? "As there are four ESPN channels in a cable package, there are also four points to the gospel"? "Speaking of life without HD . . ."? It was an unbridgeable chasm from our current conversation to the conversation I felt sure we were supposed to have. The one about God and Jesus and what's wrong with church and why bad things happen and the eternal destiny of pets. That one.

But amazingly we got there, and as it turned out, earlier that day at another repair site, the homeowner had given him an evangelistic booklet that he had spent his lunchtime reading. So it was good we got there. How we got there? Well, that's all up for discussion in this chapter. Why we need to discuss it is simple: a clear correlation between spiritual wakefulness and evangelistic willingness. The most wakeful Christ-follower is invariably the most willing witness. I don't want that statement to be true—but I think it is.

As Jesus gave shape to the contours of discipleship, the imagery never strayed far from the courtroom and the idea of bearing witness—lending our testimony to the proposition that Jesus is Lord of the universe:

"You will be my witnesses." ACTS 1:8, NIV

Always be prepared to give an answer to everyone who asks you to give the reason for the hope that you have. But do this with gentleness and respect. I PETER 3:15, NIV

As I write this, I'm sitting in the Orlando airport, and apparently my wife, Katie, has been trying to reach me for hours.

A pointless exercise, seeing as my phone's been off. Had Katie known my phone was off, I doubt she would have tried calling. And this is precisely why spiritual wakefulness is predicated on evangelistic faithfulness. Unwillingness or unavailability to be used is, spiritually speaking, having your phone off. It's not simply that you miss calls for service. In having it off, you miss calls and communication in general.

Bearing witness to the gospel, speaking about Christ, explaining our faith, responding to people critical to our faith, reaching out to unbelievers: these are challenging, but not because they're all that hard. They're challenging because we simply have no idea what we're doing.

A Seminar

In one of the 9,000 Republican debates of 2016, the moderator asked Marco Rubio about a *Time* magazine cover that once proclaimed him the savior of the Republican Party. Rubio responded:

> Well, let me be clear about one thing: There's only one savior, and it's not me. It's Jesus Christ, who came down to earth and died for our sins . . . and I've always made that clear about that cover story.[1]

The moderator said, *Oh*; the candidates said, *Oh*; Democrats said, *Oh*; the news media said, *Oh*; the 20 million viewers said, *Oh*; every atheist watching said, *Oh*. There was nothing else you could you say. He was unafraid, unembarrassed, unapologetic. There was no sign of fear, so all you could do was shut your mouth and pay respect. Who wouldn't like to respond to questions of faith like Marco Rubio?

What I think this clarifies is that this is a how-to problem, not a want-to problem. In light of that, I think a practical approach to the chapter would be helpful.

So let's place ourselves at a made-up conference. Coming out of the morning session, looking down in avoidance of between-seminar banter, you realize, to your horror, that you've left your personalized name tag and lanyard back in the room. How will people greet you?

Yes, sir, it's a pickle all right, no two ways about that. But you suspect—and rightly so—that this is an elaborate scheme of your flesh, luring you back to the room for a nap during the elective seminars. But you rebuke this foul spirit of sloth and bravely join the ranks of the anonymous: the great saints and heroes of the faith who lived and died with neither name tag nor lanyard. And so you go to Salon B, to an elective seminar given by . . . someone who's also not wearing a lanyard. The seminar is entitled "How to Give Jesus Away," which is neither funny nor clever, but whatever. Clearing his throat, the speaker begins reading Colossians 4:3-6 (NIV):

And pray for us, too, that God may open a door for our message, so that we may proclaim the mystery of Christ, for which I am in chains. Pray that I may proclaim it clearly, as I should. Be wise in the way you act toward outsiders; make the most of every opportunity. Let your conversation be always full of grace, seasoned with salt, so that you may know how to answer everyone.

Having read the passage, he introduces the seminar with this provocative statement: "Everything you need to know about being a witness for Jesus Christ is contained in these four verses." Deprived of your nap, you cynically deem this attention-getting device a "worldly" contrivance. *Well, we'll see about that, won't we?*

And so our seminar begins . . .

The first thing we notice, in verse 3, is that the apostle Paul prayed for an "open door."

Sometimes, just to feel like a part of the human race, I take my laptop to Starbucks. It's interesting to look around at all the people clicking on their laptops and strange to think of all the bits of information flying around the room. I don't understand the computerized world, so I envision it with exaggerated simplicity, like a child—webpages floating like Persian carpets; envelopes of e-mail passing through my body on the way to some meeting. It does pass through me, right? I mean, it wouldn't know to go around me, would it?

However it all works, there's an unimaginable flow of information in the Starbucks stratosphere: news, ideas, stories, e-mails, amazing pet videos. But I'm oblivious to all of it unless I answer yes to the question that comes up on my computer screen: "Do you want to join the network?" My local Starbucks frowns on squatters, so the Internet's not free; I have to decide if I want to pay the price for that exhilarating flow of communication. Sometimes I am; sometimes I'm not.

Same thing when I head out the door each day. I'm aware that God *could* lead me, use me, direct me, guide me. But I have to first decide, *Am I willing to pay the price to get that heady flow of communication?* The price to be paid is my willingness to initiate and participate in the expansion of God's Kingdom regardless of its inconvenience or awkwardness. If I say yes, the entire dynamic of the day changes, as stark as the difference between being online or off, asleep or awake. Some days I'm willing; some days I'm not.

The apostle Paul prayed, and asked others to pray, that God would "open doors" of opportunity to talk about Christ. This is the question we answer every morning before heading into the day: Am I open to God using me? Will I actively look for open doors? We make the decision every day; we need to start recognizing that we're making it if we are serious about spiritual wakefulness.

In verse 3, "the mystery of Christ" is something of a mystery. This is the opening of the letter Albert Einstein sent to President Franklin Roosevelt in the early days of World War II, alerting him to the threat of nuclear fusion:

> *Sir:*
>
> *Some recent work by E. Fermi and L. Szilard, which has been communicated to me in manuscript, leads me to expect that the element uranium may be turned into a new and important source of energy in the immediate future. Certain aspects of the situation which has arisen seem to call for watchfulness and, if necessary, quick action on the part of the administration.*[2]

Because of this letter, and who wrote it, the US government began buying up the world's supply of uranium—at least that which the Germans hadn't already confiscated. I think Einstein is the closest modern equivalent to the Daniel we see in Scripture.

Throughout the war, the government employed the best and brightest minds, and yet none of these "satraps . . . prefects . . . governors, [and] advisers," to quote Daniel 3 (NIV), could unlock the mystery of nuclear fusion. So they plucked this old man in his wool jacket and elbow patches out of the teacher's lounge at Princeton and pleaded with him to solve the mystery on which the fate of the world hung. He alone had the interpretation.

When Paul says, "We . . . proclaim the mystery of Christ" (Colossians 4:3, NIV), the word *mystery* is most certainly an allusion to the book of Daniel. The word occurs only ten times in the entire Old Testament, and all of them are in Daniel. If you remember the story, King Nebuchadnezzar's dream was a "mystery"—its meaning and imagery inscrutable apart from divine interpretation. So they send for Daniel. He alone could interpret it.

This, then, is Paul's view of the gospel, and the power of its explication. To people living apart from God, life is like Nebuchadnezzar's dream: a vivid sequence of events that appears to mean something, but apart from divine revelation, is indecipherable—an utter mystery. The gospel is the interpretation of the dream, that which makes sense of life and gives narrative coherence to human experience. To possess it, to walk around with the meaning of life balled up in your pocket, is both a privilege and a burden.

Einstein was privy to the inner working of life at the atomic level, and the weight of that knowledge and its ramifications was crushing. As Jewish writer Jacob Brackman describes, "You'd look at the portrait of this wise old Jew with long, messy, white hair, and you could see his brow all furrowed with guilt, and feel the terrible weight on his conscience."[3]

Paul does not bear this humanist burden, but he bears a burden nonetheless in having knowledge of the gospel. How can you not? What you and I could explain to someone, in minutes, could make sense of their entire life, change their destiny, and impart the meaning and purpose for which they were made.

Our excuses, even our theology, can be driven by this burden: attempting to divest ourselves of the responsibility that possession of saving knowledge entails. This is the meaning attached to "mystery": stewardship of the knowledge that's in our care—the privilege and burden of it.

And to privilege and burden we must add danger. If what we know, if what we can tell someone has such consequence, then evil needs to secure our silence. Like those T-shirts worn in the inner city: "Stop Snitching." A threat is implied. And a threat is implied in Paul's "chains."

Paul's "chains" (verse 3) for the gospel implies he's writing
from jail, and faithfulness has a price.

Erick and Elizabeth Glick work with the same ministry I do, only they're better at it. I don't have a story like theirs. Erick and Elizabeth were in Central Asia planting churches. One morning Elizabeth awoke around 4:00 a.m. and saw two men dressed in black, standing in the doorway, carrying hatchets. Elizabeth is funny, so when she tells the story, she says, "When I saw them I shouted out, 'You're here!' like they were late dinner guests or something."

The two men began to beat both Erick and Elizabeth, pummeling them with the blunt ends of the hatchets. Elizabeth remembers the conversation going on inside her head as she was being beaten, and it's easy to imagine it:

> *Where are you, Lord?*
> *Why aren't I unconscious yet? This isn't like the movies.*
> *I can't take any more, Lord, just take me.*
> [Then, thinking of her daughters] *No, Lord, don't take me.*
> *Let me survive.*

Elizabeth woke up bloody and broken. She shouted for Erick and heard an unimaginable nothing. She thought her whole family was dead. Just then Erick came in and told her that the kids were safe. Believing their parents dead, they had escaped out the window during the attack and run to the neighbors. He came over and kneeled down next to her and said, "Someday you'll look back on this as the best day of your life." She knew he meant that it's a privilege to suffer for the sake of the gospel. And it is.

Erick and Elizabeth were airlifted out for medical attention, and as the plane took off they both heard God say to them, "I want you to go back." Erick did, a month later; Elizabeth, nine months later (after she had fully recovered—she had three skull fractures). Elizabeth reflects, "The people living in that part of the world have all suffered. Their impression was that Americans don't understand. What happened to us and the fact we went back helped them understand that we are made of the same stuff."

In John 12:24, Jesus said, "Unless a kernel of wheat falls to the ground and dies, it remains only a single seed. But if it dies, it produces many seeds" (NIV). Jesus' immediate reference is to his own death, but the principle is universal. Generally speaking, this is how the Kingdom of God grows: witnesses willingly laying down their lives. As Tertullian put it, "The blood of the martyrs is the seed of the church."

This is the meaning of the enigmatic phrase in Colossians 1:24 (NIV): "I fill up in my flesh what is still lacking in regard to Christ's afflictions." Paul's firsthand observation is that in proclaiming the death of Christ, there is a kind of death to the messenger, which really shouldn't come as news. I mean, my goodness, the Greek word for *witness* is *martyr*.

We think of death as that grand moment of extinction when we stop breathing and collecting our mail. But it's the smaller deaths—the deaths to self, sin, pride, notoriety, and so on—that are the primary focus of New Testament discipleship. And when your definition of death expands to include the death of *persona*, you realize you don't have to live in Algeria to die for your faith. We all get to do that, in some form or another, to some degree or another.

Everything about the Kingdom is paradoxical, including its invitation:

> I came to you in weakness with great fear and trembling.
> My message and my preaching were not with wise and
> persuasive words, but with a demonstration of the Spirit's
> power, so that your faith might not rest on human wisdom,
> but on God's power.   1 CORINTHIANS 2:3-5, NIV

This is ironic, irony being the comic twist between surface and substance, perception and reality. What the apostle Paul explains is that the real power of evangelism is *spiritual* (resurrection) power, not the power of logic, communication, charisma, intelligence, relevance, or humor. And to get this resurrection power you need a body, a corpse—someone willing to die. A witness does that. Paul did that. He tells the Corinthians that in his willingness to be seen as a fool, an extremist, irrelevant, and a joke, true resurrection power was at work. The power of his words lay in his humiliation speaking them.

Speaking about Christ can cause fear, anxiety, embarrassment, even humiliation, to which Scripture's response is "Only if you're doing it right." No exemptions here. Paul was in chains, and while in chains, he prepared for his next opportunity.

Paul's prayer to "proclaim the gospel clearly" (verse 4) is a request for diligence, not eloquence.

If you don't know what to say, you probably won't say anything at all. That's pretty true, right? I mentioned Marco Rubio earlier. In that debate, Rubio's declaration of faith was so unrehearsed it most assuredly was rehearsed. No one sounds that natural, naturally.

Comedienne Sarah Silverstein said in an interview that she thought YouTube was killing comedy. A comedian has to appear like those brilliant lines are coming off the top of their head, but they aren't, they can't be—no one's that sharp. Jokes are rehearsed to be delivered offhand. With a litany of live performances, YouTube exposes the premeditation and forethought of stand-up comedy. Good communication is preparation to the point that scaffolds of form and structure are no longer visible, and content is freely adapted.

While the apostle Paul didn't value eloquence, he did value clarity. There are those rare individuals whose mouths are contiguous with their brain, but for the other 999 of us, clarity is the product of preparation. I think the apostle Peter was one of the 999. It's entertaining to watch him explain the gospel for the first time, to a completely non-Jewish audience. In Acts 10:36-44 (NIV), Peter is summoned to the home of a Gentile named Cornelius to explain the gospel to him and his family. Here's what he says (with emphasis added):

> *You know the message* God sent to the people of Israel, announcing the good news of peace through Jesus Christ, who is Lord of all. *You know what has* happened throughout the province of Judea.

Peter has no idea what his non-Jewish audience knows about the Jewish Messiah, so he assumes they know everything. Not a good assumption. It would be like Billy Graham saying to his audience, "Now about Jesus—I'll just assume you know what he did." But Peter can't avoid some kind of ministry summary, so he says that Jesus "went around doing good and healing all who were under the power of the devil."

That's an interesting summary. "He ate fish and wore sandals" would be equally informative. Forging ahead, Peter explains the gospel: "They killed him by hanging him on a cross, but God raised him from the dead on the third day and caused him to be seen."

"They hung him on a cross" and "God caused him to be seen." The good thing about this description is that even a six-year-old could understand it; the bad thing about it is that it sounds like a six-year-old is saying it. But no matter, Peter proceeds to present the evidence: "He was not seen by all the people, but by witnesses whom God had already chosen—by us who ate and drank with him."

Translation: "Jesus rose from the dead but no one else saw him, except me and a few friends (who also never finished grade school)." That concludes Peter's gospel presentation, not because he's done but because God can't listen to it anymore: "*While Peter was still speaking* these words, the Holy Spirit came on all who heard the message" (emphasis added).

Well, we've had some fun at Peter's expense, and in all fairness we don't know if these are his exact words or a summation, but the point still stands. Clarity matters, and clarity requires some preparation. So what does it mean to "proclaim [the gospel] clearly, as [we] should" (Colossians 4:4, NIV)?

Maybe we should start by defining the gospel. The gospel, simply stated, is the person and work of Jesus Christ, but stating it simply surfaces a glaring problem, one observed by the apostle John: Jesus did so many things that "if every one of them were written down . . . the whole world would not have room for the books" (John 21:25, NIV). But this is the miracle of Matthew, Mark, Luke, and John providing a divine summary of what couldn't fit in a world of books.

So Scripture provides us with some simple summaries that serve the purpose of communication. Summaries that distill the person and work of Christ to its irreducible essence. Think for example of this little bouillon cube: "For the wages of sin is death, but the free gift of God is eternal life in Christ Jesus our Lord" (Romans 6:23). It is the *essence* of the gospel, compact as a suitcase, made to travel across continents and down through the ages. A survey of these gospel-compacted passages yields an outline something like the following:

Who is Jesus? The Christ.
What has he done? Died and rose again.
Why? For the forgiveness of sins.
How do we know? Old Testament Scriptures and
    resurrection appearances.
How are we to respond? Repentance (Luke) and faith-belief
    (1 Corinthians).

It should be familiar—it's the basic ingredients of a billion sermons, altar calls, and evangelistic tracts. And because it is so familiar, it might be viewed cynically as simplistic or formulaic . . . because it *is* formulaic. Formulaic is the solution when accurate transmission is the problem. All of which to say, if you can write out, "For the wages of sin is death, but the free gift of God is eternal life in Christ Jesus our Lord," and briefly explain how you came to faith in Christ, then you've explained the gospel "clearly." Clear enough.

Between verses 4 and 5 in Colossians 4 is a transition in the text, moving from Paul's witness (verses 2-4) to the witness of the Colossians (verses 5-6).

I speak on college campuses pretty regularly—apologetic talks like "Does God Exist?" or "The Problem of Evil." Sometimes there's a fancy room and podium, and other times it isn't so fancy. At one university, the local ministry wasn't able to book a decent venue and, having gone to the trouble of flying me in, decided to improvise. Improvisation consisted of setting up a microphone in the main dining hall and handing me the microphone. "To what shall I liken this experience?" and "With what parable might I describe it?" to paraphrase Jesus' words. Without question, one of the most terrifying, humiliating experiences of my life. Traumatizing.

That's apostle Paul kind of craziness, and you can see why he wanted and needed prayer. In verses 2-4, Paul has been referencing *his* ministry and *his* witness. But in verses 5-6, he turns to the Colossians and *their* witness and ministry. As the name would imply, Colossae was home to the Colossians, filled with their family, friends, relatives, and coworkers. And so Paul's advice to them is about how to be a witness in that context—talking to friends and family. A lot more like the situations you and I find ourselves in. Here's what he says:

> Be wise in the way you act toward outsiders; make the
> most of every opportunity. Let your conversation be
> always full of grace, seasoned with salt, so that you may
> know how to answer everyone. COLOSSIANS 4:5-6, NIV

Let's walk one by one through the relational guidelines Paul
provides.

The opposite of being "wise in the way you act" (verse 5, NIV) is acting like a fool.

Paul does not explain what he means by *being wise*, but he sort of
does. When someone says to "be wise" with your time or money
or whatever, they basically mean "be balanced" or prudent and
avoid excess or extremes. What's profound about the advice is
that Christians tend toward the extremes in trying to represent
Christ: being too apologetic or too unapologetic, too condoning
or too condemning, too knowledgeable or too ignorant, too serious or too silly, too defensive or too accommodating. Wisdom
splits the difference.

Let me cite just one example from my personal Torah of
what not to do. Some years back, Katie and I were going to the
neighbors' for a cookout. Heading out the door, Katie looked
at my shirt and said, "Go change," in that matter-of-fact tone
you tell a child to stop sticking Jell-O up his nose. I was, as it
turned out, wearing one of those Christian T-shirts that said
something like "God's Gym" or "Got God?" or "Friends don't
let friends go to hell," and Katie was telling me, "Be wise"—
well, no, she was telling me, "Don't be an idiot," but same
difference.

Aspiring to be "unashamed" as disciples, I think we have in
our minds a spectrum where on one side is sensitivity and on
the other is boldness. But the opposite of sensitivity is insensi-
tivity and the opposite of boldness is cowardice. Boldness and

sensitivity are not opposed to each other, and here again wisdom splits the difference.

"Conversation ... seasoned with salt" (verse 6, NIV) seeds thirst for the gospel.

Salt is rock. That's pretty odd. What technically comes out of a salt shaker is an avalanche. In the 1920s the Diamond Crystal Salt Company marketed this rock with a famous brochure called "One Hundred and One Uses for Diamond Crystal Salt."[4] The list includes putting out grease fires, removing rust, killing poison ivy, and making candles so they don't drip.

The salt industry today claims the list of uses is up to fourteen thousand, if you want to consider "ant repellent" a usage, but biblically speaking it has only one. Salt kept food from spoiling, acting as a preservative in a world without refrigerators, and almost every savory metaphor of Scripture is tied to this use. In the Old Testament, salt ratified the covenant and stood as a symbol of God's sovereign power to *preserve* his covenant and his covenant people. In the New Testament, salt typifies the believer who acts as a *preservative* in the world, slowing its spiritual and moral decay.

And so the idea implicit in "conversation . . . seasoned with salt" is that conversations spoil, like lunch meat left out overnight. You see that decay in conversations as they turn from certain people . . . to what's wrong with those people; from work . . . to what's miserable about it; from spouses . . . to what's annoying about them. Vulgarity, profanity, lying, bragging, gossip—all of it rots.

Keeping conversations from decay, we serve as salt, and while that sounds perky enough, there's a reason people gossip and slander and complain. They like it. And they don't like people who keep the conversation from "going there," so friends and popularity can all be painfully lost over this, and there's nothing perky about that. Throwing your body in the path of a moving conversation takes courage. I just spent twenty minutes at the YMCA talking to some guy about the offensive "weapons" on the Philadelphia Eagles, because being in Philadelphia he assumed I was an Eagles fan. I'm not. I'm a spineless toad who didn't want to ruin our bonding experience by telling him I root for the Giants.

But to a soul thirsting for righteousness, salt seeds a thirst for God. Divine pretzels. People want more of whatever it is you have. I think it's fair to that say all of this imagery is what's being evoked by "conversation . . . seasoned with salt."

When Paul says, "Make the most of every opportunity" (verse 6, NIV), he means, "Do something."

In February 2012, over a hundred armed deputies in full riot gear were called in, as a swelling crowd inside the Florida Mall began flirting with anarchy. Then someone shoved someone, and everything went to pieces. Orlando resident Gaby Llanos, who was at the mall when the violence broke out, described the mayhem: "It was complete havoc. . . . People were running and hiding in trees so the police wouldn't find them."[5]

I personally have never experienced the horrors of a new release of a Nike sneaker, so words fail me here. But as violence fomented at stores around the globe, Nike, by and large a pacifist company, lodged a strong antiwar protest: "We encourage anyone wishing to purchase our product to do so in a respectful and safe manner."[6] Needless to say, such harsh condemnation from the manufacturer of the Galaxy shoe (priced at $220) averted what was escalating into the next Cuban missile crisis.

As retail stores across the country canceled release of the sneaker, dedicated fans stormed the Internet, where the new Nikes sold upward of $2,400 on craigslist. Those lacking financial liquidity could follow the example of one man who traded his 1996 Chevy Cavalier for a pair.

This is the picture, minus the riot, the apostle Paul paints when he says, "Make the most of every opportunity." "Make the most" translates into a single Greek word: *exagorazomenoi*. The root *agora*, hiding in the jungle of letters, carries the concepts of buying and marketplace (*agoraphobia* means "fear of the marketplace"). In context, *exagorazomenoi* means to "buy out completely" as you would an on-sale item, shoving as much of it as could fit in your shopping cart. An evangelistic opportunity is a sale, like Black Friday, patiently waiting for the doors to open.

Some metaphors need translating to a modern world. This one doesn't. We know exactly what it's like to be in a conversation when an opportunity arises to speak about our faith. For a brief, very brief moment there's an opportunity, and we need to take it—buy it out like an iPhone marked down to a dollar. You know the moments and how easy it is to let them pass. It happens to all of us, but the problem with stuff that "happens to all of us" is that it seems acceptable. Yet God has given us no indication that it is acceptable.

Luke 9:51 (NIV) says, "As the time approached for him to be taken up to heaven, Jesus resolutely set out for Jerusalem." This is a section marker in Luke, situating every discussion between chapters 10 and 20 in the context of a looming cross. These are all of Jesus' last-minute warnings and instructions, and it's here that he tells his disciples,

> Everyone who acknowledges me before men, the Son of Man will also acknowledge him before the angels of God, but the one who denies me before men will be denied before the angels of God. LUKE 12:8-9

What this passage and context reveal is the chief concern occupying Jesus as he heads to the cross: the concern that after he's gone, his disciples will be scared into silence. This would compromise the mission, the spread of the Kingdom, everything. But we *have* been silent. For days, weeks . . . years. "Fear of man" has made cowards of us all. And Jesus isn't saying that it's not understandable—of course it's understandable—it's just not acceptable.

Putting the thoughts together: As we are "wise" and our words are "seasoned with salt," opportunities will arise to talk about Christ. When they do, we need to be courageous. We need to take hold of those moments. Make the absolute most out of them. And this leads us to the last, most practical issue: What should we say?

Knowing "How to Answer Everyone": A Closing Workshop

Coming back to the premise that this is a how-to problem, not a want-to problem, we'll follow up the seminar with a mini-workshop, which you're welcome to skip if you need to go find your lanyard or something.

CoJourners

"Everyone is on a spiritual journey either moving closer to, or further from God."[7] This is how Keith Davy begins his guide to relational evangelism, *CoJourners*. In that statement, Davy reorients us to see everyone in a spiritual process (whether they're aware of it or not), and to see ourselves playing a role, helping others to take the next step toward Christ, whatever that looks like.

As *CoJourners* we approach conversations (whether with a friend, relative, or someone we just met) with a goal to explore: to discover where they are in their spiritual journey. Davy suggests having a few exploring questions committed to memory. Here are a few of his:

- Exploring their past: What's your religious background? Was your family religious growing up? What has your spiritual journey been like since then? Have you had a negative or positive experience with religion or church?

- Exploring their present: How does God figure into your thinking these days—or does he? Where are you now in your spiritual journey?
- Exploring their future: In your spiritual journey do you see yourself as moving closer to, or further away from God? Over time, do you see yourself becoming more spiritual/religious or less?[8]

Maybe you want to come up with your own, but regardless, questions like these will bring a conversation to a deeper level. Ask and listen. Listen for traces of God at work in their lives. The more you do it, the more natural it becomes.

Your Story

Having entered into someone's spiritual journey with a few well-chosen questions, it's appropriate, maybe even expected, for you to share something of your own spiritual story. So, for a minute—and no more—you can say almost anything about your own faith journey. Use it wisely.

When I was talking to the cable guy, for example, he told me that he'd been raised in a strict religious home. So in sharing my story, I told him, "I used to think of Christianity as a list of *dos and don'ts*, but it's really about what God has *done for me* in Christ, not what I *do* for God." (I stole that from Bill Hybels.) I didn't explain the entire gospel, just touched on an important element of it, using my story as a bridge.

I imagine you'd rehearse if you had an important speech to give, and it's not a stretch to consider this an important speech. So write it out, rehearse it; see what elements of the gospel you can incorporate into your personal story.

The Gospel Story

Having asked a few questions and shared a bit of your own story, there are several ways you might explain the *essence* of the gospel, ranging in risk from low to high. Here they are:

1. "Well, we don't have time for some big, religious discussion right now, but would it be okay if I e-mailed you something—an article I found helpful in explaining some of these issues of faith?" Then, look around online for a gospel/apologetic article, or write your own short explanation for use and reuse. Then e-mail it with a note referencing your prior conversation. Done.

2. "Well, we don't have time for some long religious discussion right now, but do you want to grab coffee next week?" This is a bigger step, but not too big. You're not going to try to squeeze a gospel conversation into your current conversation. Instead you're setting up a future conversation where the context has already been established—you'll be meeting to talk about issues of faith.

3. If you're truly a brave soul, you could ask permission to explain the gospel right then and there: "Can I show you something that was very helpful to me in understanding my faith?" Then you could write out Romans 6:23 on a piece of paper, explain it, and share your story. (For help explaining it, google "One-Verse Evangelism.")[9] Or you could simply read through a time-tested booklet like "Knowing God Personally," "The Bridge," "Two Ways to Live," or "Steps to Peace with God." A ridiculous number of people have come to faith through such booklets because they're clear and offer a simple way (a prayer) to respond. (You could also just give them the booklet.)

It's a very modest amount of preparation to "know how you ought to answer each person" (Colossians 4:6). And if it feels contrived, keep in mind that Jesus sent his disciples out with a memorized script: "When you enter a house, first say, 'Peace to this house'" (Luke 10:5, NIV).

Closing with a Story

Laura Hillenbrand's bestselling biography *Unbroken* tells the story of Louis Zamperini, an Olympic track star who spent the duration of World War II as a Japanese prisoner of war. For four unimaginable years, Zamperini endured the most exquisite tortures devised by Mutsuhiro Watanabe, the camp's commander. Returning home after the war, Zamperini became the face of American heroism, but in the years that followed, Zamperini's life disintegrated from the psychological damage. Money, family, sanity: Zamperini lost everything. But at the historic Los Angeles Billy Graham Crusade of 1956, Zamperini went forward and gave his life to Christ.

While many who ran the Japanese POW camps were convicted of war crimes, Watanabe escaped justice. In fact, he was still alive fifty-two years later, when Zamperini wrote him this letter in 1997:

> *To Matsuhiro* [sic] *Watanabe,*
> *As a result of my prisoner of war experience under your unwarranted and unreasonable punishment, my post-war life became a nightmare. . . .*
> *Under your discipline, my rights, not only as a prisoner of war but also as a human being, were stripped from me. . . . The post-war nightmares caused my life to crumble, but thanks to a confrontation with God through the evangelist Billy Graham, I committed my life to Christ. Love replaced the hate I had for you. Christ said, "Forgive your enemies and pray for them."*

*As you probably know, I returned to Japan in 1952 [sic]
and was graciously allowed to address all the Japanese war
criminals at Sugamo prison. . . . I asked then about you,
and was told that you probably had committed Hara Kiri,
which I was sad to hear. At that moment, like the others, I
also forgave you and now would hope that you would also
become a Christian.*

Louis Zamperini[10]

Does it seem to you that Zamperini was excited to write this
letter? It doesn't to me. Nor is the invitation to Christ flowing
with human kindness. But that's what I love about it. Here is a
faithful witness—because how he felt about performing the duty
was irrelevant to whether he did it.

EPILOGUE

IMAGINE THAT I AM A SALSA INSTRUCTOR in a universe where I go by the name of Raul instead of Rick, and as I begin to teach you how to salsa, I say, "Take three steps to the west, turn south, and move your eastern foot to the north." Using geographic coordinates would be stranger than me as a salsa instructor, because in every country and culture of the world, people use egocentric coordinates to explain such things. We say, "Take a step back," or "Move to your right"—using ourselves as a compass (a personal, relative axis) instead of the sun.

This is universal, or at least linguists thought it was. I mean, who would ever say, "Watch out for the speeding car coming from the southwest?" It turns out, the Guugu Yimithirr would—if they had cars or a freeway in their aboriginal village, but I don't think they do.

For the Guugu Yimithirr, reality is defined by the sun, not us, which is quite profound, metaphorically speaking. In their language there is no right or left—no egocentric coordinates at all, only *gungga* (north), *jiba* (south), *guwa* (west), and *naga* (east).[1] In fact, while filming his doctoral research on the Guugu Yimithirr, linguist Stephen Levinson recorded a tribal member telling him, "Look out for that big ant just north of your foot."[2]

But the tribe's heliocentric perception of the world goes far beyond giving directions: Their awareness of the sun's position and of their position relative to it extends to every aspect of life. They know where the sun is in their dreams, in their memories, indoors or outdoors, and even on television.

> When older speakers of Guugu Yimithirr were shown a short silent film on a television screen and then asked to describe the movements of the protagonists, their responses depended on the orientation of the television when they were watching. If the television was facing north and a man on the screen appeared to be approaching, the older men would say that the man was "coming northward."[3]

At some point, as children, this awareness takes conscious effort, but it quickly becomes reflexive as every experience is registered relative to the sun. In time, it becomes so natural and intuitive for the Guugu Yimithirr that they can't imagine any other way of seeing the world.

The desired end of this study on New Testament watchfulness has been to increase spiritual perception, to add new categories of observation, to open our minds to unseen realities, and to train our eyes to see what is currently peripheral and semiconscious. Spending significant time with these passages of awareness and attentiveness, I think it's fair to say that the New Testament speaks from, and speaks to, a perception of the world just like the Guugu Yimithirr, except with God as the center—where thought, speech, and actions are always coordinated, always in reference to the Lord.

The disciples and apostles didn't see this perception as odd, unattainable, overly charismatic, postmodern, mystical, monastic, Celtic, or otherwise—just the natural way of looking at the world given the fact that the resurrected Christ lives in and through us. It's this God-conscious, Christ-aware, Spirit-sensitive, New Testament way of walking through the day that has been the focus of this book. And I hope it's what you'll take away.

NOTES

CHAPTER 1: ENCEPHALITIS LETHARGICA

1. "Mystery of the Forgotten Plague," *BBC News,* July 27, 2004, http://news.bbc .co.uk/2/hi/health/3930727.stm.
2. Oliver Sacks, *Awakenings* (New York: Vintage, 1999), 23.
3. Sacks, *Awakenings,* 14.
4. William Dement, *The Promise of Sleep* (New York: Dell, 2000), 17.
5. C. S. Lewis, *The Silver Chair* (New York: Collier Books, 1953), 152–154.
6. Nathaniel Hawthorne, quoted in Julian Hawthorne, *Nathaniel Hawthorne and His Wife: A Biography, Part One* (Kessinger Publishing, 2004), 503.
7. Marshall McLuhan, *Understanding Media* (Cambridge: MIT Press, 1994), 63–64.
8. Nicholas Carr, *The Shallows* (New York: W. W. Norton & Company, 2011), 131.
9. Carr, *The Shallows,* 118.
10. Jonathan Weiner, *Long for This World* (New York: Ecco, 2010), 167.
11. Laura L. Carstensen, "The Influence of a Sense of Time on Human Development," *Science,* June 30, 2006, 1913–1915. Italics added.
12. Don Lattin, *The Harvard Psychedelic Club* (San Francisco: HarperOne, 2010), 40.
13. Timothy Leary, "Transcript," *American Experience: Summer of Love,* PBS, http://www.pbs.org/wgbh/amex/love/filmmore/pt.html, accessed April 20, 2016.
14. Susan Casey, *The Wave: In Pursuit of the Rogues, Freaks and Giants of the Ocean* (New York: Anchor Books, 2010), 87.
15. Maggie Jackson, *Distracted: The Erosion of Attention and the Coming Dark Age* (Amherst, NY: Prometheus, 2008), 34–43.
16. Sacks, *Awakenings,* 99–100.

CHAPTER 2: SENSORY DATA

1. John Sailhamer, *The Meaning of the Pentateuch* (Downers Grove, IL: IVP Academic, 2009), 217.
2. Sailhamer, *The Meaning of the Pentateuch,* 218.
3. Tom Vanderbilt, *Traffic: Why We Drive the Way We Do* (New York: Knopf, 2008), 176–210.

4. Garry Friesen, *Decision Making and the Will of God,* 25th anniversary ed. (Colorado Springs: Multnomah, 2004), 41.
5. Donald Miller, "Does God Have a Specific Plan for Your Life? Probably Not," April 29, 2010, http://storylineblog.com/2010/04/29/does-god-have-a -specific-plan-for-your-life-probably-not/.
6. Donald Miller, "Does God Have a Specific Plan for Your Life?"
7. G. K. Chesterton, "Errors about Detective Stories," *Illustrated London News,* August 28, 1920, from the American Chesterton Society, http://www .chesterton.org/errors-about-detective-stories/. Accessed April 21, 2016.
8. G. K. Chesterton, "How to Write a Detective Story," *G. K.'s Weekly,* October 17, 1925, from the American Chesterton Society, http://www.chesterton.org /how-to-write-detective/. Accessed April 21, 2016.
9. Joshua Foer, *Moonwalking with Einstein* (New York: Penguin, 2011), 3.
10. Foer, *Moonwalking with Einstein,* 91, 99.
11. Foer, *Moonwalking with Einstein,* 97.
12. Gerald Edelman, *Second Nature* (New Haven, CT: Yale University Press, 2007), 58.
13. James Geary, *I Is an Other* (New York: HarperCollins, 2011), 32–33.
14. Jonah Lehrer. "The Eureka Hunt," *The New Yorker,* July 28, 2008, http:// www.newyorker.com/magazine/2008/07/28/the-eureka-hunt.
15. Bob Sehlinger with Len Testa, *The Unofficial Guide to Walt Disney World 2010* (Hoboken, NJ: John Wiley & Sons, 2010), 77.
16. Lance Fortnow, *The Golden Ticket: P, NP, and the Search for the Impossible* (Princeton, NJ: Princeton University Press, 2013), ix, 56–57.

CHAPTER 3: HOMELAND
1. Yudhijit Bhattacharjee, "How a Remote Town in Romania Has Become Cybercrime Central," *Wired,* January 31, 2011, http://www.wired.com/2011 /01/ff_hackerville_romania/.
2. Bhattacharjee, "How a Remote Town in Romania Has Become Cybercrime Central," *Wired.*
3. Philip Goerevitch, *We Wish to Inform You That Tomorrow We Will Be Killed with Our Families: Stories from Rwanda* (New York: Picador, 1999), 27–35.
4. Bruce M. Metzger, "St. Paul and the Magicians," *The Princeton Seminary Bulletin* 38 (1944): 27.
5. C. S. Lewis, *Perelandra* (New York: Scribner, 2003), 122–123.
6. Joshua Foer, *Moonwalking with Einstein* (New York: Penguin, 2011), 64–65.
7. "The Wall: A World Divided," PBS, June 2010, http://www.pbs.org /program/the-wall/.
8. Clinton E. Arnold, *Power and Magic: The Concept of Power in Ephesians* (Eugene, OR: Wipf & Stock, 2001), 120.
9. G. K. Beale, *The New International Greek Testament Commentary: The Book of Revelation* (Grand Rapids, MI: Eerdmans, 2013), 201.
10. M. Scott Peck, *Glimpses of the Devil* (New York: Free Press, 2005), 172.
11. Peck, *Glimpses of the Devil,* 177.
12. Malcolm Beith, *The Last Narco* (New York: Grove Press, 2010), 154.
13. Beith, *The Last Narco,* 170.

14. Gregory Boyd, *Satan and the Problem of Evil: Constructing a Trinitarian Warfare Theodicy* (Downers Grove, IL: InterVarsity, 2001), 237.

CHAPTER 4: SLEEPLESS CITIES

1. Adapted from Barbara Smit, *Sneaker Wars* (New York: Harper Perennial, 2009), passim.
2. Jonah Lehrer, "A Physicist Solves the City," *New York Times*, December 17, 2010, http://www.nytimes.com/2010/12/19/magazine/19Urban_West-t.html?_r=0.
3. Lehrer, "A Physicist Solves the City."
4. Lehrer, "A Physicist Solves the City."
5. Malcolm Gladwell, "Group Think," *The New Yorker*, December 2, 2002, http://www.newyorker.com/magazine/2002/12/02/group-think. Italics in original.
6. Martin Luther, *Luther's Works, Volume 54: Table Talk*, ed. Theodore Tappert (Philadelphia: Fortress Press, 1967), 37–38.
7. Martin Luther, *The Table Talk of Martin Luther*, trans. William Hazlitt (London: H. G. Bohn, 1857), 247.
8. Recounted in Jonah Lehrer, *Imagine: How Creativity Works* (New York: Houghton Mifflin Harcourt, 2012).
9. Pete Greig and Dave Roberts, *Red Moon Rising* (Colorado Springs: David C. Cook, 2015), 77.
10. Jonathan Weiner, *Long for This World* (New York: HarperCollins, 2010), 79.
11. Ferrell Foster, "Confession, Instruction Mark Wheaton College Revival," *Baptist Press*, April 10, 1995, http://media.sbhla.org.s3.amazonaws.com/7959,10-Apr-1995.pdf. Accessed May 4, 2016.
12. For a fuller discussion see Craig Blomberg, *Contagious Holiness* (Downers Grove, IL: InterVarsity, 2005).
13. Andrew Zolli, *Resilience: Why Things Bounce Back* (New York: Simon & Schuster, 2012), 69.
14. Zolli, *Resilience*, 72.
15. Zolli, *Resilience*, 72.
16. William Hasker, *The Emergent Self* (Ithaca, NY: Cornell University Press, 1999), 90.
17. Jon Lee Anderson, "The Real 'Tower of David,'" *The New Yorker*, October 18, 2013, http://www.newyorker.com/culture/culture-desk/the-real-tower-of-david.

CHAPTER 5: RED BULL

1. W. H. Auden, quoted in Timothy Keller, *The Meaning of Marriage* (New York: Penguin, 2013), 94.
2. Jonah Lehrer, *Imagine: How Creativity Works* (New York : Houghton Mifflin Harcourt, 2012), 53.
3. Jean-Paul Sartre, "Sartre at Seventy: An Interview," interview by Michel Contant, translated by Paul Auster and Lydia Davis, *The New York Review*, August 7, 1975, http://www.nybooks.com/articles/1975/08/07/sartre-at-seventy-an-interview/.

4. Marshall Brain, Charles W. Bryant, and Matt Cunningham, "How Caffeine Works," How Stuff Works, April 1, 2000, http://science.howstuffworks.com/caffeine.htm.

5. For fuller treatment see Rikki E. Watts, *Isaiah's New Exodus in Mark* (Grand Rapids, MI: Baker Academic, 2001).

6. Paul K. Moser, *The Elusive God: Reorienting Religious Epistemology* (New York: Cambridge University Press, 2008), 107.

7. Charles Moore, "Trashed," *Natural History*, November 2003, cited in Donovan Hohn, *Moby-Duck* (New York: Viking, 2011), 44.

8. Samuel Taylor Coleridge, *The Rime of the Ancient Mariner* (New York: D. Appleton & Co., 1857), 16.

9. Brad Strait, "A Miracle Inside the Aurora Shooting: One Victim's Story," Celtic Straits, July 22, 2012, http://bstrait.wordpress.com/2012/07/22/a-miracle-inside-the-the-aurora-shooting-one-victims-story/.

10. Hohn, *Moby Duck*, 14.

CHAPTER 6: PSYCHEDELIC

1. Michael Mills, "Goof Sleuth: Unplanned Mistakes Delight 'Film Flubs' Writer," *Chicago Tribune*, December 27, 1990, http://articles.chicagotribune.com/1990-12-27/features/9004160979_1_bill-givens-film-flubs-die-hard.

2. Christopher Chabris and Daniel Simons, *The Invisible Gorilla* (New York: Crown Publishers, 2009), 6.

3. Chabris and Simons, *The Invisible Gorilla*, 7.

4. Georgia O'Keeffe, quoted in Britta Benke, *O'Keeffe* (Hohenzollernring, Germany: Taschen, 2003), 31.

5. Karyn Hollis, "Best Ever Metaphors and Analogies," http://www19.homepage.villanova.edu/karyn.hollis/prof_academic/Courses/common_files/best_ever_metaphors_and_analogie.htm. Accessed May 5, 2016.

6. Jill Replogle, "'Irvine 11' Found Guilty of Disrupting Israeli Ambassador's Speech," KPBS, September 23, 2011, http://www.kpbs.org/news/2011/sep/23/irvine-11-found-guilty-disrupting-israeli-ambassad/.

7. Winifred Gallagher, *Rapt: Attention and the Focused Life* (New York: Penguin, 2009), 2, 14.

8. American Birding Association, "ABA Recording Rules and Interpretations (version 2014b)," American Birding Association, http://listing.aba.org/aba-recording-rules/. Accessed June 23, 2016.

9. Esther Yi, "The Big Year: One Man's Race to Spot More Than 745 Birds in One Year," *The Atlantic*, October 26, 2011, http://www.theatlantic.com/national/archive/2011/10/the-big-year-1-mans-race-to-spot-more-than-745-birds-in-1-year/247214/.

10. Amy Jewett, Ruth A. Shults, Tanima Banerjee, and Gwen Bergen, "Alcohol-Impaired Driving Among Adults—United States, 2012," *Morbidity and Mortality Weekly Report*, August 7, 2015, http://www.cdc.gov/mmwr/preview/mmwrhtml/mm6430a2.htm.

11. Steve Coll, *Private Empire: ExxonMobil and American Power* (New York: Penguin, 2012), 5.

12. Coll, *Private Empire*, 7–8.

13. Coll, *Private Empire*, 1.
14. Ken Johnson, "How the Drugs of the 60s Changed Art," interview by Emanuella Grinberg, CNN, July 15, 2011, http://www.cnn.com/2011/LIVING /07/15/ken.johnson.psychedelic.art/index.html?hpt=hp_bn8.
15. Sam Sommers, *Situations Matter: Understanding How Context Transforms Your World* (New York: Riverhead, 2011), 51–52.
16. Sommers, *Situations Matter*, 199–203.
17. George Müller, *A Narrative of Some of the Lord's Dealings with George Müller* (London: J. Nisbet, 1945), 417, 420.
18. Müller, *A Narrative*, 418.
19. Mary Roach, *Gulp: Adventures of the Alimentary Canal* (New York: W. W. Norton & Company, 2013), 23.

CHAPTER 7: PERKS
1. T. S. Eliot, *The Letters of T. S. Eliot: Volume 5: 1930–1931* (New Haven, CT: Yale University Press, 2015), 210.
2. "A Nice Place to Visit," *The Twilight Zone*, directed by John Brahm, April 15, 1960.
3. C. S. Lewis, *Miracles* (New York: HarperOne, 2001), 260–261.
4. Paul Guyer, "History of Modern Aesthetics," *The Oxford Handbook of Aesthetics*, ed. Jerrold Levinson (New York: Oxford Press, 2005), 26.
5. Thomas Aquinas, *Summa Theologica* II-II.141.4, objection 3.
6. Randy Alcorn, *Heaven* (Carol Stream, IL: Tyndale, 2004), 42, emphasis in the original.
7. Kurt Vonnegut, *Welcome to the Monkey House* (New York: Dial Press, 2010), 7.
8. Vonnegut, *Welcome to the Monkey House*, 8.
9. Vonnegut, *Welcome to the Monkey House*, 7.
10. Harry Harlow, quoted in Daniel H. Pink, *Drive: The Surprising Truth About What Motivates Us* (New York: Riverhead, 2009), 3.
11. C. S. Lewis, *The Weight of Glory and Other Addresses* (New York: HarperOne, 2001), 26–27.
12. Sam Keen, *The Disappearing Spoon* (New York: Little, Brown, 2010), 67.
13. Keen, *The Disappearing Spoon*, 68.
14. Nelson Mandela, "Nelson Mandela's Address to a Rally in Cape Town on His Release from Prison," February 11, 1990, African National Congress, http://www.anc.org.za/content/nelson-mandelas-address-rally-cape-town-his-release-prison. Accessed July 19, 2016.
15. Pink, *Drive*, 145.
16. Pink, *Drive*, xi.
17. Joseph S. Nye, Jr., *The Future of Power* (New York: PublicAffairs, 2011), 10–14.

CHAPTER 8: THE SIN YOU NEVER SAW COMING
1. John S. Feinberg, *The Many Faces of Evil* (Wheaton, IL: Crossway, 2004), 170.
2. Adam Rogers, *Proof: The Science of Booze* (New York: Houghton Mifflin Harcourt, 2014), 18.
3. "NCYC 79: Saccharomyces Cerevisiae," National Collection of Yeast Cultures,

https://catalogue.ncyc.co.uk/catalog/product/view/id/122101/s/saccharomyces
-cerevisiae-79/category/250/. Accessed July 19, 2016. Price fluctuates based
on global currency exchanges.

4. *Holy Bible* (New York: P .J. Kennedy and Sons, 1950), 152.

5. *Spotlight*, directed by Tom McCarthy (Los Angeles: Open Road Films, 2016).

6. Juliet Pennington, "Mark Ruffalo Slams 'Hypocrisy' of Catholicism: It 'Chilled My Relationship' with the Church," *People*, October 29, 2015, http://www.people.com/article/mark-ruffalo-hypocrisy-catholic-church -spotlight-premiere.

7. Pennington, "Mark Ruffalo Slams 'Hypocrisy' of Catholicism."

8. Jonathan Waldman, *Rust: The Longest War* (New York: Simon & Schuster, 2015), 21.

9. Waldman, *Rust*, 7.

10. Pamela Engel, "Donald Trump Just Mocked Marco Rubio's Supposedly Big Ears at a Rally," *Business Insider*, February 26, 2016, http://www.businessinsider .com/donald-trump-marco-rubio-big-ears-2016-2.

11. Jessica Estepa, "Donald Trump on Carly Fiorina: 'Look at That Face!'" *USA Today*, September 10, 2015, http://www.usatoday.com/story/news/nation-now /2015/09/10/trump-fiorina-look-face/71992454/.

12. Holly Yan, "Donald Trump's 'Blood' Comment about Megyn Kelly Draws Outrage," CNN Politics, August 8, 2015, http://www.cnn.com/2015/08/08 /politics/donald-trump-cnn-megyn-kelly-comment/index.html.

13. Jeremy Diamond, "Trump: I Could 'Shoot Somebody and I Wouldn't Lose Voters,'" CNN Politics, January 24, 2016, http://www.cnn.com/2016/01/23 /politics/donald-trump-shoot-somebody-support/index.html.

14. Matthew MacWilliams, "The One Weird Trait That Predicts Whether You're a Trump Supporter," *Politico*, January 17, 2016, http://www.politico .com/magazine/story/2016/01/donald-trump-2016-authoritarian-213533.

15. MacWilliams, "The One Weird Trait That Predicts Whether You're a Trump Supporter."

16. David Ricci, "David Ricci," Infectious Diseases Society of America, http:// www.idsociety.org/Templates/nonavigation.aspx?Pageid=12884901901 &id=32212258927. Accessed June 21, 2016.

17. David Ricci, "David Ricci."

18. "Hunting the Nightmare Bacteria," *Frontline*, written, produced, and directed by Rick Young (October 2013), http://www.pbs.org/wgbh/frontline/film /hunting-the-nightmare-bacteria/transcript/. Accessed June 21, 2016.

CHAPTER 9: THE COMING CLOUDS

1. Tom Zoellner, *Uranium: War, Energy, and the Rock That Shaped the World* (New York: Viking, 2009), 6.

2. Zoellner, *Uranium*, 8.

3. Robert Oppenheimer, quoted in William L. Laurence, *Men and Atoms: The Discovery, the Uses, and the Future of Atomic Energy* (New York: Simon & Schuster, 1959), 118.

4. H. G. Wells, *The World Set Free* (New York: E. P. Dutton & Company, 1914).

5. William Faulkner, banquet speech, December 10, 1950, NobelPrize.org,

http://www.nobelprize.org/nobel_prizes/literature/laureates/1949/faulkner
-speech.html. Accessed June 21, 2016.

6. Zoellner, *Uranium,* 72.
7. Maggie Jackson, *Distracted: The Erosion of Attention and the Coming Dark Age* (Amherst, NY: Prometheus, 2008), 79.
8. Maggie Jackson, *Distracted,* 78.
9. Alex Stone, *Fooling Houdini: Magicians, Mentalists, Math Geeks & the Hidden Powers of the Mind* (New York: HarperCollins, 2012), 137.
10. Stone, *Fooling Houdini,* 64.
11. Ashley Parker, "Make My Bed? But You Say the World's Ending," *New York Times,* May 19, 2011, http://www.nytimes.com/2011/05/20/us/20rapture.html?_r=0.
12. Parker, "Make My Bed?"
13. Greg Keller, "France Riots Continue, Protesters Block Airports," *Christian Science Monitor,* October 20, 2010, http://www.csmonitor.com/World/Latest-News-Wires/2010/1020/France-riots-continue-protesters-block-airports.
14. John Markoff and David E. Sanger, "In a Computer Worm, a Possible Biblical Clue," *New York Times,* September 29, 2010, http://www.nytimes.com/2010/09/30/world/middleeast/30worm.html?_r=0; Tim Worstall, "Stuxnet Was a Joint US/Israeli Project," June 1, 2012, http://www.forbes.com/sites/timworstall/2012/06/01/stuxnet-was-a-joint-us-israeli-project/#1dbf63ae6f4d.
15. Elizabeth Royte, *Garbage Land: On the Secret Trail of Trash* (New York: Back Bay Books, 2005), 50–62.
16. *Newsweek,* March 28 & April 4, 2011.
17. Aviel Schneider, "The Rabbi, the Note and the Messiah," *Israel Today,* April 2007, http://www.israeltoday.co.il/NewsItem/tabid/178/nid/23877/Default.aspx. Accessed June 21, 2016.
18. Aviel Schneider, quoted in "Messiah Mystery Follows Death of Mystical Rabbi," *WND,* May 18, 2007, http://www.wnd.com/2007/05/41669/#!.
19. Douglas J. Moo, *Romans: The NIV Application Commentary* (Grand Rapids, MI: Zondervan, 2000), 379.
20. Gary Thoma, "The Return of the Jewish Church," *Christianity Today,* September 7, 1998, http://www.christianitytoday.com/ct/1998/september7/8ta062.html.
21. Barry Yeoman, "Evangelical Movement on the Rise," Jewish Telegraphic Agency, November 15, 2007, http://www.jta.org/2007/11/15/news-opinion/united-states/evangelical-movement-on-the-rise.
22. Sarah Posner, "Kosher Jesus: Messianic Jews in the Holy Land," *The Atlantic,* November 29, 2012, http://www.theatlantic.com/international/archive/2012/11/kosher-jesus-messianic-jews-in-the-holy-land/265670/.
23. Kehila News Israel, "Directory of Messianic Organizations in Israel," http://app.kehilanews.com/directory. Accessed May 26, 2016.

CHAPTER 10: METANARRATIVE

1. Dan P. McAdams, quoted in Benedict Carey, "This Is Your Life (and How You Tell It)," *New York Times,* May 22, 2007, http://www.nytimes.com/2007/05/22/health/psychology/22narr.html.

2. C. S. Lewis, *The Voyage of the Dawn Treader* (New York: HarperCollins, 1994), 247.
3. Peter J. Gentry and Stephen J. Wellum, *Kingdom through Covenant* (Wheaton, IL: Crossway, 2012), 91, 99.
4. Christopher Wright, *The Mission of God: Unlocking the Bible's Grand Narrative* (Downers Grove, IL: InterVarsity, 2006), 123.
5. Mike Bullmore, "The Gospel and Scripture," in *The Gospel as Center,* ed. D. A. Carson and Timothy Keller (Wheaton, IL: Crossway, 2012), 52.
6. James M. Hamilton, Jr., *God's Glory in Salvation through Judgment* (Wheaton, IL: Crossway, 2010), 49.
7. G. K. Beale, *A New Testament Biblical Theology* (Grand Rapids, MI: Baker Academic, 2011), 16.
8. Beale, *A New Testament Biblical Theology*, 57. Also see Beale, *The Temple and the Church's Mission* (Downers Grove, IL: InterVarsity, 2004); Michael Horton, *The Gospel Commission: Recovering God's Strategy for Making Disciples* (Grand Rapids, MI: Baker, 2011); Andreas J. Köstenberger and Peter T. O'Brien, *Salvation to the Ends of the Earth: A Biblical Theology of Mission* (Downers Grove, IL: IVP Academic, 2001).

CHAPTER 11: SPEAK NOW

1. Team Fix, "Seventh Republican Debate Transcript, Annotated: Who Said What and What It Meant," *The Washington Post,* January 28, 2016, https://www.washingtonpost.com/news/the-fix/wp/2016/01/28/7th-republican-debate-transcript-annotated-who-said-what-and-what-it-meant/.
2. Letter from Albert Einstein to President Franklin Roosevelt, quoted in Tom Zoellner, *Uranium: War, Energy, and the Rock That Shaped the World* (New York: Viking, 2009), 36–37.
3. Jacob Brackman, "Cloakroom Nightmare," *Mother Jones,* September/October 1982, 14–15.
4. Mark Kurlansky, *Salt: A World History* (New York: Walker, 2002), 5.
5. Jessica Gresko, "New Nike shoe with Outer Space Theme Causes Frenzy," *Mercury News,* February 24, 2012, http://www.mercurynews.com/ci_20039902.
6. Gresko, "New Nike shoe with Outer Space Theme Causes Frenzy."
7. Keith Davy, *CoJourners: Joining Others in Spiritual Journey* (Orlando, FL: CruPress, 2008).
8. Davy, *CoJourners.*
9. An instructional video is provided by New Vision, "One Verse Evangelism Instructions," Vimeo, November 15, 2010, http://vimeo.com/16859461.
10. Laura Hillenbrand, *Unbroken: A World War II Story of Survival, Resilience, and Redemption* (New York: Random House, 2010), 396–397.

EPILOGUE

1. Guy Deutscher, *Through the Language Glass: Why the World Looks Different in Other Languages* (New York: Metropolitan, 2010), 165.
2. Deutscher, *Through the Language Glass*, 166.
3. Deutscher, *Through the Language Glass*, 166.